ZEALS

ZEALS

A BIOGRAPHY OF AN ENGLISH COUNTRY HOUSE

JENNIE ELIAS

AMBERLEY

For my son Alexander

While every effort has been made to obtain permission from the copyright holders for all material used in this book, the publishers will be pleased to hear from anyone who has not been acknowledged and to make the correction in future reprints.

Zeals House is privately owned and there is no public access.

First published 2023

Amberley Publishing
The Hill, Stroud
Gloucestershire, GL5 4EP

www.amberley-books.com

British Library Cataloguing in Publication Data.
A catalogue record for this book is available from the British Library.

ISBN 978 1 4456 7821 4 (hardback)
ISBN 978 1 4456 7822 1 (ebook)

1 2 3 4 5 6 7 8 9 10

Typesetting by SJmagic DESIGN SERVICES, India.
Printed in the UK.

Contents

List of Illustrations

Map of Wiltshire.

Introduction

The house is big and offers a confused picture, owing largely to ample Victorian additions. The DOE sees medieval features in it. It ought to be studied properly.

Nikolaus Pevsner[1]

Zeals House lies empty and neglected. A pair of derelict Grade II listed gate lodges known as Black Dog East and Black Dog West announce the northern entrance to the estate. High stone gate pillars are surmounted by pier finials of talbot passant dogs from the coat of arms of the Chafyn family. The straight north drive with symmetrical three-hundred-year-old lime trees on either side is underplanted with grass, unattended. Sweeping southwards along the drive a Grade II listed dilapidated early eighteenth-century roofless orangery is nestled into the undergrowth and ahead stands the forlorn picturesque stone manor house of Zeals.

This rambling L-plan house is a jumble of architectural periods from medieval beginnings, through seventeenth- and eighteenth-century additions and a dominating nineteenth-century extension. It is set in a landscape of chalk downs overlooking the edge of the Blackmore Vale in the south-west corner of Wiltshire, in the parish of Mere. There is a lake, a boathouse, mature trees and an extensive park. The manor house, Grade I listed, is tucked away from view amongst the trees and fields divided by park railings and the crumbling remains of the ancient estate wall.

The story of the Chafyn and later Chafyn-Grove family who lived there is one of spectacular fortunes and misfortunes, their personalities ranging from utterly charming to severely haughty.

Zeals House east elevation, 1994.

The family typically moved from merchants to landed gentry. Following the dissolution of the monasteries they subsequently prospered through land purchases that incorporated the village of Zeals and beyond.

Zeals House has a rich history of involvement with the prominent architects of their respective generations: possibly local mason-architect William Arnold for the medieval house and Nathaniel Ireson for the early eighteenth century. This was followed in the Regency period with alterations made by Joseph Saunders. The largest part of the house was added by the prominent Victorian architect George Devey. In published references to Devey's work, Zeals House only registers briefly, overshadowed by his much larger houses and his aristocratic and banker clients. His visits and overnight stays are documented and although he was jovial, his reception was treated in a business-like manner. Zeals House is unseen from roads but is arguably Devey's best integrated house and one of the prettiest.

At the time of writing, the current owners of Zeals House do not live there, leaving the melancholy of an abandoned dwelling. Its future is uncertain, but behind these walls lies the narrative of its architecture and the social history of the ancient family who lived there.

The Chafyn family survived through the turmoil of the Civil War, helping King Charles II on his flight from Worcester between

Trent House in Dorset (formerly in Somerset) and Heale House in Amesbury, near Salisbury.

Rooted in country life and country sports, the family negotiated the social, ecclesiastical and political changes of the times. Their excursions to Egypt, Spain and France were documented in previously unpublished diaries highlighting the joys and pitfalls of travel in the mid-Victorian years. A voyage to Australia, Ceylon and Bombay was adventurous, but was undertaken without setting a foot outside the British Empire.

In the course of its history, Zeals House was run by three women, the first a Chafyn heiress who married a Grove and added his name to hers. The second was a Regency widow who controlled the house for thirty-nine years, and the third a Victorian spinster, for twenty-six years. Over the generations, the occupants, being a county family, had civic responsibilities, as leaders of the local militia, justices of the peace, deputy lieutenants, sheriffs and as members of parliament. As well as being rural landlords, they served in the army, navy and the church.

The story of Zeals House is predominantly a Victorian tale of lives and generations long gone in a quiet backwater in the West Country, just inside Wiltshire, bordering both Dorset and Somerset. The family lived close to the soil of their English country house through the generations, immersed in their immediate domain, in the beautiful landscape. As the seasons changed, they lived through the harsh trials and joys of an agricultural community. Human nature in all its strengths and weaknesses is documented, as well as the necessary adjustments having to be made through cultural and political transformations, which closely mirrors the country as a whole.

In the updated edition of *The Buildings of England, Wiltshire*, Julian Orbach refers to Zeals as a 'fascinating house'.[2] Its future is in the balance as it is registered by Historic England as a Building at Risk. The Chafyn-Grove family lived there for five hundred years and it is part of the legacy of George Devey.

All ancient houses have their secrets, and Zeals is no exception.

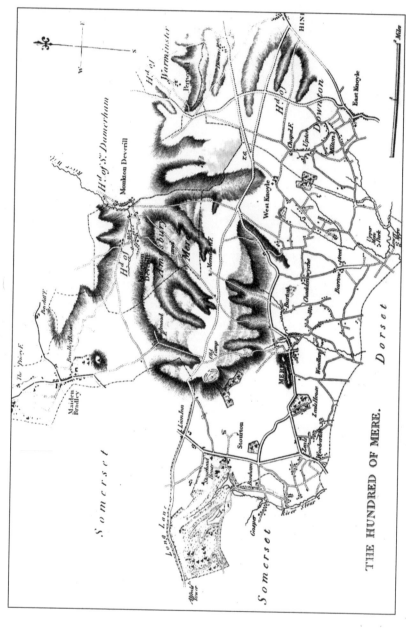

THE HUNDRED OF MERE.

Map of Mere with Zeals House, 1820s.

PART I

HISTORY

CHAPTER ONE

Tudor

Black Dogs gate piers and lodges.

'Life is going so well for him,' wrote Julia Chafyn-Grove.[3] She was referring to her younger brother, William Chafyn-Grove, known as Chafyn, who was celebrating his 21st birthday at Zeals House on 25th September 1861. Two years previously, he had inherited the estate from their father, also named William. Chafyn was celebrating not only his landmark birthday with all his life ahead of him, but freedom from the guardians and trustees he had before he became of age. But as so often happened to this family, events spiralled in unexpected directions.

Julia and Chafyn were descended from the Chafyn family of Warminster and Salisbury with a likely former spelling of Chauvin, indicating a Norman descent. Related families in the area, like the de Grove family, share this Conquest heritage. The early Chafyn family, also spelt as Chafen, Chafin, Chaffyn or Chaffin, were established in the Wiltshire County town of Salisbury as wool and cloth mercers. After the Black Death swept north through Salisbury from Weymouth, the town of New Sarum in the fourteenth century became a thriving city dominated by its early thirteenth-century cathedral with its landmark spire. With a rising population, most residents were employed in the wool industry. The Salisbury area was known for raw wool from old Wiltshire horned sheep that roamed in large numbers on Salisbury plain. In the fifteenth century, the emphasis changed to the production of wool which was transported to the south coast ports of Southampton and Poole by teams of pack horses and shipped to Flemish towns to be made into cloth by expert weavers.[4] The Chafyns emerged as a prosperous merchant family who owned many tenements and a property in Crane Street, now known as Church House.[5] They took part in civic life as mayors, and members of parliament and may have represented New Salisbury in the Parliament of 1472-5.[6] A John Chafyn was elected Mayor of Salisbury in 1461.[7]

Through commercial success and opportune marriage, the family became members of the new gentry, well placed to take advantage of the rapidly changing rights of property and the ecclesiastical land made available by the dissolution of the monasteries in 1536. In addition, lawyers were finding ways of selling crown feudal land.[8] Following the decline in the wool market the family moved their investments away from sheep and into land that could be enclosed and tenanted. In the area of Mere, a small agricultural market town in the district of Warminster, there were two major estates: Stourhead to the north-west and Longleat to the north-east. The Chafyn family who purchased and lived at Zeals House were to have dealings with both.

The Zeals estate takes its name from an early owner, the de Seles family, but the earliest record of a manor house in Zeals, a tithing in the parish of Mere, is in 1304 when it appears to have been surrounded by a moat. It is likely that the present Zeals House was built on this site of limestone rubble stone with slate roofs, stone stacks and moulded cappings by Matthew de Clevedon, in 1380.[9] The north wing and the great hall probably date from this time.[10] The estate contains two ancient manors, Zeals Clevedon and Zeals Ailesbury, named after previous owners. Thomas Chafyn of Seales – an earlier spelling – was living in the manor of Zeals Clevedon in 1534, although the Chafyn family were known to have lived at Zeals House from at least 1452.[11] The walls of the manor house at this time would probably have been hung with cloth, the hall and better chambers in tapestry depicting hunting or religious scenes. To keep themselves amused in the winter months, playing cards was popular, the court cards in the deck being similar to today's pack. Cards provided an alternative opportunity to gamble instead of dice.[12]

The 8th Baron Stourton of Stourton House (now Stourhead) was a major landowner and prominent resident. His family had been overlords in the Mere area for several generations, an ancestor being steward to the Prince of Wales. The first encounter between Stourton and the Chafins concerned Zeals Ailesbury, the home farmland of the estate which Thomas Chafin held on a lease for the lives of himself, his wife Margaret and their son Thomas. Lord Stourton (Charles) demanded the return of the land as he held the freehold, so Chafyn withdrew payment of rent. Stourton was not easily satisfied and 'thrust Chafyn out of possession', but he was reinstated by order of the Star Chamber.[13] In the fifteenth century 'perpetual law-suits about title to land, often dragging on for years without settlement, [...] especially when both claimants for a manor sent in armed men and extorted the rents by force.'[14]

The second encounter involved the ownership of 200 acres of demesne farmland, property of the manor and park of Mere occupied by Chafyn. In February 1551, Lord Stourton and his men attacked Chafyn's servants with weapons, stealing and driving 1,200 sheep, cattle and horses to Stourton House, impounding them before returning some and selling others at market as strays. In May of that year, they assaulted Thomas Chafyn's son Leonard and others, beating them, taking away iron bars and money. Leonard was taken against his will and shut in a prison at Stourton for several days before release. In another burst of aggression in August, Lord Stourton and his men threatened to slay or hurt Thomas Chafyn.[15] Stourton won his lawsuit as his father's lease from King Henry VIII took precedence over Chafyn's, which was from Prince Edward, King Henry's son, as Duke of Cornwall.[16] But Lord Stourton's behaviour towards another neighbour was to prove fatal.

In 1556 his victims were William Hartgill and his son, of Kilmington in Somerset. The dispute centred on a long-standing grievance and he and his men took both Hartgill men prisoner and beat them with clubs. Then Stourton ordered his men to cut their throats. On the 6th of March 1556 Lord Stourton and four associates were hanged together in Salisbury marketplace for murder, the only difference between them being that the peer was suspended with a cord of silk. He was possibly interred in the cathedral.[17]

In 1563, Sir John Thynne (1515-1580) had been steward to Edward Seymour, Lord Protector and first Duke of Somerset, and a powerful influence in the area. In this role he gained favours and benefitted financially from the connection. Thynne held lands in Longbridge Deverill near Warminster where he was to start building Longleat House on the site of a small Carthusian priory. In the social hierarchy of the time, it was important for country squires in small towns to be of use to influential landowners.[18] William Chafyn, son of Thomas, attached himself to Thynne as his 'true and lawful attorney'.[19] Sir John Thynne was granted the Chantry of Mere upon the dissolution of the Chantries, which he assigned to Thomas Chafyn. The Chantry land included the aisle and south chapel of St. Michael The Archangel Church. Built in the mid-fourteenth century, the former catholic church's chapel holds entombed generations of Chafyns of Zeals with their hatchments, helmets and memorials, inside what is now the Anglican parish church. The long lease, later purchased, also included the lands owned by the Chantry together with 'messuages, cottages, orchards, lands, meadowes, pastures, feedings, rentes, tenures and occupations'.[20] The Chantry House remained in the hands of descendants of the Chafyn family until they left the area in the mid-twentieth century. It was often leased. Once, in 1639, to a widowed Mrs Martin who was summonsed for cock fighting, and in the nineteenth century to the poet William Barnes.[21]

William Chafyn, being Sir John Thynne's attorney, would have met William Arnold as the mason employed at Longleat and Arnold may well have been an early architect at Zeals House. Features specifically indicating Arnold's work include a string course, and tall chimneys set in pairs placed on the gable ends, unusual at that time. These elements are apparent in the medieval part of Zeals House. Alterations to the house that took place at this time probably included the enlargement of the windows, the addition of the chimneys and the building of the dovecote in the service courtyard.[22] The dovecote is square, not unusual for Wiltshire, and resembles the two square lodges at Cranborne Manor in Dorset twenty-five miles away, which were built by William Arnold.

In the 1565 Visitation, William's son Thomas is listed as of Seales Clevedon in the parish of Mere. The coat of arms is surmounted by a black talbot passant. This now extinct dog also guards the two gate piers of the northern drive. The Chafyn family had another Visitation from the heralds in 1623 in a century of political and religious turmoil.[23]

CHAPTER TWO

Stuart

Rural Wiltshire was predominately on the side of King Charles I in the civil war, but it appears that the Chafyn household at Zeals, although Royalist, mostly kept a low profile and avoided being compounded of their estates. Another Chafyn heir called William, son of Thomas, who married a daughter of William Willoughby, had died in 1626 leaving two surviving brothers. Richard Chafyn, who would later inherit on his father's death, was granted a commission in 1627 from the Earl of Pembroke to 'his very loving friend, Richard Chafyn, Esq.', appointing him captain of a Company of Foot in the County of Wiltshire.[24] Richard's brother, Thomas D.D., was Rector of Mere from 1630.[25] He had spoken against Parliament in a sermon in Sarum Cathedral but it was decided not to fine him, as was usual, but to imprison him. On another occasion it was said that he added to the Litany, 'From all lay Puritans and all Parliament men, good Lord, deliver us.'[26] Towards the end of the civil war in 1645 he was dragged from his house by parliamentary soldiers and abused by one of the soldiers who 'kick'd him in the Privy members and then forced him to mount a horse without saddle, where he was led away to Fisherton prison in Salisbury'.[27] He stayed for a few weeks before becoming weak and was sent home. After a few days he died of his injuries, suffering the anguish of seeing his house, stables and all

Engraving of Mere Church, 1820s.

his goods and horses plundered, leaving his family in a desperate situation.

A few years later Charles II was escaping from the disastrous Battle of Worcester in 1651 on his flight to the coast. Hutton, in his *Highways and Byways in Wiltshire*, suggests that Charles II slept one night at Zeals House when in hiding.[28] There was an oak four poster bed with its alleged original silk damask drapes preserved in a bedroom in Zeals House called the Charles II room in the mid-twentieth century, but this panelled former billiard room is not where he rested, it being unlikely he would have slept so openly there whilst in flight. He spent most of the nights on his dramatic journey from Worcester to the coast with known Catholic families whose houses had priest holes. Zeals, being an ancient dwelling, had a priest hole and this is where he crept in, avoiding servants, to take refuge as is described in a later chapter. The king arrived from Colonel Wyndham's Trent House in Somerset (now in Dorset) where he hid at Zeals House, but there may well have been an alarm as he appears to have left in a hurry, leaving behind items of clothing.[29]

The group then rode to the George Inn in Mere to take refreshment in the cellar.[30] The inn was owned by the Chafyn family so the landlord would have been trusted, whereas they may not have had full confidence in the loyalty of the servants at Zeals House. Accompanied by Henry Peters, Mrs Julian Coningsby and

Colonel Phelips, the king would have ridden through the Zeals estate on the Monarch's Way track, which still exists, on his way to Mere, 'going into Mere which would have been on the left hand'.[31] It was not a difficult journey by way of Wincanton and Mere to Heale House, and Phelips, who lived nearby at Montacute House in Somerset, was a good friend of the Chafyn family. 'Knowing all that country perfectly well [Phelips] brought them in such private ways that they came near very few houses, only the king being hungry would needs go into Mere and there at a true local Innkeepers they dined.'[32] 'His Majestie' was disguised as a servant and unknowingly, the landlord said, 'Thou lookest like an honest fellow, here's a health to the king.'[33] They raised a glass to the amused monarch.[34] The journey then took the king onwards to stay with the Hyde family at Heale House in Amesbury, near Salisbury, where he remained for several days.

When Richard Chafyn died, his son William inherited Zeals. The Chafyn family may have avoided open participation in the Civil War, but their Royalist leanings surfaced in an uprising in 1655, which was to affect the Zeals household. Hugh Grove, known as Hugh Grove of Chisenbury, became William Chafyn's son-in-law when he married his daughter Dorothy, who died childless. Hugh married for a second time Jane Grove of Ferne. In 1655, Col John

Engraving of Hugh Grove.

22

Penruddock of Compton Chamberlayne near Salisbury, with Hugh Grove, led a group of followers to proclaim for King Charles II, but they were discovered by parliamentary troops at South Molton in Devon. Both were imprisoned. Later they were publicly beheaded at Exeter on the 16th of May 1655, the execution warrant being personally signed by Cromwell as 'Oliver P'. In a speech from the scaffold Hugh Grove said:

> I dye a loyal subject to King Charles II, my undoubted sovereign, and a lover of the good old laws of the land; the just privileges of parliament; the rights and liberties of the people; for the re-establishing of all which, I undertook this design, and of which I am now ready to lay down my life. [...] Now God bless the King, and all those that love him; and turn the hearts of all of them that hate him! God bless you all, and God be merciful unto you, and to my soul. AMEN.[35]

Broadsheet of execution at Exeter, 1655.

In happier times, Charles II revisited Mere on several occasions and may have stayed at Zeals House. He toured the places that helped him in his escape from Worcester, presenting gifts to those who had helped in his escape. To the Chafyn family it is understood he presented a magnificent silver salt, as a centre piece for the dining table. The town of Mere was also included in his generosity.

'One of the church bells bears the date 1670, and it is generally supposed to have been presented to the inhabitants on the restoration of Charles II for their loyalty to their lawful, much beloved, though unfortunate sovereign, who concealed himself about this part of the country, and frequently honoured Mere with his royal presence.'[36]

In later life, as his family's status required of him, William Chafyn became high sheriff for Wiltshire and deputy lieutenant. His claim for expenses in the role of Sheriff in 1684-1685 is revealed in a document discovered at Zeals House by Edward Troyte-Bullock, a much later descendant. It included 'wine (and hams), ten gallons of Claret, three hoxeds of Claret, a hoxed of Shery Sacke, sixteen galons of Wite Wine, twenty galons of Claret'.[37] The total amount of the year's expenses was £282 16s. 9d., revealing that public money was spent freely. To put this sum into context, the total average yearly income at this date of a gentleman's family is listed as £280.[38] It is interesting to note that another expense was for putting the coach into mourning with black cloth upon the death of Charles II. There were also presents for the judge and retainers including lobsters, salmon, turces (possibly turtle doves), poulets and canaries.[39]

A year later a warrant was issued to 'distrayne the goods of William Chafyn, Esq, for his not sending out a horse to the King's militia [...] to suppress the late rebellion in the West'.[40] This was a reference to the Monmouth rebellion. The claim was dropped when Pembroke declared himself satisfied that William was otherwise engaged on the business of being High Sheriff for the County. Although William Chafyn was a comfortable squire of his manor house, head of his family and Lower Zeals village, he was still accountable to an overlord. In his case it was the Earl of Pembroke at Wilton House near Salisbury.

Inside Zeals House at the time there was a two-storey great hall fully panelled in oak and a flagstone floor leading to the servants' quarters. To the right of the building, facing a kitchen garden known as the nunnery, there was an adjoining courtyard.[41] To add to the provisions gained from his expenses, the servants in the kitchen would have prepared beef, lamb, rabbit, hare, chicken and trout from the round pond in the grounds. As a delicacy, there were pigeons from the dovecote.[42] Mary Chafin's recipes from 1698 provide an overview of late seventeenth-century cuisine in the English country house. She was a distant cousin, living at the Tudor Chettle House in Dorset before the current house was built. Mary's book reveals that very few vegetables were grown or eaten at this time, but there would have been a herb garden for remedies of common ailments. Potions were made from wild flowers, herbs and oils. Vinegar was used extensively to preserve meat and fresh summer fruits were preserved for winter use.[43] The netting of partridges on the ground was a fashionable sport, often carried on with dogs who pointed the game concealed in the grass.[44] The incumbents of Zeals would also have enjoyed hunting, mainly for roebuck, and they would have had large white hunting dogs called talbots.

William Chafyn died in 1695 aged fifty-six. He is entombed in the family chapel in Mere Church, under a marble slab on the east side wall with the unsentimental inscription: 'The ancient possessor of the manor of Zeals, served as high sheriff of this county in the year 1685, left good husbandry in plantations, improvements of land, scarcely to be paralleled.'[45]

William was survived by his wife Mary ([née Freke), two sons and one daughter. Their son Harry Chafyn married the widow of Colonel Bullen Reymes, a trusted Cavalier who was a loyal friend of Charles I, fighting alongside Prince Maurice, and of Charles II. In later life, before becoming a member of parliament for Weymouth and Melcombe Regis, Reymes was a diplomat in Paris, Venice and Tangier. His mother was connected to the Coker family of Mappowder in Dorset. The description of Coker Hall as having 'sixteen chimneys, a wide gateway with two stone pillars each formerly surmounted by a head of a blackamoor' is all that remains of this Tudor manor house.[46]

Robert Coker's daughter Ann married Thomas Gerrard who owned three estates in Dorset – Waddon, Trent and Broadwey – and had three co-heiress daughters. As they married, their husbands inherited the estates on the father's death. Anne married Colonel Francis Wyndham who inherited Trent and Bullen Reymes married the eldest daughter, Elizabeth, in the 12th-century Mappowder church, inheriting the Waddon Estate.[47] It was subsequently on Harry Chafyn's marriage to the widowed Elizabeth Reymes that the Chafyn family inherited the Waddon Estate in Portesham, on

Colonel Bullen Reymes.

the Dorset coast. Two centuries later, in 1859 the Bullen Reymes diaries were removed to Zeals House and turned into a book by an American academic.[48] As Harry Chafyn's marriage to Bullen Reymes widow was childless, The Zeals and Waddon estates were passed to his brother Thomas.

CHAPTER THREE

Queen Anne

The Chafyn family continued investing in the accepted way for gentry, by increasing land holdings. Records show that land was purchased in 1648, in the form of a house in Mere and land in Mere and Broughton.[49] A bundle of deeds relating to houses in specified streets in Mere from 1537-1794 comprises forty titles.[50] Another purchase was for a house in West Waddon near the manor house.[51]

At Zeals House, sometime during the seventeenth century, there were additions to the main structure. The medieval range is to the right, facing north-east. The additions were asymmetrical and the façade is plain, having few architectural details or embellishments. The central range has 'three light and four-light mullioned and transomed casements to ground and first floors, two attic gables with three light ovolo-mullioned casements, Tudor window hoods and coped verges with ball finials'.[52] Harry's brother Thomas sought to make further additions and repairs to Zeals House. But it must have been apparent to him that the Tudor style of house was unfashionable in the reign of Queen Anne.

Just across the border at Chettle in Dorset the family's kinsman George Chafen, who shared the same lineage and coat of arms, whose forebears had branched off from Zeals House, was building a baroque mansion to replace a Tudor house. Designed by the architect Thomas Archer, it was of brick with stone facings and 'the plum among Dorset houses of the early eighteenth century'.[53] Meanwhile, George Bubb Dodington, who had challenged George Chafen to a duel following an altercation about dogs, was building the enormous Eastbury Park in nearby Tarrant Gunville.[54] Dodington chose the prominent baroque architect Sir John Vanbrugh to design his new mansion and estate.

The fashion was for baroque architectural detailing, as instigated by Inigo Jones at the Queen's House at Greenwich in East London, where panelled lofty rooms with large sash windows replaced Gothic or Tudor mullioned to let in more light. Rooms were set in a square or rectangular order, high-ceilinged and more formal for elegant living. Although not as theatrical as Continental baroque, the whimsical use of stone dressings on brick mansions with stone balustrades at roof level was considered attractive. Architectural tastes were evolving.

Access to London was limited, but style changes slowly filtered through to the West Country. With the extra income from the tenants on the Waddon Estate, at Zeals the Queen Anne-style Manor Farm House was built in Flemish bond brick, with evidence suggesting the work of Nathaniel Ireson.[55] The five-bay symmetrical house stands adjacent to Zeals House with access from the service drive parallel to Black Dogs. In later years this house was considerably enlarged to include extra accommodation, outbuildings, barns, and a walled garden. At 660 acres, the home farm gained a reputation as one of the best managed farms in Wiltshire.[56]

The Queen Anne-style Manor Farm is delightfully well proportioned, lacking the more flamboyant stone dressings of larger houses of the period, either due to budget restrictions or with the intention of creating a more appropriate appearance for an estate farmhouse. Fragments of plans remain, together with receipts from the Wincanton-based architect and mason 'Natt' Ireson. The plans are internal and appear to have been of a kitchen and service area. Handwritten receipts to Thos. Chafyn give an indication of the considerable quantity of work undertaken. Ireson was not an educated man, and his poor English is reflected in his writing, but he was a prolific builder and architect in the West Country. Ireson's architectural approach appears to have been to follow a rural version of the English baroque and Palladian styles he had been exposed to. He had worked on Thomas Archer's Hale House in Hampshire. As an accomplished mason, he may have worked as the builder or mason at Archer's Chettle House in Cranborne Chase, Dorset.[57] Ireson's Ven House in Milborne Port on the Somerset/Dorset border near Sherborne, built in 1725, shares a resemblance, although without Archer's assured facility with classical Baroque architectural detail.

The orangery, snuggled into the foliage at an angle to gain a southerly aspect, is in the Queen Anne mode. The picturesque outbuilding is also by date and style the work of Nathaniel Ireson. The architect's final receipts are dated 1722. From the top of the hill on the parkland to the east, the orangery sits at a perfect angle in relation to the eastern façade of the house. Built in Flemish bond brick with a gabled parapet, a coped verge and end piers with an oculus, it is adjacent to the front entrance. The contrast of the brick orangery next to the stone manor house is striking.

At the same time, the successful banker Henry Hoare purchased the Stourton Estate, demolished the medieval house of the ancient Stourton family and embarked on the building of a new house. He chose Colen Campbell, an early pioneer of the English Palladian house who had designed Burlington House in Piccadilly (now the Royal Academy) for Lord Burlington. To build the house, Campbell also turned to the local Somerset master builder Nathaniel Ireson in 1720, the date parallel to Ireson's work at Zeals.

The Chafin family were friends and close neighbours of Henry Hoare and a client, the Zeals estate banking being carried out from Hoare's headquarters. Hoare's builder Ireson lived in Wincanton in Somerset two miles from Zeals House, and Stourhead was a similar distance, so it was possible both projects were undertaken at the same time. With Ireson busy with the building of Stourhead, which was a considerably larger undertaking than work for Thomas Chafyn, the work at Zeals was not progressing as planned. As Ireson was unable to satisfy Chafyn's demands, there was a disagreement. After two payments of fifty guineas to end the dispute, the agreement ended. In October 1722 Ireson scribbles: 'It is agreed this day and an end to be out of all desputes bewen Tho Chafin esq and Natt Ireson that the said Mr [Chafin] doth take the finishing of his house to himself and that the said Natt Ireson upn som controvsey doth promise to up hold the stack of chimneys and the arch of the sd seller for seven years and to pay for the altering of the oven when done.'[58]

Complaints appear to be a constant problem for Nathaniel Ireson. He had also fallen out of favour with Thomas Archer on the building of Hale House. Despite Ireson's considerable talents, dealing with clients does not appear to be one of them. There seems to have been a missed opportunity to update the Tudor Zeals House, but if more substantial alterations were discussed, Thomas's age and the dispute may have put an end to any further work.

Thomas died childless and passed the house to his sister Mary, who was now in possession of the Zeals and the Waddon Estates. She was the first of three women to inherit these extensive lands. She married John Grove of Ferne House, Donhead St. Andrew, Wiltshire, near Shaftesbury. He was the son of the Cavalier Hugh Grove from the latter's second marriage to kinsman William Grove of Ferne's daughter Jane. John Grove had been given a 'richly carved wooden comb and pincushion' from Charles II for Mary.[59] Following this marriage, the Grove family were now related, near neighbours and would connect socially and through marriages to the Chafyns for several generations.

A William Grove who purchased Ferne House in 1568 had been the fourth generation of Groves to live in Wiltshire, where his father Robert Grove was member of parliament from the county. William also became a member of parliament for Shaftesbury and a barrister at Gray's Inn.[60] The succeeding generations of male heirs conform to this precedent and leave an impression of a family of highly educated professionals who went into politics, law, medicine, the army or the church and performed civic duties. From the time of Mary and John's marriage, their family would be known as Chafyn-Grove. It was a merging of two landed gentry families which would intermarry and straddle the Wiltshire/Dorset border for the next three hundred years.

CHAPTER FOUR

Georgian

A period of stability began under the Hanoverians, after the turbulent Stuart years. By the 1720s great changes were taking place in architecture. In central London, tastes for housing were rapidly changing. Aristocrats, having viewed Palladio's villas in the Veneto on the Italian Grand Tours, brought back with them ideas of the clean lines and square symmetrical plan of a new classical order. One of the instigators and taste maker was Lord Burlington who had Chiswick House in West London built as a replica of a Palladio villa. Palladian houses were taken up by the Whig party as their style for the shires, but not by the Tory gentry who preferred English Baroque.

John and Mary Chafyn-Grove had five children: Hugh who died before his father, Jane, Mary and Robert, who became a parson, and the heir called Chafin Grove. The Revd Robert held two livings. He was Rector of Manston in Dorset and also of Wootton Rivers in Wiltshire. As the parishes were sixty

Engraving of Zeals House, 1822.

miles apart the bishop questioned whether it was tenable to be in two places on the same day. To prove it was possible, Robert organised a relay of fast horses and galloped furiously between the two churches on inadequate roads. The bishop was impressed and allowed Robert to keep both livings.[61] Robert's brother Chafin Grove succeeded their father, having married Ann Amor. The family was by now prosperous, holding substantial investments in land in Zeals, Mere, Waddon and elsewhere in Wiltshire, Dorset and Somerset.

Life for country squires revolved around horses, dogs and drinking, as opposed to the excessive gambling with cards and dice in the towns of London, Bath and Tunbridge Wells.[62] Coffee houses emerged in London, Whigs and Tories favouring different establishments in bustling St James's, precursors to the gentlemen's clubs. A revival of an interest in religious doctrine ran alongside a culture of drunkenness, duelling and the taking of snuff. In the country, field sports with packs of hounds were the predominate leisure occupation of the gentry. It was social, a good opportunity to share sport with neighbours, show off estates and enjoy being outdoors riding on one's own land.

An aesthetic interest in gardens emerged at this time. In Dorset, Capability Brown was landscaping Milton Abbey for Lord Milton in a twenty-year mid-century project. To reach a steep, high viewing point he designed an innovative grass 'staircase', which still exists. His signature 'natural' parkland was enhanced with lakes, bridges and clumps of trees inside iron park railings to keep deer and sheep in, the latter being used to 'mow' the extensive lawns. Later in the century, Humphrey Repton was commissioned to redesign the gardens at Longleat near Warminster. Visiting gardens became as interesting as viewing houses.

Before these projects at Stourhead, the Hoare family moved their focus to laying out the grounds in the 1740s. Henry, grandson of Richard Hoare who purchased the estate, shared the culture of his contemporaries. It was the age of the Enlightenment, a passion for literature, art and science. The formal gardens of flowers and parterres of past generations made way for a contrived naturalness, shifting the landscape subtly to form varying vistas to heighten all the senses. Paths would weave in and out of beech and fir with new visual distractions entwined in the foliage. Items from the Grand Tour of Italy and Greece, like stone urns on pedestals, temples and grottos, were placed strategically as focal points for the eye. The idealised landscape paintings of Claude Lorraine and Richard Wilson would also have stimulated ideas.

Zeals, being so close to Stourhead, shared the same landscape of gently rolling hills and extensive views towards Dorset. Chafin and Ann would have frequently visited Henry Hoare and watched the development of the grounds. It is very likely that the Zeals parkland was laid out at this time, on a much smaller scale and budget. The elements of a green garden, grass, mature trees and water, were already there. The substantial lake was either natural or an ancient quarry but had existed for many generations and the remains of a stone structure of a former fountain and waterfall are still there on the south side. The south drive leading from the Gillingham Road lined with pairs of horse chestnut trees may have been added at this time. It led through a beech wood, an icehouse and a two-storey gazebo, now called the folly, built on elevated land as a viewing point to the Dorset Blackmore Vale, before winding through woods around the side of the lake. This route gave visitors a sense of arrival when they swept up to the front elevation of the house.

Chafin and Ann would have walked along the paths through the woods, covered in the spring with bluebells, and in white towards the summer, with the pungent scent of wild garlic. Following Chafyn's death, his widow Ann lived to be eighty-three. She died in 1794, outliving all of her children but having seen her eldest son inherit. His name was William Chafyn-Grove, (1731-1793).

'A typical bucolic figure of a squire is exhibited in the rendering of that former Wiltshire worthy, William Chafyn-Grove, who represented Shaftesbury in 1768-74 and his very comely lady make an agreeable pendant.'[63]

William Chafyn-Grove's portrait depicts him flush with prosperity and confidence, a county squire, solid and respectable; an accomplished eighteenth-century gentleman. Having been called to the Bar in 1756 after six years at Middle Temple, he became a member of parliament for Shaftesbury in a contested election but did not run for the seat again as it would have been too expensive. Instead, he successfully sought the seat of Weymouth and Melcombe Regis in an uncontested election.[64] Waddon Manor in Portesham, which William had also inherited, was in the latter constituency. He held the seat, formerly held by Bullen Reymes, until 1781, but his career was undistinguished, as he consistently voted with the Opposition. Although he became a Deputy Lieutenant for Dorset and Poole and High Sheriff of Wiltshire, the *English Chronicle* described him in 1780 as: 'An invariable and inveterate advocate for Administration, but not distinguished in any particular degree for any other quality either good or bad'.[65] William had married his

Portrait of William
Chafyn-Grove.

cousin, Elizabeth Grove of Ferne, twenty-five years his junior. She,
too, was painted by Romney, twice, in 1779 and 1780, one portrait
hanging at Zeals, the other at Ferne.

Towards the end of William's life in 1791 some modernising was
carried out to the porch at Zeals House. There are architectural
drawings with detailed measurements of 'frontispiece to entrance
from Garden for William Chafyn Grove esq. at Zeals'.[66] The work
was carried out by Joseph Saunders of Edgware Road, near the
Oxford turnpike, Middlesex. Saunders' work at Zeals is modest and
includes the addition of the porch with the Georgian fanlight over,
seen in the 1820s engraving of the house.[67] Although fashionable at
the time, it was unsympathetic to the original architecture.

The marriage of William and Elizabeth was childless, but William
appears to have adored his glamorous young wife, providing her
with beautiful clothes as seen in her two Romney portraits. As a
former barrister, William's will is a lengthy and detailed document
in exquisite handwriting on large sheets of parchment.[68] One
of his executors was Elizabeth's brother Thomas Grove Snr of
Ferne, a Major in the Wiltshire Yeomanry Cavalry and Master of
Foxhounds.[69] He was William's brother-in-law, cousin, and close
friend. Elizabeth was permitted to stay for life at Zeals House
where she remained for another thirty-nine years, the second of
three women who would inherit the estate.

She was also left money and William's coach and horses. Because Elizabeth was both a Chafyn-Grove and a Grove, she was in close contact with her Grove family and engaged in the life of both households. It was Elizabeth, following William's death, who was to take the family forward into the nineteenth century, and into the manors and manners of Regency England.

CHAPTER FIVE

Regency – Elizabeth

George IV was Regent from 1811-1820 following the decision that George III was unfit to rule. The reign of George IV began in 1820 on his father's death. But what is commonly known as the

Portrait of Elizabeth Chafyn-Grove.

Regency period in art and fashion effectively began in 1783 when the younger George became of age.[70] This was the same year he first encountered the small Sussex village of Brighton where he would later build his extravagant Pavilion. The birth of neo-classicism began with the influence of George IV and would fade from 1837 following the death of William IV and the beginning of the long Victorian era. Domestic architecture, however, which evolved rather than being transformed, continued in the Regency mode into the 1840s, particularly in the rural areas where fashionable styles filtered through slowly from the cities and towns.

Elizabeth Chafyn-Grove was thirty-nine when she was widowed and was well placed to enjoy the prosperity and cultured leisure of the age. Palladian houses were being redecorated in vibrant colours, with furniture in mahogany, rosewood or satinwood, enhanced with ormolu features. Windows were dressed in silks with elaborate fringed swags, tails and tassels on pelmets. A celebration of the anniversary of Admiral Lord Nelson's Battle of the Nile in 1820 coincided with Thomas Hope's interest in ancient Egypt.[71] Hope, Thomas Sheraton and other furniture makers produced tables with tripod legs, which complimented the sabre-legged Trafalgar chairs. Egyptian heads, sphinxes and motifs were added to furniture including console tables made with marble tops.

Alongside the Egyptian style was a Grecian theme with Greek key motifs, brought from France by Hope and George IV's architect, Henry Holland. A favourite scheme for drawing rooms was a combination of light blue walls with crimson drapes, and a revival of small pieces of chinoiserie furniture. Leisured ladies in the Regency period would have subscribed to Ackermann's *The Repository of Arts,* a journal with instructive hand-coloured plates for furniture, window treatments and room settings.[72] If Elizabeth decorated Zeals in this fashion, (she appeared to favour clothes and jewellery) nothing would have remained after the later substantial Victorian additions to the house took place.

Beautifully dressed in silks, Elizabeth took advantage of her position and used Zeals House for her entertainment, and when a change of scenery was desired, she would head for Bath, handily only twenty-five miles away. Here she would be amongst friends, neighbours and family members enjoying all the frivolous pursuits of this spa town, which was at the height of its fashionability. She could stroll under a parasol in Sydney Gardens, accept invitations to tea, write letters, read, go to theatrical performances in the

Assembly Rooms, balls, and to improve her health she could have 'taken the waters'. There were private and public dances in the Upper and Lower Rooms. Elizabeth was the hostess of the Pump Room, above the old Roman baths, a daily meeting place to drink healing water and exchange gossip.

Elizabeth saw little of her unmarried sister Philippa (known as Aunt Grove) who was living at Netherhampton on the outskirts of Salisbury, but she was very close to Ferne and her brother Thomas Grove Snr, and the Groves' ten children. Being widowed and childless, she naturally gravitated towards two of his daughters, Charlotte and Harriet Grove. Both girls wrote diaries which have been transcribed and published. It is through these diaries that the life of Elizabeth Chafyn-Grove can be glimpsed. She was known in the family as 'Aunt Chafin'.[73] A typical entry by Harriet Grove in 1809 reads: 'Arrived at Zeals. My aunt Chafin received us most cordially and kissed both of us. We went to church in the great lumbering coach. Came back to Netherhampton. Aunt Chafin accompanied us. We saw fern [Ferne House] at a distance and met Mr. [William] Beckford's dwarf.'[74]

Harriet's diaries written when she was eighteen reveal her teenage romance with her young cousin Percy Bysshe Shelley, to whom she referred as her dear Bysshe in a constant exchange of letters throughout 1809.[75] In March 1810, Shelley sent Harriet and her sister Charlotte copies of his first published prose work, the Gothic novel, *Zastrozzi*.[76]

Aside from the romance, Harriet's diaries provide a detailed account of trips to Zeals House to visit Elizabeth. In 1810, on a visit with sister Charlotte and her brothers, they were received by Aunt Chafin in her 'usual form' and 'walked to Mere, where brother George was nearly run over as being so riotous, he nearly spoilt the Musical Clock'.[77] Sojourns to Zeals would have been welcome as the Groves had moved to temporarily to Donhead St Andrew rectory, now Donhead House. The girls' father had discovered that 'Old Fern will tumble down as the front is cracked all the way down.'[78] Ferne House was subsequently demolished. The architect engaged to draw up plans for a new mansion was sixty-one-year-old Weymouth builder and mason James Hamilton. An odd choice, as he was best known as a purveyor of bathing machines and for designing a statue of George III in Weymouth.

By early 1811, when sister Charlotte took over the diaries, it was agreed in the family that Aunt Chafin would entertain the two sisters in Bath to console them following romantic disappointments. Harriet had become aware of Shelley's elopement with Harriet Westbrook and Charlotte's beau had died. As the two girls prepared for their trip at the end of February, Charlotte was well aware of their provinciality. 'Last day before our Bath expedition. In a bustle, packing up. A great event to us rusticks.'[79]

As portrayed by Romney, Elizabeth Chafyn-Grove was elegant and dressed in the latest fashions of the season from London. With the improved turnpike roads, it was easier to travel to 'town'. In her own coach complete with coachmen in the family livery of scarlet and white, she would have appeared glamorous to her two nieces. She received the girls in Bath and took them on an endless round of visiting and entertaining friends, relatives and neighbours. They wore embroidered empire line dresses matched with bonnets tied under their chins with wide ribbons. In a gig, a fly, a barouche, a phaeton, or in Aunt Chafin's coach with her coat of arms emblazoned on the doors, they were constantly on the move. They also enjoyed gossiping, seeing their friends such as Elizabeth Penruddock, and cousin Elizabeth Shelley, and going to Church on Sundays. Games were played – Crambo, Dumb Crambo, Chess or Battledore – and when entertaining Aunt Chafin played carols. In quieter moments Charlotte read *Marmion* by Sir Walter Scott to her aunt. Then there were the balls in the Lower Rooms for cotillons and country dances.

In the manners of the times dancing, once one had been introduced, was an acceptable way of meeting young gentlemen. They were sorry to leave their Aunt Chafin when they had to return home in the spring. Reading Shakespeare in the carriage on their homeward journey they arrived at their temporary accommodation for dinner, finding their parents and siblings well.

That evening, the family had a pleasant conversation about atheism, prompted by the news of cousin Bysshe's expulsion from Oxford – and a discussion about pocket books. Their father declared that they were mostly used by old maids. Soon the sisters would resume their rural life, walking regularly in the sweeping landscape of Cranborne Chase, and in April listening out for the cuckoo.[80]

Escaping to Bath had restored the spirits of Charlotte and Harriet, but their mother was anxious. She was growing impatient to move into the new Ferne House. The building work was taking longer than anticipated, but by the end of August they visited the house to place their beds and saw the marble chimney piece for the drawing room.[81] They began packing up and then the wagons were going off, one overturning coming down Ashcombe Hill. Finally, in September they moved in, to great excitement. Charlotte proclaimed, 'May the owners of this charming mansion enjoy years of happiness within these walls'.[82] There was happiness when Harriet married William Helyar, a friend of her brothers, but flaws in Ferne House soon appeared. The library chimney caught fire and the drawing room chimney was so small 'a boy could not get up it'.[83] A photograph reveals an old-fashioned provincial design suggesting budget restrictions or lack of creative inspiration.

Charlotte returned to Bath with Aunt Chafin on several occasions, being an ideal companion for the older woman. But she found Bath flatter without Harriet and her friend Elizabeth Penruddock and cousin Elizabeth Shelley. She spent evenings reading to her aunt and making notes in her pocket book.

Although Elizabeth Chafyn-Grove enjoyed the gaiety of Bath and beyond, and being with her Ferne family, she had to oversee the household affairs of Zeals House. For the running of the estate, she relied upon her nephew, Major William Chafyn-Grove. Eventually he would inherit Zeals on the death of his childless cousin Chafin Grove in 1851.

Charlotte Grove, the eldest of the ten Grove children, had been the last of the siblings to leave Ferne House.[84] A new Rector for the Church of Berwick St John on the Ferne estate had arrived and married Charlotte. At forty-three years of age, she became Mrs Richard Downes. She was delighted to move into the attractive Berwick Rectory in the grounds of her former home.

On Saturday, 9th November 1833, an express arrived for Charlotte from Zeals.

My father and I set off directly, driven by Tom. My aunt very glad to see us but very ill and in great pain. Major William Chafyn-Grove arrived. I sat up at night. My aunt remained in a stupor all day. Mr Newman the apothecary came. He said hers was quite a decay of constitution from old age. My dear Aunt Chafin died without a struggle. William C. G. a great comfort to both my dear father and myself. The former is left sole executor to her Will.[85]

In the following days,

My father found about £800 in my aunt's bureau.[86] He returned to Ferne. My aunt told me she left all her wardrobe to me the Saturday I came. In a drawer of the bureau, I found the jewels that are left to Mrs William C. Grove, an heirloom to Zeals, also a quantity of banknotes and gold which quite frightened me. My father, and my brothers George and Charles came. In the evening we counted the money which amounted to £1,915.[87]

No explanation is given for the substantial amount of money. It was presumably left for her by her late husband.

Village gossip circulated in Mere that the poet William Barnes may take over Mrs Grove's Zeals House to enlarge his boarding school, which he was running at the Chantry. This was unsubstantiated and Barnes stayed on at the Chantry until 1835, then left to go to Dorchester to set up a larger school, where he befriended Thomas Hardy.[88] On leaving the Chantry he wrote a poem:

Sweet Garden: peaceful spot! no more in thee
Shall I e'er wile away the sunny hour,
Farewell each blooming shrub and lofty tree;
Farewell the mossy path and nodding flower;
I shall not hear again from yonder bower,
The song of birds or humming of the bee,
nor listen to the waterfall, nor see
The clouds float on behind the lofty tower.
No more at breezy eve or dewy morn
My gliding scythe shall shear thy mossy green;
My busy hands shall never more adorn,
My eyes no more may see this peaceful scene,
But still, sweet spot, wherever I may be,
My love-led soul shall wander back to thee.[89]

Thomas Grove Snr was the chief mourner at his sister's funeral, leading his children and many poor people from the village who gave their respects to their late benefactress. Charlotte wrote, 'My dear father gave us aunt Chafin Grove's carriage. We returned home in it driven by her coachman and horses which were left at Ferne afterwards.'

Following Elizabeth's death at the age of seventy-seven, Zeals House passed into the hands of the fifty-three-year-old Chafin Grove, member of parliament for Weymouth. Major William would wait nineteen years before he inherited from his childless cousin and had to fill the time.

CHAPTER SIX

Regency – Major William

Major William had been in the 20th Foot of the Wiltshire Militia in Spain fighting in the Peninsular War against Napoleon under the Duke of Wellington.[90] His daughter and son would later visit San Sebastian and the surrounding area of Northern Spain reflecting on their father's time spent on military duty in 1813. To celebrate the end of the Napoleonic Wars after six years of British involvement, there was 'Peace Rejoicing' in Mere. Revealing the glaring social divide, *The Salisbury and Winchester Journal* of August 1814 reports.

A festival in celebration of the peace commenced at Mere on Thursday 11th August and continued for four days. On the first day a dinner of roast beef and plum pudding, with good strong

Major William
Chafyn-Grove.

beer was served up in a large field at the foot of Castle Hill, to nearly 2000 persons. The most respectable part of the inhabitants dined in a pavilion, and the poorest part were regaled at tables in front of it. In the afternoon there were rustic amusements, and a dance on the green in which all classes joined. On the second day there was a grand match of singlestick.[91] It was well contested, though chiefly by young players; and in the evening there was a ball at the Ship [Inn], which was attended by more than 100 respectable people of the town and neighbourhood. [...] On Sunday after evening service, the principal inhabitants met again in the pavilion, and the ladies were regaled with tea, syllabub, &c. The whole was extremely well conducted.[92]

Although the Regency period was a time of prosperity, the plight of the agricultural community contrasted sharply with the life of the leisured ladies of Mere and Bath. The celebrations at the end of the Napoleonic Wars were short-lived. Focus shifted towards domestic issues. The west country landscape where Zeals was situated was ideal for sheep farming, as it had been for centuries. The enclosed land was suited to dairy farming, from where milk and cheese were sent to London. On the edge of the chalk downs of the Blackmore Vale, the plains along the banks of the River Stour were mostly used for arable farming. The import of European corn having been disrupted by the war, recommenced, undercutting the prices of the domestic yield. Cheap grains like wheat were imported from America. To combat the price differences, tariffs were installed to protect English farmers, becoming known as the corn laws. Buying expensive English grain caused hardship for the poor as the price of bread became prohibitive, but it benefitted landowners. This was compounded by having to feed larger families because of a surge in population. Riots ensued; in some areas those who were instigating civil unrest were hanged or transported. The aristocracy increased their land holdings, but the gentry also gained. The smallholders sold their land to larger estates and rural poverty took hold, Wiltshire being particularly badly affected.[93]

Major William soon settled back into life in Wiltshire. His role as Commander of the Mere branch of the South West Wiltshire Militia overseen by the Earl of Pembroke at Wilton House was not full-time employment, so he occupied himself in the gentleman's pursuit of hunting. As a young man he would have given chase to roe and fallow deer with William Chafen's hounds at Chettle House, at the heart of the forested hills and valleys of Cranborne

Chase with his good friend Thomas Grove Jnr. Sometimes they were joined by Thomas's brothers, William and George.[94] They hunted woodcock, hare, pheasant, rabbit and partridge.

In 1819, William married. His wife was twenty-year-old Eleanor Michell, the daughter of Thomas Michell of Standen House near Hungerford, Berkshire. It is possible they met at Compton Chamberlayne, the Penruddock's family estate (known as Compton) as the Penruddock and Michell families were close.

Following their wedding, they travelled to Italy, France and Switzerland. This would be one of many excursions William would undertake to Europe, to discover the continent in peace time. They stayed in Paris for five weeks, William wrote: 'We will never tire of Paris – nor, I hope, of each other.'[95] Moving on across France to Switzerland, some of the journey was through woods filled with wild boar and wolves. William disliked being jolted in the 'cabriolet or gig' and preferred to ride behind it, leaving Eleanor in the crammed carriage. The top was piled with their luggage and a man was employed just to keep an eye on it.[96]

The newly married Chafyn-Groves were away for ten weeks. There was happiness the following year with the arrival of a son called John. This would have brought the family both joy and relief. After so many generations of childless marriages and sideways moves from cousins and nephews (Major William's father had been a fifth son) to source a close male relative from the family pedigree, there was continuity at last. The heir now had an heir. The future of Zeals House was assured. Although christened John, William and Eleanor would refer to their new son as Chafin.[97]

After another excursion to Paris three years later, they rented a house called Slades in East Knoyle, best known as the birthplace of Sir Christopher Wren.[98] It was a handsome house on the estate of Clouds, Major William now having the owner, his friend John Still, as a neighbour and landlord. The following year, on 24th January 1825, through the thick snow typical of the harsh Victorian winters, William walked to Hindon after breakfast. 'Mr Armer came and dined with me and about half after 7 in the evening – Eleanor was brought to bed of a daughter.'[99] Her given name was Julia Elizabeth.

With their household established, situated between Zeals and Salisbury for easy access to both, the young family carried on a rural life of visiting and receiving friends, going to church on Sundays and country walks. William noticed that young Chafin was fond of seeing stagecoaches 'as I used to be, and he seems

to enjoy singing'.[100] As well as his Wiltshire Militia duties and
attending freemason meetings, overseeing estate management for
the aging Aunt Chafin at Zeals took more and more time. He dealt
with matters as they arose. On one occasion an old woman from
Black Dog lodge at Zeals was robbed. The robber came before
Thomas Grove Snr who committed him to Salisbury gaol. William
would ride around the estate visiting tenant farmers to discuss
farming conditions, which changed frequently with the weather.
He also organised repairs to the cottages, fences, gates and barns as
needed. There were accounts to be handwritten in ledgers, banking
at Hoare's and decisions about stocking of animals with the tenant
farmer at the home farm, called Manor Farm.

Sporting activities were also a regular feature of William's life.
Thomas Grove Jnr was a regular hunting companion and having
married, had rented Wincombe Park near Shaftesbury from Major
Gordon.[101] '25th May. Dinner at Wincombe. Farquarson, Burlton,
Capt. Benett, Mr and Mrs and Miss Helyar (dull as ever) William,
George and Charlotte Grove and Mr and Mrs Michell were there.'[102]
Major William also often went to Ferne for dinner with Thomas Grove
Snr, and the Grove boys would go to Zeals to dine with Aunt Chafin.

With a young family, William's life was now settled. Before the
Peninsular War, he had been an Eton scholar, and later became
a Fellow of King's College, Cambridge. The family lived in The
Close, Salisbury, where his father Dr Charles had practised as a
physician. His widowed mother (Elizabeth née Acland) remained in
Salisbury at Odstock close to William's younger brothers, the Revd
Charles and his wife (who were childless and lived in the Rectory
at Odstock), and Harry (Henry Thomas) who was only three when
his father died. Sister Maria lived in Mere and in 1826 married
George Bullock of North Coker Manor, near Yeovil in Somerset.
Unmarried Fanny (Frances Harriet) who was William's favourite
sibling, lived at Zeals House with Aunt Chafin.[103]

Mother Elizabeth was hoping to have the companionship of her
daughter Fanny when the elderly Aunt Chafin died. But sweet-
natured Fanny, aged forty, announced in 1828 that she was to marry
Charlotte Groves' brother, William Grove, who was living at Ferne
House, aged thirty-eight. Aunt Chafin would have been delighted
that her Chafyn-Grove niece was marrying her Grove nephew, but
both sides of the family had reservations. Charlotte wrote, 'The old
lady [Mrs Charles Chafyn-Grove] demurs about the match. My
father similarly curious.'[104] The pair had been close friends since
childhood. The title 'Commander William Grove R.N. Retired',

sounded more accomplished than the reality. William made a promising start to his career on the *Orestes* when it was recaptured from the French. However, when in the East Indies, instead of being promoted at the taking of Batavia, he underwent a court martial, for 'behaving in a cruel and oppressive manner to the company of HMS *Hecate*, contrary to the 33rd Article of War'.[105] A letter from Lord Pembroke to his father reinstated him in the Navy, but at the bottom of the list of lieutenants. He joined the *Primrose* sloop off the downs and was retired early. As a third son on half pay, his marriage prospects were slim.

In October 1831, Major William was stationed with his family in Salisbury as a special constable. The County suffered periodically from agricultural distress in the Swing Riots due to poor working conditions for farm labourers, and the use of farm machines. There were arrests and deportations to Australia. Civil unrest again erupted, this time over electoral reform. It was gaining momentum across the country as the second Reform Bill had been voted down by the House of Lords. Charlotte Grove recalled in September, 'There have been many ricks of wheat and barley burnt at Broad Chalke,' and in mid-October, 'The rioters have been attacking Lord Digby's and the clergymen at Sherborne, and at Yeovil sad riots, where the yeomanry at last fired on the mob and dispersed them.'[106] The protestors wanted greater representation for the industrialising towns and to get rid of the rotten boroughs. In Salisbury, Major William wrote, 'A great influx of people into the town, all went off quietly.' Duty not required, he dined at General Michell's. 'The Michells on their way to Compton stopped with us for an hour, and Mrs Michell being unwell remained the night.' The following day, 'Laetitia Penruddock came for Mrs Michell and I set off in a one-horse phaeton hired of Garrett after breakfast for Zeals. On my way I called on Mr John Still. Walked to Mere, and rode to Captain Hoare's and back. Left Zeals at half past nine. Stopped an hour at Knoyle and paid visits, got home to dinner.'[107] The following day, 'The Miss Penruddocks [Laetitia and Elizabeth] came to us, Elizabeth, Julia and I went to a moving panorama at the assembly rooms in the evening.' Towards the end of the month, all was peaceful in Salisbury, 'walked with Julia over Harnham Hill'.[108]

On 29th October, Major William wrote, 'A fine dry morning. A fine day ensued.' Meanwhile, Bristol was besieged by an angry mob of up to five hundred mostly young men when an anti-reform judge arrived in Queen Square for a dinner in his honour at the Mansion House. The local militia and civil authorities were taken by surprise and charged into the mob, escalating violence, which ended in the death of a member of the public. The judge and mayor were stoned and sought refuge in the Mansion House. Many constables abandoned the fight and late into the night the rioters stormed the Mansion House, the local dragoons shooting two men dead, the judge and mayor escaping over the roof to a safe house. The building was looted, the wine cellar emptied and then torched. On the second day, the civil authorities being unable to control the crowd, sought military back-up. Confusion over the roles of the military and civic authorities caused chaos. The 3rd Dragoon Guards were sanctioned by Home Secretary Melbourne, who was loath for the mob to be charged unless absolutely necessary.[109] There were memories of the Peterloo massacre. The Guards arrived under Colonel Brereton but had no orders as they had to come from Bristol Corporation and Mayor Pinney, so he did not deploy his men. The local 14th Dragoons charged a mob entering the Customs House and killed two men, but the militia were overwhelmed when defending the city's gaols, and prisoners were set free. The mob, armed with torches, sticks and looted railings, caused extensive damage, mostly in Queen Square. Burnt-out buildings included the Customs House, the New Gaol, which was attacked with sledgehammers, the Bishop's Palace, warehouses, townhouses, and the excise office. 250 people were injured. As the riots in Bristol ran out of control, on the last day of October, the Mayor, Charles Pinney, finally gave the orders for the Square to be cleared after a night of drunkenness and looting and deaths.[110] Isambard Kingdom Brunel became special constable for Bristol.

In Salisbury, Major William was dealing with his demanding mother who was staying at Odstock. 'Julia [aged 6] walked to Odstock and back with me and was not at all fatigued. I saw only my mother, my brothers being in Salisbury. She had planned to go to Coker [North Coker House in Somerset] to visit her daughter Maria, but was then not well enough to travel to Yeovil.'[111]

'Part of the 52nd Light infantry under the command of Colonel Fergusson which only landed from Halifax on Saturday last at Portsmouth marched in today on their way to Bristol, where the riots have been destructive to property and life.' But Major William seemed to have other things on his mind that day. 'We had a dinner party with Mr Jacob, Miss Broadhurst, Miss Eyre, Mr Grove and my brother Harry. This day the purchasing of game is lawful and we took advantage of the new act of Parliament.'

Life carried on peacefully in Salisbury, and while Eleanor, heavily pregnant, and Julia visited Major William's mother in Odstock in a fly, brother Harry having gone fox hunting out of the area, he reflects,

> Heavy baggage of the 52nd came in today. I went out at night as Special Constable in The Close – all was tranquil and at 10 o'clock the police constable was dismissed. The disturbances at Bristol, Worcester and Coventry have proved the good spirit of the military, and ought to be an encouragement to the citizens of towns to unite against every beginning of rioting.[112]

While Bristol was still reeling in the aftermath of the destruction of their corporate buildings and loss of life, the Salisbury Corporation held a reception for their local dignitaries. Major William was entertained in the Council House.

> Exclusive of the members of the Corporation there were present only Lord Radnor and his brothers, the Messrs Wadham, Wyndham, Jacob, Fowler, Grove, Ambrose Hulsey, and one or two others whose names I did not know.[113] The party altogether amounted to between fifty to sixty; it was the first civil feast I had attended and altogether I passed a very pleasant evening – the wine was good.[114]

But by mid-November, 'The public mind is now occupied with the Cholera which has shown itself in Sunderland,' wrote Major William. The conversation at Ferne was also focussed on this new health concern with Charlotte Grove adding, 'flannel round the loins is recommended.'[115]

The Chafyn-Grove family had decided to go to Bath in December for six months and they settled on a house in Russell Street. With Eleanor preoccupied with the forthcoming birth, William arranged his own social life, enjoying playing commerce with his army friends and going to the race meetings at Lansdowne, preferring the company of Old Etonians. Invited to many parties and balls, he attends but generally lacks enthusiasm. 'Went to Lady Acland's [his mother's family] and thence to a large party at Lady Bateman's – of the gaiety of it, my being home by 10 p.m. will be a proof. Other events he did enjoy: 'Dined with Lord Carrington at his Hotel, and went to the theatre to hear that wonderful and non-human creature, Paganini – Lady Stanhope, Wm Somerset, Capt Courtenay and Mr Cooke accompanying us.' He also accompanied Mr and Mrs Buthill, who 'took one to Mr Beckford's tower.[116] 'The inside of this structure consists of a few <u>very</u> small rooms, ornamented with some pictures and china.' During the day, William walked with Julia in Sydney Gardens, and to the Penruddocks, and in mid-December, the 12-year-old Chafin arrived by the Reading coach. He had been collected from his boarding school in Richmond and arrived with the Michell family who lived at Speen, near Reading. Major William 'took Chafin to the circus in Monmouth Street where there was some good riding and loose rope swinging'. Julia meanwhile was being invited out by her parents' friends to dinner and went to a ball.

Christmas having 'ushered in a fine dry day', Major William went to Bristol. A Special Commission would open in the New Year. Mayor Pinney was to be tried for incompetence, and Colonel Brereton had been court-martialled for failing to instruct his men. 'I saw the demolition of Ireson's [Queen] Square, The Bishop's Palace, the Jail, with feelings of shame and sorrow of such wanton destruction.[117] I called on Mrs Pinney.'[118]

After walking with Chafin to the ball ground, at 12 o'clock Major William attended a small dull party at Lady Acland's, where the family 'learned of Colonel Brereton's death'. Charlotte Grove's diary, is more forthcoming: 'Poor Colonel Brereton shot himself, his conduct being enquired into during the late Bristol riots from derangement.' Major William wrote, 'Chafin and I were taken by Mrs Pearce and her son to Bristol, we drove about the town for two hours and then returned to Bath and accepted her offer to dinner.'

Chafin had to get back to school. He went to Speen by the Reading coach, 'his uncle Michell accompanying him, tho' nearly being too late, as usual. Four men hanged today at Bristol for riots.'[119] William then went to Bristol, 'to attend the Court Martial of Captain Warrington 3rd Dragoon Guards which was much crowded, and it was not without difficulty that I obtained a division, his defence was proceeding. I called on Mrs Pinney and left Bristol of 5 p.m. by York Road.'[120]

On 24th February, 'Palmer acquainted me with the birth of my daughter. Mr Cam attended Eleanor for about an hour: I was imposed much today in writing letters, and then dined with Lady Acland meeting her nephew Capt Lewis.' Julia, aged seven, and her father dined at various friend's and relative's houses in the next few days when 'Mr Cam visited Eleanor assiduously.' Mostly, William spent the next few days quietly walking, to the ball ground, a long walk in the direction of Box, and with Major Dashwood to

Claverton and Coombe. He also went to the Abbey and had 'a good swim in the Bath solo'. As Eleanor recovered, she went out in Lady Acland's carriage and Mrs Michell called.

Now the baby was born, Major William was able to leave Bath. Duties had to be attended to at Zeals and he needed to check on his aunt.

> ...set off by the Pool[e] coach at 9 o'clock for Zeals – got down at Stourton and called on Capt. Hoare and Sir Richard – walked to Zeals and found Mrs Chafyn-Grove well. Walked to Bayford [adjacent to the Zeals estate in Somerset], saw Mr N Messiter [family solicitor of Wincanton] and heard a bad account of his wife – in my walk home I called at Silton [adjoining estate to Zeals, in Dorset] and found the Revd. Harry Martin in a very invalid state.

The following day Major William went to church at Mere where there was a full congregation and 'fair clergymen'. Busily engaged in business in Mere, he then rode Mr. White's mare to Knoyle and Shaftesbury and home to dinner at Zeals.[121] With his love of walking, and in the warm evening sun, he called on Harry Martin again.

Before returning to Bath, he went to stay with his friend Captain Henry Hoare at Stourhead, where they strolled in the picturesque grounds in the crisp spring landscape.[122] As return visits were the custom, Henry and Richard Hoare and others were added to a dinner party at Zeals the following day. Sir Richard Colt Hoare knew Elizabeth Chafyn-Grove well. When he was compiling *The History of Modern Wiltshire* a decade earlier, he spent time with her, evaluating the family pedigree and looking at the Zeals portraits. He was interested in a miniature painting of Hugh Grove and the story of his beheading, so he borrowed the painting and had it engraved so he could use the picture in his history of the county.[123]

Once back in Bath, Major William found the town dreary. Although he went to the Pump Room, he was uninterested in gossip. He went to a christening party at the Penruddocks but 'turned my back soon on the company', followed by a visit to the Abbey where he heard a 'tiresomely long sermon from the Bishop of Bath'. Following the announcement of the resignation of Lord Grey's Ministry and Julia's vaccination against smallpox, there was the christening of their new daughter, to be called Maria Catherine.

After the service at Walcot Church the Chafyn-Groves held a party at their house.

Another opportunity to leave Bath arose when Mrs Still needed a 'conducteur' to accompany her in her carriage to London. 'Went by Chippenham and Calne and stopped at Speen to see Mrs. Michell. Arrived in town 6.30 p.m. Took up quarters at Hatchett's in Piccadilly.'[124] Whilst in town, he visited Hoare's in Stone Square, dined with the Hoare family in Eaton Square, went to a Levee in St. James's, visited shops and saw his friend Penruddock. He took time to go to Richmond to see young Chafin, taking him to Twickenham where he bet on 'Copland'. After lunch with his son, Major William took the boy back to school at Richmond. He returned to town, and subsequently to Bath where the coach arrived at the White Hart in the evening.

Towards the end of the family's stay in Bath there was a meeting on the High Common of the Political Unions of Bath, Frome and Bradford (on-Avon). The procession through the street consisted of about fifteen hundred persons. It went off peacefully. Still fearful of a revolt on the scale of the French Revolution, in 1832 The Reform Bill was finally passed. After a final walk in Sydney Gardens with Julia, Major William went back to the house to pack.

The following year, in the middle of the summer of 1833, William and Eleanor's world was turned upside down. Fifteen-month-old Maria Catherine was thriving, and Julia was a joy. Their hope for the future of Zeals was with their twelve-year-old son Chafin – John Chafin. But they suffered a tragedy that befell so many Victorian families. On 9th June, William's heir, his playful son Chafin, died suddenly.

Being a military man, William liked to have a plan. Julia, as his elder surviving daughter would have to be well educated, and he would take her with him when he visited tenants on the estate. Perhaps he could allow her to live in Zeals House for life with the same rights as a widow, although as a woman she would not be able to own property. Until she married and had children of her own, his heir was George Troyte-Bullock, the son of his sister Maria Caroline and her husband George Bullock. Neither of William's two brothers Charles and Harry had children, and his sister Fanny married William Grove after her child-bearing years. After losing John/Chafin, he would have reflected that of his parents' five children, only one grandson had survived, although he and the Bullocks both had daughters.

At the end of May in 1838, when Julia was thirteen years old, younger sister, Maria Catherine died at the age of six. To help the family in their grief, Major William planned an excursion to Europe. They set off for Italy in August that year, travelling through France and Switzerland. Unlike a Grand Tour of the aristocracy, the journey would not be about collecting, but of sight-seeing, visiting places of interest. Included would be historical churches, houses in a variety of architecture, and walking in the Alps collecting wild flowers. They soaked up the cultures and landscape of a peaceful Europe and were away from home for fourteen months.

The future of Zeals House was at risk. Major William had no choice but to place all his hopes and dreams for the future in Julia.

PART II

VICTORIAN

CHAPTER SEVEN

Church

At the beginning of 1840, in the year Queen Victoria married her cousin Prince Albert of Saxe-Coburg and Gotha in St. James's Palace, Aunt Chafin's formidable sister Philippa (Aunt Grove) died. Major William was pleased to learn that his sweet sister Fanny and her husband William Grove would inherit Philippa's Netherhampton House on the outskirts of Salisbury. Charlotte, who was close to Aunt Grove wrote, 'Accompanied Franny Grove from Netherhampton to Odstock to see her mother, Mrs Charles Chafyn-Grove. She is very well, the same age as my father. It will be a great pleasure to her, Fanny living so near.'[125]

Major William could not have predicted the next turn of events for his family soon after their return to Wiltshire from their Continental tour. He was to be a father again at the age of fifty-four, but more worrying was that Eleanor was forty-one. The chances of having an uncomplicated birth in Victorian England in 1840 at that age were low, but on 25th September a healthy baby was born in Clifton, Bristol, possibly in the Georgian Hospital there. It was a boy. The baby was baptized William Chafyn-Grove although, once again, within the family he would be known as Chafyn, but with a different spelling than his late brother John Chafin. Life would change again for William and Eleanor, for fifteen-year-old Julia – and eventually for Zeals House, which they were yet to inherit from cousin Chafin.

Although cousin Chafin had inherited Zeals, it is likely that Major William continued helping his cousin with the running of the estate as he had grown to know the farmers, groundsmen and the land management under Elizabeth. Continuity and stability were important to tenants. With his love of the countryside, being tall, slim and fit he walked long distances, and continued his evening

Zeals Church.

saunters past the lake through the Zeals parkland laid to lawn with mature trees. Across the fields over the border into Dorset by the River Stour he would arrive at the adjoining two-thousand-acre hamlet of Silton, later to become part of the Zeals estate. He enjoyed the company of the cultured and artistic Harry Martin at The Rookery, now Lower Silton. They were both Cambridge men at differing times. Harry was from a family of clergymen, his son, also called Harry, becoming Rector of Silton Church.

Cousin Chafin's family were clergymen as well. His father the Revd Hugh Chafyn-Grove (known as Hugh Grove) and Chafin's brother William Frederick Grove, were both Rectors of Melbury Abbas Church across the border near Shaftesbury in Dorset, the latter for over fifty years.

In the new Victorian Era, the gaiety of the Regency period was replaced with a more sombre outlook. Religious seriousness became pronounced with acceptance of virtue and temperance. The gentry became more regular attenders of church services, and they expected their tenants to follow their lead. Although the gentry subsidised their churches, there was a shift from the estate workers towards non-conformist alternatives, notably the Methodists, based for the most part on the preaching of John Wesley in the preceding century. The movement took hold in the industrialised towns and gradually spread to rural areas. Although the gentry tolerated their tenant farmers' and their families' non-conformist faith, there was the risk of a bandwagon for the evangelical faiths threatening the control the landlords enjoyed and promoting free-thinking.[126] There were also Roman Catholic reading rooms, but they were in the minority and ignored, their followers receiving no visits from their landlord's family. In Mere, the Primitive Methodist Chapel on North Street was opened in 1846. The Plymouth Brethren met in a room in the Ship Inn, and a substantial Congregational Chapel was planned, which eventually opened in 1868.

Mere Church of St. Michael the Archangel, a handsome mid-14th century parish church with Norman origins in the gothic style, was built with the traditional north and south chapels in the late medieval style. The tall spire is a landmark seen from many miles away. It was a mile and a half from Zeals village, and although the inhabitants of Zeals House would arrive for services by carriage, it was a long walk for the tenants and their children, especially in bad weather. But the rise of competing faiths was the overriding issue. The campaign for a church or a chapel-of-ease for Zeals village was first proposed by Chafin's brother, Revd William Frederick Grove, in 1845.[127]

Having established some public subscriptions, William Frederick gained approval from the Dean of Salisbury for a new church. It would be dedicated to St Martin, after a former chapel known to be in the village in 1220.[128] Also on Zeals Green would be a parsonage house and school. The cost was £3,000, but as the village was poor, the benefice of the vicarage was modest.

The architect engaged by the Church of England to design and build the new church was George Gilbert Scott, who had been working in Wiltshire and Somerset with his then partner, William Moffatt, building workhouses. A decade before they had built the workhouse in Mere in the Tudor style.[129] Scott's brief was for a church for three hundred persons with extra seating in a gallery for fifty. When working on Zeals church, Scott was introduced by Major William's friend Harry Martin to a young artistic village boy from Silton called Alfred Bell. Impressed by the young lad, the architect offered him a place in his studio in London.[130] Once there, Bell met Richard Clayton and they formed the partnership of Clayton and Bell, becoming successful Victorian stained-glass makers. Later, in Scott's Albert Memorial in London's Hyde Park, Clayton and Bell produced some of the decorations.

Zeals Church, with a stumpy tower – the spire which was not added until 1876 – was consecrated in 1846 by the Bishop of Salisbury.

Mere Church.

Following the opening, the Dean and one hundred guests were invited by William Frederick to his brother Chafin's Zeals House for a celebration.[131] Unwell, William Frederick died the following year.[132] The school room was built by Scott and Moffatt at the same time, but it would take another two decades before the rectory was finally built.

An early career work of Scott's, Zeals Church is high-Victorian Gothic in the Decorated style, lofty, with an unembellished interior set in a churchyard, later extended. For the Chafyn-Groves of Zeals House, as benefactors, it effectively became an estate church and gave them more power over the tenants' ecclesiastical and economic lives, as well as the ability to choose the clergy.

William and Eleanor with their family were living at Corsham in Wiltshire when Chafin died in 1851 at the advanced age of seventy-one. In later life he was cared for by two loving nieces, daughters of his sister Jane. The two girls commemorated their uncle's life in Mere Church, 'In memory of their beloved uncle Chafin Grove, this window was restored by his affectionate nieces, Jane Auber and Johanna Maria Harvey.'

Major William learnt of his inheritance in an unusual way. On 17th June a local farmer, William White, who had long wanted to take the tenancy of Zeals Farm, was told by the agent that the letting had already been agreed. This was true, but Chafin had not signed the papers. On hearing of Chafin's death, White immediately galloped across Wiltshire to see Major William in order to plead for the tenancy, to which William graciously agreed.

The family moved in to Zeals House in June, in the middle of the bustle of haymaking on the farms. On Sundays, the family went in their carriage either to St. Michael the Archangel in Mere, or St Martin's in Zeals. Sometimes they worshipped in both, with matins in one and evensong in the other. Dressed in a Sunday bonnet, Julia loved going to church, as much as young Chafyn tried to avoid it.

CHAPTER EIGHT

Family

William and Eleanor and their two children settled into living at Zeals House. For Julia and Chafyn there were endless walks, boating on the lake, the horses in the stables and dogs kept in the kennels alongside. But Chafyn's dog ran in and out of the house.

As a father of an eleven-year-old boy, Major William would most likely have sent him to the boarding preparatory school in Richmond previously attended by John/Chafin. He would have taken him out of school for outings when business took him to town, as he did with his late son. As an army officer who liked discipline, in his advancing years Chafyn may have tested his patience. A strict code of behaviour encouraged by the queen, and especially Prince Albert, was one of conformity and austerity. He was doubtless a good father, instructing his son in the ways of the countryside and the intricacies of farming, but controlling the boy was not made easy by his loving mother spoiling him and letting him do as he pleased. Chafyn would have bonded with his father while hunting and shooting. Dinners would have been serious affairs for friends,

William Chafyn-Grove
(Chafyn).

relatives and neighbours, with discussions on local and national politics – the family being shire Tories – country matters, farm yields, and hunting adventures. Chafyn would have taken part in these discussions at a young age as part of his education, his father aware of his own advancing years. After dinner was served, Julia was pushed out to the drawing room with her mother and with the other ladies present while the men passed the port.

Despite the generation gap, Julia and Chafyn were always close and the relationship between the two was more important to them than any with their individual friends. An impression emerges of a daughter close to her father and a son close to his mother. There is evidence for this supposition which would surface much later, when a pair of portrait oil paintings were removed from the Zeals House drawing room, one of Major William, the other of Julia. They may well have been commissioned before Chafyn was born or was away at school, but a lack of a matching portrait of Eleanor is unusual, although there was an oil on board portrait of her playing the mandolin. This woman with long, wavy light-brown hair was a proficient pianist. Although it was customary for girls to learn the piano, Chafyn was also taught to play and inherited his mother's musical genes. The well-used Bechstein grand piano was in a corner of the hall.

Julia sang, enjoyed going to church, and followed the acceptable manners of the times, but she was happiest when she was outdoors. She loved the freedom this allowed her. Being an expert rider, she never felt more unleashed than when she was galloping on the downs alone, sometimes in raw weather, enjoying the changing rural scenery. She would relax, let herself go and relied on her horse to navigate its way through the stones on the rough tracks and the flocks of south downs sheep. Returning home, she was exhilarated.

Trapped by the proprieties of Victorian virtues of moral duty and modesty, options were limited for Victorian women. Julia envied Chafyn's freedom to choose his career, to harness his talents and to be able to fulfil his dreams and make a difference in the world. She was unable to go to London spontaneously without the cumbersome procedure of arranging an escort, and a ladies' maid to accompany her, while Chafyn could jump on a coach to town on a whim.

Knowing that the only option open to Victorian woman was to marry, she rebelled against it. She rejected the idea of a man to look after her while she looked after his house, as her life would be severely curtailed by a husband who was her master. And she would never find a man who lived up to her idealised father. The alternative was to be an old maid, a burden to her family, or being a companion to her mother as she became elderly, but she did not think that far ahead.

Julia showed no inclination to find a partner for life, and if suitors were suggested or put in her path, a mixture of parental control of potential suitors or her avoidance put an end to it. There was a story from the village that Julia was to become engaged on her coming of age to a young farmer, and that the engagement was hastily untangled because he had 'got a girl into trouble'.[133] She may well have been flattered by the attentions of a young man flirting with her as she grew into a young woman. The family would surely not have approved of any suitor for their only daughter unless he was from a neighbouring estate or a cousin. If the story is true, the ending of the dalliance would not have been a sufficient reason to forgo any subsequent marriage, as no damage would have been done to Julia's reputation or her heart. It is also significant that if this incident took place, it could not have been at Zeals. She did not move into Zeals House for another thirteen years after her coming of age. Being an attractive, accomplished woman with a good dowry, she would surely have had many chances.

Julia Chafyn-Grove, *c.*1855.

At times, Julia was riddled with self-doubt and occasionally her confidence slipped, but although irked by her restrictions, she had no choice but to comply with the customs and conform to her pre-destined position in life. She was born too soon to benefit from women pushing the boundaries. The stirrings of female emancipation were thirty years away. She did needlework, painted, sketched. She was well travelled and spoke fluent French. But although formal education for girls was poorly provided for, Major William would have located a good governess to tutor his beloved daughter to widen her world. Julia developed an enjoyment and knowledge of art, architecture, theatre, opera – and books. The library at Zeals House was well used by her. In mid-Victorian England she was not restricted like Charlotte Grove, of her father's generation, to reading Walter Scott and Jane Austen. There were Tennyson's poems, Macaulay's *History of England*, an original edition of Chaucer and novels in French to absorb, the house library being a source of inspiration and self-education. She learnt about the Napoleonic Wars in great detail, imagining her father's involvement, which gave her comfort. Even before she lived at Zeals she was interested in religious works, copying extracts of theological and moral works into a notebook.[134]

Julia was intelligent but she was not socially confident. She had underlying insecurities that would surface from time to time throughout her unfulfilled life. She was also headstrong and knew what was best, but not necessarily best for herself. Having periods of introspection and doubt, Julia also had a total lack of awareness of how she was perceived. She was not welcoming or warm with people and raised unnecessary barriers. She generally thought the worst of everyone until they proved to her that they were worth knowing. 'They grew on acquaintance' is a common thread throughout her diaries, and once they had grown on her she would allow herself to be friendly. Always immaculately dressed, she loved shopping for the latest fashions, making several trips per season to London and absorbing the latest trends when in Paris. Although she enjoyed her trips to town for a change of scenery, she was always happy to leave the city and return to Zeals House.

Despite her irritations, Julia was contented with absorbing country life at Zeals House, with the scenic walks, with wandering to the stables to talk to the grooms and to give treats to the horses, which she loved. Within the confines of the estate, she could be outdoors, teaching Chafyn the flora and fauna of the changing seasons. They would have crunched through the beech leaves in the wood and picked up acorns and conkers in the autumn. In winter, dressed in warm scarves and gloves they would have snowball fights and watch the groundsmen breaking the ice on the lake, taking it to the icehouse. Then there were the first signs of a seasonal change as the first snowdrops forced their way to the surface. In spring, Julia would pick posies of primroses for her mother to put into vases. Chafyn would climb trees, the gardeners may have made him a tree house so he could observe the green and spotted woodpeckers and the tawny owls in the dusk. Chafyn's love of botany would remain with him for life. As a child when visiting Uncle Chafin with her father, Julia would have walked through the meadows, making daisy chains, looked for four-leafed clovers and played in the two-storey gazebo by the south drive. She would climb to the top of this garden folly to take in the sweeping views and read peacefully. Chafyn also liked the folly. He would take his shotgun to reduce the astonishingly high population of rabbits. The Zeals parkland is laid to lawn with ancient beech trees and a view of the lake to the south. The folly and the icehouse sit by an ornamental dry stone arched bridge towards the south drive, later to be restored. It is a copy of one at Stourhead, indicating an eighteenth-century picturesque design, although no records of the garden layout have been traced.

Major William was concerned about how Chafyn would turn out as an adult. The boy was so mischievous and full of fun and pranks that he doubted he would make a responsible estate owner, while Julia was strong and capable. But the father misread his son's character. Later he was accused of being immoral and unspiritual, but he was also responsible, disciplined about work, a natural leader and very careful with money. He had an energy and enthusiasm for every new adventure, an aptitude for music and was a gifted writer. Julia seldom deviated from being serious, while Chafyn did not take himself seriously and could see the humour in some of the situations they found themselves in.

Julia wanted this idyllic family country life to go on forever. But it did change. Still determinedly single at the age of thirty-four in 1859, her father died in London on 25th June. Chafyn, nineteen and at Cambridge, inherited the estate.

Chafyn came home immediately and took charge. Journeys to Zeals were now quicker since the Salisbury and Yeovil Railway Company had opened Gillingham Station a month previously, with a new line from Salisbury. It made it easier to visit his mother regularly. He knew the tenant farmers and the villagers well; his father would have seen to that. Visiting them at this sad time and doing the rounds was important to give farmers reassurance that nothing would alter. Once again, continuity and stability were important. At the end of the university term Chafyn spent time going through the estate papers. On 28th July, a month after his father's death, Chafyn set off for Waddon Manor in Portesham, Dorset, to inspect the Waddon Estate he had also inherited.[135] He climbed up into the attic to retrieve all the stored papers, including the Bullen Reymes diaries from the time of Charles I, which had survived for over two hundred years and were in good condition.[136] He also took a portrait of Bullen Reymes and one of Anne Coker, together with two seascape oil paintings by the 17th-century Flemish painter Jan Van Kessel of Antwerp, books and a sun-dial.[137]

During the summer Chafyn visited Ferne House where Thomas Fraser Grove was now running the Ferne Estate. The Groves had experienced their share of upset when Charlotte's brother, the eldest son Thomas Jnr died two years before his father, Thomas

Snr. Second son, John M.D., who was living in Close Gate in Salisbury practising as a physician had to abandon the career he loved to take over the estate before he, too, died. Thomas Fraser Grove (Tom Grove) was his eldest son.

It was an important meeting for Chafyn at Ferne as Tom Grove was one of his trustees until he came of age. His other trustee was originally his mother's Michell brother, but this had been changed in a codicil either through the death of Michell or a change of heart. Instead, George Troyte-Bullock had been added as a trustee, and until Chafyn had children of his own, would be the next heir to Zeals. It was normal for heirs of heirs and sometimes more generations to be mentioned in wills, every precaution being taken to secure the future of the house. Major William's wife Eleanor was made the sole executor of her husband's will. It is a very short, business-like document made two years before he died, with Julia being able to stay in Zeals House with her own income, and also receive his widow Eleanor's income upon the latter's death. Everything else was left to Chafyn.[138]

Being brought up in the company of older parents and because of the age gap with Julia, effectively Chafyn was like an only child. He would therefore have spent more time than most children in adult company, resulting in him being confident and opinionated. By the time he went to Eton College he was more mature than most of his contemporaries. His fun-loving disposition belied an underlying intelligence, an acute observation and a perception of people far beyond his years. By the time he arrived at Trinity College, Cambridge, he was a fully formed adult. The choice of college is a diversion from the normal family route to St John's. This could have been Chafyn's choice so he could be with school friends who were heading there, as he had no siblings at the university. Although young, he was ready to take over the estate and knew exactly what he would do when he came of age.

Aside from taking charge of the estate and the house, Chafyn also took charge of his own life and had already decided on his career after he graduated. Like his father, he wanted to enter the services by becoming a Guards officer. He did not want Zeals to be a full-time occupation, so to give him the freedom to pursue his favoured course he employed Mr E. P. Squarey of Rawlence and Squarey of Salisbury as his land agent to collect rents and take charge of banking and accounts, instead of his father's land agent, Messiters.

E. P. Squarey.

To have a break during the summer and for Julia to deal with her grief, the siblings took a two-week holiday in August, travelling to Hamburg and then to the pretty villages on the banks of the Elbe, before reaching their destination of Heligoland.[139] The two had visited the island in a paddle-steamer from 'Hamburgh' before, with their parents when Chafyn was a very small boy. Popular as a holiday destination for Germans, the island had no horses, but plenty of bathing machines. The small population spoke 'low German' but was strangely a British territory for most of the nineteenth century.

Even before his twenty-first birthday Chafyn had taken charge of the local Mere Rifle Company formed in 1859, which helped to provide references for his chosen career. A letter addressed to The Officer Commanding, Shaftesbury Volunteers, Shaftesbury, went by penny post from Mere on 7th September 1860. It was written on Zeals House notepaper, embossed with a talbot passant in an oval surround, and read:

> Sir, I should be glad to know if your company will attend the review at Salisbury on the 26th. If so, should you feel inclined to join with our company (and that at Gillingham if possible)

in chartering a special train to take us to Salisbury which will be cheaper and more convenient than going up by the common trains, especially as having to be at Salisbury at 11 we should have to start by the early up train. Yr. Obt. Servant, W. Chafyn Grove, Commander, Mere Rifle Corps.[140]

On 25th September 1861, Chafyn came of age. He was still studying at Cambridge but came home for a big celebration for this special birthday. Hosting the party with his mother and Julia, guests included neighbours, family friends and his own friends. Cousins George and Alice Troyte-Bullock were there, Tom Grove and his wife Kate and other Groves from Ferne (but not Charlotte who had died the preceding year), Michell and Acland relatives, his father's brothers Uncles Charles and Harry from Salisbury, as well as Aunt Fanny and Uncle William Grove from Netherhampton. Nearby landowners would have been invited, the Morrisons of Fonthill and the Hoares of Stourhead, the Penruddocks of Compton Chamberlayne, but possibly not the Arundells from New Wardour Castle because they were Roman Catholic. Another family who would become increasingly important to Julia would be there – cousin Charles-Henry Grove with his wife Eliza, and the three eldest of their six daughters.[141] Uncle Harry, who even in his advanced years attended dances in Salisbury, danced all night. Neither Julia nor Chafyn liked dancing, but Julia made an exception for this momentous occasion. She watched her happy brother and reflected with pride, 'things are going so well for him.'

Chafyn lost no time and immediately became an Ensign and Lieutenant in the Coldstream Guards, and he had joined the local Mere freemasons.[142] His best friend was Arthur Myers, two years older than Chafyn, who joined the Army Medical Corp in the Coldstream Guards. Whenever Chafyn went to London he would see Myers as well as other friends, but doubtless it was Myers who mentored him to join the Coldstreamers. Although still at Cambridge, Chafyn met and befriended the other officers and was looking forward to an exciting career. He was already very well-travelled; his restless father having taken the family abroad on many trips across Europe to fashionable destinations.

The 1860s were a profitable and stable time for agriculture, the gentry being totally dependent on farming income for the upkeep of their manor houses and their way of life, as opposed to the aristocracy who spent more time in town, using their country Palladian mansions and vast estates for entertainment, sport and political status. Many aristocrats had supplementary income from land holdings in London and elsewhere. Chafyn, therefore, did not have to do too much management of the estate, although there was a constant buying and selling of small parcels of land, mostly for convenience. Selling more remote acres and buying adjoining smallholdings made management easier.

In the summer months, Julia and Chafyn would take the boat out of the boathouse or picnic on the small island in the round pond, which was filled with trout for the house. The island had been designed with arbour arches and planted with climbing roses. The Zeals gardeners would pick roses for the house and deadhead the withered ones. It was labour intensive to keep it in perfect order, but the family and future generations loved it.

By 1862, Chafyn had graduated from Cambridge with a BA in Classics.[143] As so often happened in his family, joy was followed by sorrow. On 11th November, his mother Eleanor died. It was devastating for Chafyn to lose his beloved mother, and Julia was very sympathetic. Later he would build a row of almshouses in Zeals village dedicated to Eleanor – notably, not to both parents. It ended an era, and the grief lingered for both Julia and Chafyn. Together they set up a charitable foundation to help the poor and needy in Zeals and Mere as well as for good causes elsewhere. But the loss destabilized the balance of the house. Eleanor had been in charge of running the house and pastoral care of the village. Julia would walk to visit the poor with baskets of produce from the kitchen garden and game after shooting parties. Comforting the sick, Eleanor would often be accompanied by Julia who would now take on this role.

Discussions had already taken place between the siblings earlier in the year about how they would live together at Zeals. Julia wanted to stay in the house, so they were stuck with each other. Chafyn was very happy with this arrangement, as he loved his sister and she would look after the house and the staff while he looked after the estate, with the help of Squarey. But the layout of the Tudor house did not lend itself to having separate parts. Zeals House had not undergone changes for many years. Both Chafyn's father and uncle inherited late in life and lacked the enthusiasm for making changes to the house or carrying out disruptive repairs.

Chafyn often visited neighbouring landowners and they would have visited him. He regularly went to Ferne to see his cousin Tom Grove, as Tom had inherited a year before Chafyn on the death of his own father, John Grove M.D. They were both adjusting to their responsibilities. Tom, four years older than Julia, had married Katherine O'Grady (Kate) the daughter of an Irish aristocrat and had children, but he had much in common with Chafyn. Both were in charge of their branches of their local Wiltshire yeomanry and were often invited to the same hunting and shooting meets. The two of them would walk around the Ferne estate shooting rooks. They had both lived under strict fathers who expected them to conform to a rigid existence, so were now unleashed, and both knew what they wanted to do to their houses the moment they took over. As soon as Tom Grove inherited, he left the rented Seagry House near Chippenham. On his way to move into Ferne he collected the architect John Henry Hakewill from Wilton House. Extensive alterations were planned and were executed immediately. Chafyn had to wait until he came of age, but seeing Ferne House enlarged would have helped to form his ideas about substantially enlarging Zeals. As the estate was prosperous and well able to support the cost, there seemed no better time to create an enlarged house when he had all his life ahead of him, with Julia in her own quarters.

He wanted the house to remain in the Tudor style and to integrate the new part to match the old. He also wanted a new, large drawing room facing south towards the lake, and to create a comfortable residence for his generation. He needed a renowned architect, and he knew where to find one.

CHAPTER NINE

George Devey

When Chafyn visited the Fonthill estate, ten miles from Zeals, he walked around the with owner, Alfred Morrison, also a client of Rawlence and Squarey, who had witnessed the new estate buildings being built at Fonthill, followed by a visit to the Beckford Arms.

William Beckford had left the estate and his disastrous folly, Fonthill Abbey, in 1825, described by Kenneth Clark in *The Gothic Revival* as 'architecture meant to make one's hair stand on end'.[144] The estate was sold to James Farquhar and subsequently a part of the former estate was sold to the Marquess of Westminster so he could take advantage of the two rotten borough Parliamentary seats on the estate at Hindon.

James Morrison, a successful London haberdasher, purchased a portion of the Fonthill estate consisting of one thousand acres. His son Alfred inherited it from his father and embarked on a rebuilding programme including estate buildings and cottages which had been left neglected by Beckford and were in disrepair. Some of this work was carried out by J. B. Papworth, but they fell out over another Morrison property, Basildon Park in Berkshire. The architect he chose was George Devey. In *Fonthill Recovered*, Caroline Dakers suggests that Morrison chose Devey because of a lack of confidence in his own social status.[145] George Devey had been working with the de Rothschild family and the 2nd Duke of Sutherland, whose sister was married to Morrison's neighbour

George Devey.

the Marquess of Westminster, so Morrison may have liked the association of Devey's connections.[146] Mostly, Devey's clients were Whig aristocrats and friends of Gladstone.

George Devey had just finished a lodge on the Fonthill south drive opposite the Beckford Arms with high-pitched gables, a tightly packed thatched roof and tall diagonal chimney stacks – a typical Devey feature. The use of the charming half-timbered tile hung Old English Weald style would have been familiar in the home counties but unusual for Wiltshire and not generally taken up in the West Country. Chafyn was impressed by its charm and loveliness.

Alfred Morrison's next commission for Devey was to enhance the north entrance to the estate into an even more imposing one to give a sense of arrival for visitors and a sense that Morrison, too, had arrived. The architect added imposing, enormous urns and walling to give more substance to the existing monumental arch. Given a free hand, with no budget restriction, Devey built some quaint gabled cottages and estate buildings at Fonthill over many years. They were far removed from the local style of low-built humble brick and flint banded cottages.

Chafyn had no interest in the architect's clients but was excited to learn that George Devey was a prominent Victorian architect known for building country houses in the Tudor Gothic style. A meeting was arranged for Devey to visit Zeals House to carry out an inspection. By the end of 1862 plans had been proposed and approved and work had begun to create a substantially extended manor house for the twenty-two-year-old Victorian gentleman. Devey would have been shown every part of the existing Zeals House including the stables. The architect, being a lover of country life and sport, understood country people's love of horses. He kept a carriage and four roan horses himself, to which he gave a good deal of attention. Julia would have been consulted about her own rooms in her part of the house and appreciated the architect's love of horses.

Devey rarely kept his sketches, but he would have produced detailed artistic drawings in ink or watercolours of the proposed house to show Chafyn his ideas. Three-dimensional models made of cardboard were sometimes produced as an alternative to drawings, but they were fragile and would have failed to survive.

The skills Devey used at Zeals House were a culmination of astute observation, a deep knowledge of historic principles, and his imagination. He built in local materials, respected local traditions and wanted his houses to fit naturally into the surrounding landscape.[147] His first choice of career was to be an artist, and it was to painting in watercolour that he turned. Whilst at King's College School his tutor was John Sell Cotman, a prominent member of the Norwich School of Artists. Cotman worked in watercolour, and importantly for Devey's future career, architectural drawings favouring historic vernacular buildings.[148] Devey was later tutored by James Duffield Harding who taught drawing from nature and was admired by John Ruskin.[149] The lessons of watercolour painting and draughtsmanship never left him.

Chafyn and Devey both had an easy manner and were prone to making sarcastic remarks. They discovered a shared passion for weapons. Chafyn collected miscellaneous arms, including daggers, pistols, guns and swords. Devey's maternal grandfather Durs Egg, born in Basle, was gunmaker to George IV.[150] There were artistic genes in his family, too. Devey's maternal uncle was the Victorian artist Augustus Egg, R.A., who painted scenes of moral Victorian decline as seen in his triptych Past and Present, executed in 1858, now in Tate Britain. As Egg was only four years older than Devey it is more than likely that Devey was exposed to his uncle's art world and influenced by it. Young George's father, Frederick Devey, was a solicitor and encouraged his son to go into a profession. Being an artist was not viewed as a respectable career, so Devey chose architecture.[151] A pupillage was found for him, followed by a continental tour before he set up his own practice at 16 Great Marlborough Street in London. When his solicitor father was left a house in Hastings in Sussex, his son George lived and worked extensively in the County. Devey's launch commission was for Lord De L'Isle of Penshurst Place, cottage building in the Weald style, which led to extensive rebuilding of the house.[152] Then he was introduced to Sir Walter James, who had purchased Betteshanger House, a two-storey Regency villa in Kent.

James engaged the architect Anthony Salvin, 21 years older than Devey, for internal alterations and estate buildings but abandoned him in favour of Devey in 1856.[153] He had seen Devey's work and wanted an older looking house. The work of the Middle Ages appealed to Devey, his artist's eye appreciating the detail and designs of the early Renaissance.[154] Anthony Salvin's interpretation of the Tudor Gothic was influenced by Elizabethan mansions. They were built with symmetrical detailing, whereas Devey's country houses have an asymmetrical plan. Heavier Jacobean details appear in Salvin's work and although he created high ceilings and well-proportioned rooms the visual resulting scale appears solidly Victorian, even though his picturesque Mamhead Park (1825-1838) was mostly built in the late Georgian period.[155] Devey formed a longstanding friendship with Walter James, a Whig MP and friend of Gladstone, working on additions at Betteshanger until the end of his life. He understood the vanity of his clients. They wanted a large house to define their role in society but did not want a formal symmetrical building or a monstrous edifice. The sensitivity of the artist in Devey produced picturesque buildings that had a delicacy as well as fine attention to historic Tudor Gothic elements. It was his preferred style, which he saw as freer and more suitable for the needs of the nineteenth century than merely copying work of the Gothic period.[156] The Tudor Gothic style evolved and became popular for country houses due to a cultural and architectural shift away from what was considered to be an arid classicism.[157] His brief from Sir Walter James, later 1st Baron Northbourne, was to turn this thirty-year-old house into something which was to look as if it had stood and been subjected to additions over some hundreds of years.[158] It was the opposite of Devey's work at Zeals House, which had stood for some hundreds of years, where the substantial additions were to look integrated. Betteshanger House became a model for the designs of Devey's future country houses including Zeals House, which it closely resembles.

Betteshanger House, Kent.

Recurring devices in Devey's country houses of this mid-career period were used at Zeals House. Both houses have informal massing, steeply pitched gables, lofty chimney stacks, crenelated towers and tall clock towers surmounted by timber painted lanterns. Despite these recurring themes each house had its own individuality. The style drew the eye vertically creating a romantic skyline. Devey built in stone, brick, or diapered brickwork patterning with stone window facings in asymmetrical elevations. These features were used extensively in his country house practice in the 1860s and the 1870s. An oriel window was often incorporated, as at Zeals, to enhance a medieval appearance.

The double square bays to the drawing room at Betteshanger House remodelled by Devey were reprised at Zeals to create a spacious drawing room and encourage light through large triple-aspect casement windows. To focus on differences, Betteshanger has curved Flemish gables to create movement in the facades, which was a feature in many of Devey's country houses. At Zeals the gables are pointed to match the existing medieval ones. At Betteshanger there are a jumble of styles and focal points, while at Zeals, six years later and on a much smaller house, he shows more restraint.

Devey's design for Zeals House was in limestone with mullioned and transomed windows in the picturesque Tudor Gothic style (not the Gothic of Pugin with ecclesiastical motifs of ornamental trefoils, quatrefoils and ogee arches). The building work was done in 1862-1863, but Devey still visited the house in 1864 to oversee internal work, the latter stage being carpentry and internal fixtures. During the summer, Chafyn with Julia visited Fonthill House where Julia toured the Owen Jones-designed interior, marvelling at the 'wonderful china heaped about the house and a row of lovely caskets set with jewels on the chimney piece', while Chafyn and Alfred Morrison went to the Beckford Arms.[159]

In 1865, when Chafyn was away travelling, Devey visited Zeals House while working on the almshouses in Zeals village commissioned by Chafyn after the main house was completed. Sometimes he stayed the night at Zeals, or on one documented occasion arrived with Alfred Morrison.[160] To build the house, he liked to choose his contractors locally and they would report to him. At Zeals, he chose Mr Coakley and often met him at the house for updated reports, following complaints from Julia about the slowness of the progress.

Experienced at developing friendly relationships with his clients, Devey would have expected young Chafyn to rely on the older architect's experience and expertise to guide him through the process of rebuilding Zeals House. Devey was known to be good humoured, and 'always turned business into pleasure'.[161] Chafyn appreciated architecture and his preferred taste, highlighted in his diaries, leans towards the picturesque.

A modest man, clients were attracted to Devey because of his discretion. He was not inclined to write about his achievements or his clients in the *Architectural Review* or *The Builder* or to advertise his services in any way. His clients liked him because they were also averse to any personal publicity. But one device which Devey used in his practice was to have photographs taken of his buildings in the process of being built, complete with scaffolding poles. In High-Victorian England this was unusual. The photographs were more accurate than sketches. They would have provided the architect with a visual assessment so that adjustments could, if necessary, be made. Devey used the architectural photographic practice of London-based Bedford Lemere for some of his houses of this period.[162] The photographer would return to take photographs of his finished work. Devey derived pleasure from the recording of the process of bricks and mortar taking shape.[163]

Zeals House under construction from the south-east.

Zeals House under construction from the south-west.

From the south-east one can see two new square bays, designed to let in as much light as possible for the new drawing room. The windows on the right are smaller with the gable in place, whereas the left-hand bay with large and low casement windows awaits the building of a gable. Designing different window treatments for the two bays adds to the asymmetrical look of the elevation. On the right of the photograph is the medieval part of the house, the great hall and the service wing.

Behind the white horse in the second photograph taken from the south-west is a thick hedge that separates the kitchen area from the family rooms. From left to right the square bay with windows on all three sides is the office, the gable under construction with exposed joists. Between the library and the drawing room the lower levels of the tower are underway. In the foreground women appear to be carrying laundry. The grass is uncut during the building work.

Devey respected local traditions and wanted his houses to fit naturally into the surrounding landscape.[164] He may have looked at other houses in the area to ensure the new Zeals House included regional detailing. Athelhampton House near Dorchester has a curved oriel and battlemented porch stylistically similar to the one Devey added to Zeals House.

Having demolished the existing porch with its out of place Georgian fanlight, the replacement was in Devey's typical Tudor Gothic mode. An angled porch with a side window and an arched oak entrance door was Devey's solution to add authentic looking detail. To emphasise the early origins of the house, the porch was surmounted with atmospheric battlements. A stone coat of arms is nestled into the masonry above the door, which adds Tudor detail and satisfied Devey's habit of applied decoration. The heraldic symbol gently integrates, appearing subtle and discreet.

Zeals House was a successful example of a compact integrated Victorian country house. George Devey synergised the medieval, seventeenth-century, eighteenth-century and Victorian elements in his substantial rebuilding and extension of the medieval house, so that it blends into one picturesque mass. Over time, the old and the new have mellowed together. Both Zeals House and Chafyn's future were taking shape.

Zeals House porch under construction.

CHAPTER TEN

Zeals House

Everything was going well for Chafyn, he was an officer in the Coldsteam Guards and Commander of the Mere Rifle Company formed in 1859, overseeing Devey as work progressed on the house, and thinking about extending acreage of the estate to make it more manageable. An opportunity arose when the Duke of Somerset put the estate of Silton up for sale. Chafyn asked Squarey to do a thorough survey of the hamlet including all the stock, rent revenues, houses, cottages, Silton Church, the Rectory and Manor Farm House, extending to approximately 2,000 acres. Chafyn walked across the fields and over the river Stour, from Wiltshire into Dorset, to take in his ideas, the same route his father would have taken to visit his friend Harry Martin. As the estate adjoined Zeals, management would be easily centralised and because it was heavily wooded would be ideal for a shoot. The fields were well irrigated by the river, and the flatter land was ideal for arable farming and for the Zeals' prized Hereford herd. Squarey advised an offer of £60,000, to which the Duke agreed.[165] At the time, the Zeals estate owned Fairfield, an estate very close by but just across the border into Somerset and much larger than Silton, which Chafyn was thinking of selling for considerably more than the purchase price of Silton. The spare funds from the sale would be invested in case there was a downturn in farming fortunes.

At Ferne, Tom Grove had also employed a land agent and purchased a larger estate than Silton, but did not sell anything else to pay for it. Having spent almost £10,000 enlarging Ferne into a mansion, he now sought to be a major landowner and bought the Winterslow estate near Salisbury for 50,000 guineas, half the sum borrowed. Tom spent most of his time taking part in field sports. Known for his prowess with a rifle and being personable, he was often invited to shoot on aristocratic estates. Hosts like Lord Bruce, the 3rd Marquis of Ailesbury, were influential. Through moving in aristocratic circles, Tom Grove wanted to escape the religious morality of the Tory gentry that he was born into.

Zeals House from the south.

The Whig Party aristocracy were not compelled to attend Church unless they wanted to, their constituents being predominantly non-conformists. He could see that their looser behavioural code gave them more freedom. They made the rules for others to follow, whilst they could do whatever they liked. They were the ruling class. He had also been spending time with Sidney Herbert, The Earl of Pembroke, at Wilton House, often staying overnight helping Herbert campaign to become a Tory Member of Parliament for the Wilton constituency. Tom Grove admired the life that Herbert had. With an enlarged landmark estate and an enhanced mansion, then he, too, could become a Member of Parliament, aim to become a Baronet, and be part of the exclusive aristocracy.

Whereas Chafyn was very careful with money, sometimes excessively so, bartering over pennies, Tom Grove was not financially astute. Unlike Chafyn, he had never been groomed to take over an estate, his doctor father unexpectedly inheriting Ferne late in life. Herbert was persuaded to propose his ambitious neighbour for a parliamentary seat, but Grove failed to win on this first attempt and instead Colonel Bathurst was elected. He would try again, but he was forty when he inherited so there was no time to waste to achieve his ambitions.

Ferne House, Donhead St Andrew.

As Devey worked on the building of Zeals, sectioning off rooms so the house could still be occupied, Chafyn regularly travelled to London to see friends, leaving Julia on her own, although she was kept busy with her church and schoolroom activities.[166]

At Zeals House in April 1863, after a mild winter the daffodils were blowing in the strong winds and the leaves were bursting from the trees. Chafyn had been feeling unwell and he would make a discovery that would change his and Julia's lives forever. Rather than see his local physician, he went to London with Julia to consult his London doctor in Manchester Road for a health assessment. He had caught an infectious disease of the lungs which would shorten his life span and was given strict instructions on how to manage it. Chafyn was to check outside temperatures regularly and not get too hot or too cold or be in a draught. The disease was progressive and there was no cure, but once it had taken hold it could no longer be contagious, so he was not restricted in his movements. It was a solemn train journey to Gillingham station on their way home, with Chafyn closing his eyes, which he liked to do when he was thinking. They were picked up in their carriage by their coachman and driven through the iron gates of the south drive along the chestnut avenue, past the folly and the wood, disembarking at the entrance where Chafyn's dog Tip greeted him enthusiastically.

In his headstrong way, Chafyn made instant decisions. If his life was to be shortened, his first responsibility was to secure the succession of Zeals House. Considering his marriage prospects, he thought it may be difficult to find a wife who would marry a man with an incurable disease and a reduced life span, and there seemed no immediate prospect of a cure or a wife.

Over dinner that evening in the dining room he was alone with Julia and confronted her about her future: Julia would have to get married and have children. He argued that she was thirty-eight and there was still time, after all, their mother Eleanor was forty-one when Chafyn was born. Julia resisted, emphasising that a husband would take over the estate if it was hers and he would be her master. Her brother, frustrated with her stubbornness, pointed out that if he should die before marrying and producing an heir, she would be all alone and have a very isolated life. Although Great Aunt Chafin was alone at Zeals for nearly four decades she had the status of a widow, which Julia would not enjoy. Chafyn was optimistic about the prospect of having nieces and nephews but in Victorian England his mother's example of a late birth in her forties was an exception, and he was not only her third son but her fifth birth.

The following day Chafyn went to Wincanton to see Messiter, the family solicitor. He had discussed his plan with Julia and she asked him to add to his will legacies for the vicar at Mere, the vicar at Zeals, and also the clothing and coal clubs for the poor, as well as other religious causes. The will covered every possibility and following the pattern of his father's. Julia could stay in the house for life and if unmarried, then cousin George Troyte-Bullock would inherit the estate. He then optimistically made arrangements for Julia's marriage and children. Her husband would change his name to Chafyn-Grove and if Julia died before him, he would be found accommodation on the estate. Any children of the marriage would inherit Zeals House, sons first in order of birth, followed by daughters and if a daughter succeeded to the house, her husband was to change his name to Chafyn-Grove. Julia's wishes regarding legacies were also included in the will.

Julia was beside herself with worry. She turned more and more to religion for comfort. God had taken away brother John/Chafin when Julia was twelve, brother Hugh when she was three, which she could not remember, and little six-year-old Maria Catherine when she was thirteen. Her beloved father had been taken from her and her dear mother. She prayed for Chafyn to be spared. Her pleadings to her brother to go to church were ignored. Despite Julia's strong religious beliefs, Chafyn had no wish to attend church services and did not feel that God could help him recover.

Julia and Chafyn planned their summer. They would go to Switzerland for a few weeks when Chafyn had leave from his Guards' duties. The crisp air and the sun would be good for Chafyn and Julia would be there to care for him. But although he sometimes tired easily, he felt well and did not want his sister treating him like an invalid.

By September, to his great disappointment Chafyn was compelled by his illness to resign his commission in the Coldstream Guards, having only been able to serve for two years of what was supposed to be the start of a career of active duty. During those two years he witnessed both sorrow and joy for the sovereign he served.

The Coldstreamers were based at Wellington Barracks where Guards were occasionally supplied to Kensington Palace, the British Museum, The Tower, and Dublin. The latter was given up as a Guards' station the year after Chafyn enrolled. During training Chafyn would have had instruction in gymnastics, musketry and horsemanship. Shooting and riding he already excelled at. Country house shoots for game were established for sport but also with an eye to training young heirs and spares for military service. When the National Rifle Association was set up by the Guards, the shooting competitions proved to be very popular.

Only a few months after Chafyn enrolled in December 1861, the country was plunged into mourning for the death of Prince Albert. The Coldstream Guards had lost their senior Colonel, whom they much admired. As part of the Queen's household, they were in deep sadness for their sovereign. But there was joy in 1863 when H R H The Prince of Wales married Princess Alexandra of Denmark. They were married at Windsor, but the Guards were providing a guard of honour near the palace in Waterloo Place when Princess Alexandra arrived in London ahead of the ceremony. A few months later, the brigade held a ball in the exhibition buildings in honour of the prince and princess.[167]

At Zeals, towards the end of the year, the building work was nearing completion, and Devey again had the house photographed. He must have been pleased with the result as he placed the photograph in an album to keep as a permanent record of his work.[168] There was a ladder on the parlour wing and building rubble still outside the house.

Repairs were also needed to the original house, so these were tackled after the new section of the house was completed. In the

Zeals House near completion, 1863.

1820s engraving of the house there is a hipped roof on the medieval gable. This was altered into a matched gable with a ball finial and Tudor window hoods to assimilate with the end gable and the new rooflines. The grey sky and watery lawn indicate the photograph was taken in winter.

Devey had completed the masonry and the external works at Zeals House, but there was still interior work to be completed. There is no apparent client influence in the choices of internal fittings of chimney pieces, oak panelling or ceiling decorations. None of these show major stylistic architectural diversions from Devey's earlier country houses. Arched doorways without doors to let light through was his standard practice, as was the recessed staircase to make more space in the hall. Devey did not move on stylistically from his standardised internal designs, but in his later Tudor Gothic country houses he used semi-circular bays instead of square triple aspect windows for reception rooms to soften a long range, as seen at Wilcote House in Oxfordshire, in 1866-1870.

To avoid the cold weather the Chafyn-Groves planned a winter excursion for several months. It would be a break for Julia who had become very anxious for her brother, and good for Chafyn's health. With the reliable Squarey, who was popular with the tenants, left in charge of the estate, they embarked on a journey to Egypt for a cruise on the Nile accompanied by Chafyn's friend Myers. Starting the journey by embarking on a steamer from Southampton to Alexandria, they arrived in Luxor on 1st January 1864.

PART III

THE DIARIES

CHAPTER ELEVEN

Egypt

Chafyn, with his friend Arthur Myers, at the time Assistant Surgeon in the Coldstream Guards, arrived in Luxor with Julia at about 11.30 pm 'just in time to save the old year who gave us a parting nip of no pleasant nature, the thermometer having gone down to forty-two degrees last night, being the lowest point at which it has been since we have started'.[169]

To escape the cold, damp English winters, the aristocracy, who usually hired two boats, had made cruises on the Nile popular, and although they would accept gentry on to their boats out

A dahabieh on the river Nile, Egypt.

of courtesy, they would not be invited to dine. Class distancing applied in Egypt as it did in the English countryside. The social order was like the current of the water on the river Nile, always running below the surface.

In the mid-Victorian period, these excursions would be considered adventurous and would not necessarily run smoothly. The biggest danger was negotiating the cataracts, rapids made hazardous by rocks and boulders. The crews were experienced in manoeuvring the vessels through this part of the Nile, but it was only achieved by hauling the boats upwards on ropes, and on the descent finding one narrow passage with little room to spare on either side. Chafyn had hired a dahabieh called the *Clara,* a wooden, shallow-bottomed barge style boat of which there were many sailing up and down the Nile in the winter months to and from Cairo. They were used for excursions to see the various temples and attractions on the route to Aswan and Luxor. There was also a small rowing boat with a sail called a sandal to reach the shore. Each dahabieh had a captain, called the Reis, who was also an officer of the state, in charge of hiring the crew and sundry help when needed. The guide and interpreter, called the dragoman, who features often in Chafyn's diary of the voyage, was the highly strung Mohammad. Other crew members included Hammad, and the unreliable pilot, Khaleel. It was the custom to be civil to guests on other boats, many were English, some previously acquainted, but socially the excursion was not plain sailing.

On the first day of the New Year there was only one other dahabieh in Luxor beside the *Clara*, the Duke of Rutland's boat starting its downward journey. Chafyn and Myers went ashore to go to the Consul's to collect letters and read an *Illustrated*. There was a letter from Zeals telling Chafyn there had been a fire in White's rickyard at Manor Farm.[170] Having found no other news of importance, they went to visit the Temple of Luxor. The pair were surprised to see a third of the height of the obelisk and other buildings buried in the ground. 'The obelisk in question is the twin brother of the one in the Place de la Concorde at Paris. It is covered with very deep and sharp hieroglyphics, but does not come up in appearance to its Parisian brother, lacking the latter's French polish.' While walking around they met the Governor Abdullah Pasha sitting outside the Russian and Prussian Consulate, where they were invited in for pipe and coffee. Afterwards, it was a very hot ride to the 'beautiful relic of antiquity', the Memnonium.

'In company with us were Mr Tooke, Young, who was with me at Cambridge and two Lubbocks. We met them in the Temple their boat having arrived at Luxor this morning. Tooke is a Salisbury clergyman and knows Townsend having done duty at Mere just before he left England.[171] Young and one of the Lubbocks are evidently invalids, the latter I had not seen since I left Eton.'

Having read classics, Chafyn was enthralled to see the Egyptian relics, comparing the entablature to the Greek classical, in awe of the scale and quantity of the temples, and at the same time saddened to see the dilapidated state of these treasures. Detailed notes were recorded and absorbed. 'The great hall must in its perfect days have been a magnificent object indeed with its central aisle of 12 fine pillars with papyrus capitals and its forest of simpler ones in the side aisles. [...] In the evening the two Lubbocks came and we played a rubber of whist, not of a very strict nature, as the younger Lubbock would, like a schoolboy, pour forth anecdotes of Tooke, whose presence he seemed to find rather irksome. They seem to be a rather incongruous party, Tooke being evidently rather absurdly strict in his notions.'

On the morning of Sunday 3rd, Tooke went on board the *Clara* after breakfast for service on the quarter deck, which had been decorated with carpets borrowed from the Consul's, and after luncheon Chafyn and Myers went on donkeys for a view of the immense ruins of Karnak. After spending three hours amongst the ruins and the vast space covered by the temples, the pair rode back across the plain of Luxor. 'In the evening six dahabieh came up amongst us amid much firing of guns. Of these Lady Herbert has two, Lord Howard and Lady Manx two, the remaining two being Americans. Lord Howard and his fair partner are moored close to us but their doctor, who is in the other boat, is sent to Coventry the other side.'

Lady Herbert (Elizabeth) was the widow of Tom Grove's political friend Sidney Herbert, who had died three years previously. She was accompanied by her 14-year-old son George, who had inherited the estate of Wilton near Salisbury in Wiltshire with the title of Earl of Pembroke from his father's half-brother who had died a year after his father in 1862.

On returning to the boat we entertained at dinner Mustapha Agha and the Governor, Abdullah Pasha. They were both very well behaved and gentlemanlike though the latter was not very skilful with his knife and fork, notwithstanding which he contrived to put down quite his fair share of dinner. I was amused at the bitter way in which he spoke of the French and said Pasha's predilection for them. The poor Egyptians will see that coalition day. In the evening the Lubbocks came in to whist. They brought very bad news which they had heard from Lady Herbert viz: that Lord Elgin is dead.[172] Sir J. Lawrence appointed Governor General, and that a routing has broken out in the Punjab, 14 officers having been killed. It may be that the latter is only an isolated case and will not spread. Whatever it be, it is a matter which must be dealt with, with vigour and decision. No mercy for the sufferers. The gossip of Luxor is now Lord Howard's row with his doctor, a Greek, who he engaged at Cairo and furnished with a small dahabieh. The doctor, it seems, thought Lord Howard married and did not find out who the Lady was until nearing Thebes, whereupon he wrote to Lady Manx saying he had found out who she was, and should give warning at Thebes. Lady M is said to have exclaimed that she didn't care who knew who she was. On making Thebes Lord Howard turned the doctor out of the boat and refused to pay him anything as he had broken his contract. The doctor appealed to the Consul and there at present the matter stands.

About 10 o'clock on the following morning a steamer arrived from Cairo with about eighty or ninety passengers, 'from their appearance principally foreigners'. After being in Luxor for a few days, they would go up the cataract. 'On their return Myers will go down in her, his leave being now up.' Chafyn and Myers went on board to have a look around and see if there were any letters for them – only two for Julia. Satisfied that the boat appeared to be clean and fairly comfortable, they picked up a *Times* dated 14th December but there was no mention of the supposed Indian mutiny, so Chafyn hoped the rumours were false. After another hot donkey ride to the tombs of Sheikh Abd Goorneh honeycombed over a whole hill, they arrived back in the evening to the *Clara* to find 'Mohammad illuminated the sandal and rowed about with all the crew singing poems, much to the astonishment and as he said admiration of the world at large.'

To avoid the excursionists from the steamer, 'perambulating Luxor with hand books, a prey to the "antique" sharks who had come out in numbers', Chafyn and Myers rode to Karnak.

As we were riding home, we met Lord Pembroke and young Cameron his tutor who both turned and rode back with us.

They were on two of Mustapha Agha's horses which were very decent looking nags all things considered, though perhaps their appearance was improved by the good English saddles and bridles they wore. Young Pembroke seemed to be a decent sort of boy, and not much of an invalid. In the evening Mohammad repeated his fond illuminations with ten thousand additional lamps, while Herberts set up a responsive illumination which gave a very gay effect to the bank. They all came on board while we were out today and stayed for about an hour conversing with Mohammad who was full of it on our return.

The following day the excursionists had commandeered the best donkeys, so Chafyn and Myers had to be content with 'three very indifferent quadrupeds', ferried over from the opposite bank. Chafyn was guided by *Murray*, which often took the pair into deep water.[173] Wading through the river near the landing place on the other side, Myers' donkey quietly gave way beneath him and left him standing in the water 'colossus-like above his beast'. He was picked up and put on a stronger beast and then they rode on past the Memnonium to their destination, the tombs of the assessors.

> Myers made some explorations and found a valuable "antique" in the shape of a human skull with a quantity of coarse grey hair attached. Truly we might say with the grave digger "Alas! Poor Yorik", that this poor old skull should after two thousand five hundred years be disturbed by barbarians and carried off in the pocket of a shooting coat. This ended our sightseeing for the day. In the evening two dahabieh came up having on board Lord Newry, Col. Moore and others.

On discovering from her son, Lord Pembroke, that the Zeals family were on the *Clara*, Lady Herbert visited Chafyn and Julia on several occasions as they were neighbours in Wiltshire and the Chafyn-Groves had been in charge of the Mere branch of the local militia for centuries under the jurisdiction of the Earls of Pembroke. Her affability was natural to her as her late Peelite Tory politician husband Sidney Herbert had always aimed to nurture the support of the local gentry.[174] 'Lady Herbert and company came on board and brought us a quantity of newspapers which were very acceptable. As soon as they left us, they sailed off with such wind as there was.'

As Chafyn awaited the arrival of the steamer which would take Myers away, his leave being up, he casually dropped in to see

Mustapha Agha and found him entertaining two Englishmen who had just arrived who were 'dallying coyly with the messes into which the old Consul was plunging his fingers most unhesitatingly. I was obliged to join, but could not bring myself to dipping into the meat and fish messes, so confined myself to forking up bits of omelette, which was greasy but good. Luckily all the dishes were served up at once, so that I was not obliged to partake of everything but could pick out what was least objectionable.' Having mentioned that he and Myers intended to ride to the tombs of the kings, Mustapha Agha sent his dromedary and his horses for the excursion.

> The horses were not bad animals, though from having been so much ridden with very sharp bits, their mouths required careful handling. After passing the Temple of Goorneh, the way to the tombs is up a dreary, arid valley bounded on both sides by limestone precipices probably honeycombed with tombs yet unexplored. Returning to the light of day from the temples we encountered our spirited steeds and made home, getting a good gallop on the sands where the sandal was moored.

Chafyn and Myers also took advantage of the loan of the horses to go pigeon shooting. 'We got some splendid rocketing shots by standing on a spot past which they flew continually. It was very good fun and we killed eighteen. We did not find much good cantering ground though we managed to go sufficiently fast to leave behind Mustapha's groom who ran by Julia's horse until the pace became too good.'

A quiet day followed, being a Sunday. Letter writing was the order of the day so that the post could go with Myers on the steamer, and there were letters to collect for Chafyn from George Bullock and Uncle Charles which 'gave no news of importance'. The Beaumonts' dahabieh arrived. Beaumont and his wife, an invalid, went on board for Sunday service. 'She looks more of an invalid than when we met in Aswan.' Julia had befriended the Beaumonts who 'improved on acquaintance'. Resourceful, she organised her own excursions while Myers and Chafyn looked at temples and artifacts, visiting bazaars for shopping accompanied by her maid, Ann England, and making her own friends. Although the Beaumonts were a respectable couple, they were unlanded and were honoured to be invited on to the *Clara*, even if it was for Sunday service rather than a social occasion. They boldly invited the Chafyn-Groves for dinner, apprehensive about whether they would accept an invitation to a much smaller boat.

'In the evening we had a very good dinner at the Beaumonts and plenty of draughts both of air and wine. Their cabin is very small for 5 people and the divans absurdly high. It turns out they were staying last summer at Maiden Bradley, having actually passed the Black Dogs. They are at present living in Somersetshire – near Crewkerne'.

But if the Beaumonts hoped to move past the Black Dog gates towards Zeals House on their return to England, no invitation appears to have been extended.

Myers was to sail early next morning. 'I am very sorry to lose him as I shall have no one to join me in shooting excursions etc. and he is always so cheery. I fear that he will hardly catch the P & O steamer of Jan 19th from Alexandria. He went off about 10 o'clock to the steamer after a most affectionate and tumultuous farewell from all our crew, who will miss his doctoring very much.' Immediately after Myers left, Hammad fell ill and was given Dover's powder to set him straight.

The *Clara* left Luxor in a gale. Not much progress was made and the lurching discomposed the furniture in the cabins. They had to stop as there was a bend in the river, where the crew dragged the boat slowly against the wind. There were two dahabiehs ahead of them and one behind, so Chafyn anticipated some good racing for the following day. They awoke to find they had reached Esna, moored close to the Pasha's villa. In the afternoon the crew were investigating a nasty smell in Julia's cabin, 'supposed to arise from poopas of <u>the</u> rat, who fled in that direction one day severely wounded according to Hammad. Two men crawled about below and others poked sticks about down the window slides but failed to find "el far".'

Eventually, they set sail two hours behind the other two boats, who having smaller crews contrived to get ahead with their bread collection before the *Clara* arrived. 'Mohammad has promised them a sheep if they pass all <u>four</u> boats, very improbably, seeing that two of them have a twenty-four hour start of us.' The water was now calm and they tacked on to Edfu, where they stopped to replenish their stock of charcoal, Chafyn going onshore with his rifle, shooting a buffalo bird. When the wind picked up again, they headed without incident towards Aswan. Lady Herbert's two boats were moored on the same side of Elephantine Island as the *Clara*. After working two hard nights in succession, the *Clara* crew were quiet in the evening, making no attempt to answer the singing of the boats on the opposite bank. 'Ahmed the cook's mate is worse with his scurvy eruption which Mohammad thinks is turning into something infectious, so he has been sent on shore.'

Awaking after a quiet night, Chafyn wandered around Elephantine Island in a blowing day with clouds of dust, and as he could not find the milometer he was looking for, returned to the boat. Lady Herbert arrived on board in the afternoon and stayed for some time. 'She is a most agreeable woman. She told me that they had some Soudan sheep at Wilton formerly and that they throve very well, which is satisfactory as I have bought a pair. Lord Pembroke and Cameron are going in a cargo boat to shoot crocodiles.' Lady Herbert, friendly and charming, regaled them with stories: 'Lady Duff Gordon has taken a villa here for four months on her own' and 'Lord Scarborough shot a crocodile.' She would have been regularly invited to dine on the boats of her social contemporaries and would have returned the invitations. But she would not have invited Chafyn and Julia into the exclusive group of aristocrats and the Chafyn-Groves would not have expected it.

The *Clara* started the following morning with Chafyn and Julia hoping to see the boats go up the cataract, but there being no wind when they reached Mahattah, the village just above the cataract, they went on to Philae. They paid a visit to a convent on the bank, a Roman Catholic one with an Italian Franciscan monk and two little black boys, a dog and a monkey. After a short stay at Philae the wind rose and the boat headed towards the cataract where they found Lady Herbert and her party had been there some hours. There were up to one hundred and fifty men pulling on ropes over difficult rapids while 'on a high rock stood an old Dervish, distinguished alike by his age and dirt, who waved a tattered white flag and shouted prayers and invocations for success.' Both men and the boat went through the first door without mishap save for a broken rope.

There was a long wait caused by an argument amongst the Reis of four boats, each vying to go up the cataracts either first or two at a time, and when the *Clara* did move it was to put into a sandbank for their night. Chafyn invited Pembroke and Cameron to dine as Lady Herbert had gone to Philae 'with her very fat French maid riding au cavalier on donkeys' to stay the night at the convent.[175] 'Mohammad was much annoyed at my not having given him any notice in the morning, but I pointed out to him that as we generally have dinner enough for ten, the cook need make no additions for these young gentlemen. Lord P is I think a niceish boy. He is still at Eton but absent on long leave, and is a pupil of Billy Johnson's, whom he describes as madder than ever and at odds with all the masters.'

While waiting for their turn to go up the cataract, Lady Herbert returned and came on board the *Clara* with a book called *Four Months in a Dahabieh* by Miss Carey. She thought it would amuse Chafyn and Julia because Miss Carey's dragoman was their Mohammad. 'He appears continually in her pages, and from it I gather one or two hints as to the way to treat him when fractious.' Despite having to deal with Mohammad's fluctuating emotions, they would not have wanted Lady Herbert's dragoman. 'According to Cameron, he did Lady Herbert out of £500 at one coup, having been entrusted with this sum to buy things at Cairo, and it being found on enquiry that he made away with the money in other ways and paid for none of the things.' During the sunset, Chafyn and Julia went for a sail round Elephantine with Mohammad as pilot, 'a duty which he really performed very well.'

Shortly after the *Clara* got off, we reached the "first door", a rapid studded with some nasty looking rocks just showing above the water. Here three unsuccessful attempts were made by the Hubrians to carry a rope to the rocky island. Boldly they plunged in, the rope in their teeth, but each man was forced to drop it by the weight of the water. It was at last thrown to them and after attaching it to a rock the pull began by about 10 people on deck. Mohammad and all joined in and with a hard pull they had to get us up, accompanied with much shouting and screaming of orders by the 2 Reis. Heavy as she was, the boat went steadily into smooth water beyond, and went on until we reached a sandy spot where they dead cleverly ran us ashore and refused to proceed any further for that day, now but 1.20 p.m.

In the afternoon we went on board the *Pera* and sat for some time with Mr and Mrs Cunliffe.[176] The latter is nice looking and far less vulgar than her husband, who looks and talks rather like a respectable shop keeper. However, they are both unassuming and good-natured people, and moreover English, which makes their society pass more than its real value in this world of scruffy Arabs and Hubrians. Mohammad considers that we have gone very pleasantly and quietly so far because he has not yet been brought to tears. 'Last year between my master and the Reis I stand in the bow of the boat and cry like little child.'

The cataract Reis and the men arrived for their work in the morning, despite their previous threats. The rest of the rapids were negotiated satisfactorily, until the last but one called the 'Bab el Sogheir'. Chafyn and Julia were watching from the shore from where they saw 'a great deal of shouting and stamping while the ungainly Mohammad leaped about the rocks like a huge baboon'. The rapids were ascended on ropes fixed to rocks by the Hubrians, some on deck stripped and ready to go into the water at a moment's notice. 'The channel is narrow, the men pushing with poles and dragged by people on shore while "the Reis" danced about. Our own Reis, his moustache bristling with rage, stood in the bows pushing and working like twenty men.' More men were brought in from the *Pera* 'and at last the ropes were manned by two hundred people, many of them boys, and with a shout of E'Shekayla, the great boat went up, Mohammad looking awfully solemn and praying away, calling perpetually on E'Seydse.' Chafyn came to the conclusion that the long and tedious job could be cut short inexpensively by blowing up some of the rocks creating 'here and there capstans which would greatly accelerate the whole job'.

They sailed on by the beautiful reaches past Mahattah to Philae, mooring on a sandy bank close to Pharoah's bed. Mohammad was on a sharp lookout for thieves, declaring that the Hubrians would take things through the windows off the rocks.

Accordingly, he appeared hanging on the ledge outside the cabin windows when the boat was about three or four yards from the rocks, and no one could possibly have entered. After this display of zeal he retired again to the deck, resuming his former aspect of solemn fear. In the evening Mr and Mrs Cunliffe came to tea and accompanied by Julia took a moonlight walk among the ruins, attended by two torch bearers, who were, however, more in the way than anything else. Pharoah's bed looked beautiful in the moonlight from the cabin windows. Mohammad was very sulky tonight and declared that he was sick and could not accompany the party.

The journey through the Nile was stop and start with either too little wind or too much, but they reached Kom Ombo where Chafyn enquired about Khaleel, the Hubrian pilot, and was informed that he had been 'drawn for the conscription and could not come with us'. Chafyn and Julia walked through Kom Ombo and saw 'one or two caravans encamped and some ruffian-like army soldiers, whom Mohammad informed us that the Pasha had engaged to fight against the Xians [Christians] in Africa, whoever they may be.'

The boat is very quiet without the ceaseless jingle of his melodious voice, and the waiting progresses in Mohammad's hands far more satisfactorily than in K's. Mohammad has since passing the cataracts displayed a sprightliness and affability quite unusual, and at dinner he literally bounded up and down the little passage between the deck and the saloon. The scenery is much more cultivated than the last few days, and the hills in the distance are curious resembling stoppered pinnacles, sometimes flat on top (or as Mr Cunliffe, bored by Egypt, unromantically described them, gigantic ash heaps).

The morning stoppage was prolonged today by the cook who had to kill and disembowel a sheep, which he performed with great adroitness. While we were waiting, Khaleel appeared dragging along a lean sheep, some hard dates and an ebony club as offerings to me. He then departed with his train laden with oranges and other delicacies which he had brought up from Cairo for his relatives. About 2 o'clock the wind got up sufficiently for us to take advantage of it. We passed within hail of Daraw but the faithless Khaleel did not appear so we went on without him. A little before dinner two crocodiles were reported on a neighbouring sand bank. Before however we could get within decent range, they saw the sail and with great discretion retired from public view.

The breeze forming into a gale, the *Clara* floated as it was too rough for rowing. 'Just as we were starting Lord Spencer's two boats arrived bringing the deserter Khaleel, who brought tremendous accounts of his Lordship's stores, below they have twenty-four barrels of beer, thirty hams besides the English provisions to the value of £700, which impressed the said K very much.' It was the first day of Ramadan, and the Reis had been very sulky the day before.

On coming on deck, I was surprised to find the Reis quietly smoking as usual. On enquiry, I found that he had availed himself of a legal quibble, and denied that Ramadan had begun because he had not seen the new moon himself last night. The crew don't seem to have seen the new moon either for they all, but one or two, partook of their breakfast in their usual cutlet fashion. In the evening the crew began rowing until midnight, screaming and shouting the whole time in chorus as they headed slowly towards Cairo. Mohammad went to a market but only managed to find 6 fowls and a seedy sheep for the Ramadan feast after sunset, the *Clara* setting off again without Khaleel who went ashore and had not returned. The poor cook must find it hard to keep his fingers out of the saucepans. The Reis' temper is certainly not improved by fasting. What hits him hardest is the loss of his pipe which he was previously never without.

While docked, Chafyn walked round to General Dixon's boat to try and get some newspapers, but he had lent all his to the Spencers. He told Chafyn the Prince of Wales had a son. It was a crowded boat with the General's relatives, Mr and Mrs Wynne and two nephews Dixon and Edwards. The former is in the 25th Regiment and is a very nice fellow. They took a walk where Mrs Wynne poured out all her troubles to Julia. In the evening the two nephews 'came on board and we played a not very scientific rubber, conversation being more attended to than the cards. It is calm tonight.'

Descending the cataracts was much easier than the ascent but the boat had to be rowed by twenty-four men and boys at a careful angle to glide down seven rapids rolled into one. It was precarious because of the narrow width with the vicious looking rocks protruding either side and because of the screeching of orders and counter orders from the two Reis. The boat filled with an 'odoriferous throng of old men' for no apparent reason other than that they were one family and had been doing this for fifty years and were praying. 'It is very exciting work sweeping through the great door. The waves were much higher than I expected to see and lashed into the boat two or three times. I saw and felt two distinct drops each time of about 3 feet. On getting safely through great congratulations took place on every side.' The crew rowed quietly into Aswan where Chafyn and Julia walked around the bazaar and saw a cargo of animals from Soudan being loaded for the Pasha consisting of a young 7-month-old leopard, a donkey with horns like a deer and a bird resembling an eagle. 'Mohammad has been seized with a fit of liberality and has been at intervals bringing us in small presents all day, I suppose, as peace offerings.'

Chafyn's pair of Soudan sheep had to be picked up at Kom Ombo. They had been grazing at the Reis's village in very good care, and were taking up their new accommodation in the sandal. 'They are not at all wild, so I hope they will get safely to England.'

They reached Esna late that night, and moored close to the palace.

> We have to stop here for the men to replenish their stock of bread. The space before the palace was filled with a crowd mostly of women, relatives of the conscripts whose names were being drawn in the Governor's office. The women kept up in incessant wailing similar to that at funerals, some walking about with a hopping step, others waving their arms in the air, and many apparently in hysterics. Presently, the conscripts, 40 in number were marched out into a boat waiting to take them to Cairo. With few exceptions they seemed very indifferent, and took but little notice of their weeping relations, who crowded round, notwithstanding the efforts of the officials with sticks. As soon as the recruits, many quite boys and all of the lowest class, were huddled together on board guarded by three or four ill looking ruffians with pistols and whips, the boat pushed off to float to Qena where it will be taken in tow by a steamer. It was a melancholy scene. If in England any such occur, as they do of course, when a body of recruits is marched off, one has the satisfaction of knowing that the men are volunteers, and not torn suddenly from their homes by an arbitrary government. However, a country must have soldiers, and if the people will not volunteer, they must be made to go.

The *Clara* reached Luxor in the afternoon, where the quantity of letters awaiting the Chafyn-Groves fell short of expectations. They were expecting to find a whole packet of newspapers as they were being sent from England from 1st January. Instead, there was only a two-and-a-half-month-old *Salisbury* paper. Later that night, Julia went off with England to see the bazaar during Ramadan but did not return much edified.[177]

The boat got underway in the morning and after stopping to pick up some dates they headed towards Cairo, but the force of the wind was holding them back and there was a possibility that they would not get to Cairo in time for Eid Sogheir festivities to mark the end of Ramadan. Chafyn wanted to stop at Abu Shusha but Mohammad would not allow it, as the neighbourhood was bad and that they would likely be attacked by Bedouins. 'He said that 2 Americans were murdered here last year, and that the dragoman, Reis and the crew were in consequence thrown into prison where they still lie!!'

Slow progress was being made, the crew, according to Mohammad, anxious to get to Cairo for their 'Xmas Day'. To get some exercise, Chafyn and Julia walked along the shore, a good straight walk of seven miles, and being picked up at the end. During the walk, 'I saw a large field of poppies all in bloom, containing, I should think, opium enough to stupefy half the population of Jirja.' They managed to get some good rowing in but when they started to drift they pulled into the bank so that Chafyn could take his Soudan sheep for a walk to get some exercise, 'which they seemed to enjoy amazingly'. Julia accompanied him. They saw 'large numbers of sheep, cattle and camels grazing in the fields of clover which was growing very thickly, and sometimes making unrestrained incursions into the green wheat, indeed our sheep munched the ears off near the path as they walked along without any objection being raised by the inhabitants. I suppose it is the remnant of the old patriarchal custom, for the crops are always eaten away sometimes for several feet on either side of a pathway, the passing donkeys and cattle being allowed to take a nibble as they go along.'

The journey appeared to be on course to arrive in Cairo with time to spare before the great celebrations. They went for a walk with the Cunliffes, Mr Cunliffe managing to slip off the plank on leaving his boat, 'mauve stockings and all in the mud'. It was their last night sleeping on board and the most wretched. The wind was blowing violently and the sandal bumped against Chafyn's cabin, although for dinner they had their preserved plum pudding originally intended for Christmas day but not produced on that occasion out of consideration for the cook's feelings. 'It turned out very well indeed.' As fog covered the whole river, they secured donkeys for a pleasant ride into Cairo as they heard the guns announcing the commencement of Eid Sogheir.

The roads and streets were full of people in every variety of new and gorgeous attire assumed for the occasion, and driving through them numerous carriages with gorgeously laced officers going to or returning from the Pasha's house. As we rode by Shepherd's Hotel, which is brim full, our letters appeared in the hands of Mohammad's guide Hassan, who got them out of Briggs & Co.[178] We got literally the last two rooms at the Hotel D'Orient and are to be changed with better tomorrow. Well! I am not sorry to get into a room with four walls again. Cairo looks wonderfully European after the cities of Upper Egypt, and the people amazingly fair. I later called at Shepherd's Hotel where I found E M. Young still, as well as Heathcote and Jebb and Casey who have been up the Nile together. H and J are now Fellows of Trinity and I think par consequence more or less priggish in their ideas and habits. I find this a very decent hotel, the people civil, and the dinner pretty fair.

After breakfast, Julia went to the pyramids with the Cunliffes and Kennard while Chafyn went to Briggs and to Mr Rowlett at the Bank of Egypt, to settle the account for the boat, he being Mr Flemings' reference in Cairo, which was settled without difficulty. On his return he found the crew, the cook, Khaleel and all except Mohammad lined up in the port corchère of the hotel 'with bakshish intent'. Later, having dealt with the crew, he waited with Julia for Mohammad who was supposed to accompany them to the Shobra Gardens, but they set off on donkeys without him. Mohammad turned up during the afternoon 'in gorgeous array with patent leather boots, sent to him from England as he pointedly informed me by his master of last year, Capt. Barton'.

In the crowded streets, Mohammad took them to the home of the Dreuse and to the 'Bab el Nasr' in a 'sandy and glaring expanse covered with tombs of all sorts and sizes, from the mock like erections of the rich surrounded by a wall to the humble tombs of the poor'. They visited the burial place of Mohamed Ali and his family. 'There are about twenty-five tombs all of white marble covered with paint and gold with the usual Egyptian taste in such matters. But everywhere and in fact all over Egypt the same dilapidation prevails, not the respectable antiquity of an old English ruins, but a sort of debauched seediness very characteristic of the country.'

They set out for Suez with the Cunliffes and Mr Marston.

There is only one passenger train a day each way and the train from Cairo is advertised to start at 7.30 a.m. Accordingly, we got up early, hurried over breakfast and started off to the station where we found a hideous scene of dirt and confusion. With some difficulty obtaining tickets we got into our train, and about 8 o'clock made a start, unluckily a false one for after going for ¼ of a mile we stopped and were backed into a siding, where we remained till ten o'clock waiting until the special train with the India mail, timed to start at nine, had got clear off. [...] The carriages are very comfortable being English built and lined with leather, which is far fresher and less frowsty than the cloth of our railways. Between Cairo and Suez are nineteen or twenty stations at equal distances. They consisted of a few mud huts where the people who take care of the line live, who are dependent for their supplies of water on the trains. At No. 8 and 14 there is a larger establishment, an English refreshment room at which P & O stores could be obtained, arrangement for watering the engines and for trains to pass each other. As we passed through the desert, we all agreed it was far pleasanter to be going through it in the railway than on the back of a camel. The bright blue of the Red Sea was very different and most refreshing was it to the eye. We arrived at Suez 5½ hours late and found the Hotel full of passengers just preparing to go off in the tender to the Indian steamer. The Hotel is very good, the servants are all Bengalese who wait well and quietly, but look very meek and downtrodden.

We started after breakfast today for Ani Mura, the 'Wells of Moses' where tradition asserts that the Israelites stopped. I believe it is satisfactorily proved that they did not do so, still the tradition makes an excuse for a pleasant excursion. After luncheon in a mud summer house, we set off again to the boat, in which we all got safely embarked finally reaching the Hotel after a very pleasant day at 7.30. As concerns the much-vexed question of where the Israelites crossed the Red Sea, the most likely spot would seem to be opposite the headland of El Akaba which is on the W side.

The following morning after breakfast:

We set off to see the fresh water canal which has lately been completed and now supplies Suez with what was greatly needed before, viz: good water. The breadth is about twenty yards and its depth about seven feet. The banks of the canal were well cut, but even now the water seemed to be beginning to eat them away. This, it seems to me will prove the great, or rather one of the great difficulties in the Ship Canal, as they will hardly get the banks to stand the wash of steamers unless they are cased with masonry. We had not time to visit the Ship Canal as the part where they are at work is fifteen miles from Suez. There are twelve thousand men at work there and we saw a large number going there. Each set of men work for a month and they get no pay save rations of bread. Such is the system in Egypt. The fresh water canal is it seems to irrigate the land near the Ship Canal so as to bring it into cultivation as, I am told, by the law of Egypt all land so reclaimed becomes the property of the irrigator, so that the French will doubtless get a considerable territorial acquisition in these parts. The P & O company have an extensive depot here and are building new storehouses. The coal was piled in mountains.

At 2.30 p.m. Chafyn and Julia were on the train to return to Cairo. They reached their hotel at 1.30 a.m.

Sightseeing resumed, Chafyn, Julia, the Cunliffes, Marston and Miss Kennard walked through the narrow dusty streets or rode donkeys. The group went to see the Dervishes perform. They walked into a room surrounded by a heel kicking expectant crowd of Turks. Presently the Sheikh of the Dervishes entered, bowed to the company and took his seat on the divan where he was supplied with coffee and pipe 'which delicacies were not extended to us "pigs of visitors". He was a fine-looking old fellow and wore the usual felt hat of the Dervishes with the distinction of a green roll round the bottom of it. After having gazed for some time at the operations of the great man, a supernatural impulse seized us all, and we sneaked out leaving him alone in all his glory.' The group descended into a room where the performance was to take place, being seated 'outside the magic circle, the performers entered one by one, each in his Dervishes cap and cloaked. After bowing to the East they squatted inside the railings. 'They were of various ages, some being old and grey, others in the prime of life. Some of their hats were very much the worse for wear, reminding me in one or two cases of that garment as worn by the car drivers of Dublin. After 4 dances, each of about 5 minutes duration, they saluted the Sheikh and the performance concluded. I was glad to have seen them, for in few parts of the world if any would one meet with a ceremony of this sort in the way of a religious rite.'

It was time to send baggage off to Alexandria. After an hour of confusion at the station, the bags were weighed, registered and paid for. In the afternoon Chafyn went with Julia to the Turkish bazaar to shop. 'We found a man who sold the Damascus silks cheaper than the people in the Syrian bazaar. He was more civil than the generality of Egyptian shopkeepers and succeeded in drawing several pounds from me for various things.' After church, where they listened to a nervous young parson with a meek voice, they went on donkeys with Mr Marston to Heliopolis.

There was nothing left except an obelisk with the oval of Amun Ib I. The sycamon nearby, under which the Holy Family are said to have rested in the flight into Egypt, was surrounded by an orange grove and olives. Marston is a very gentlemanly Yankee of which one may call the conservative party. He lays all the blame of the war on the hasteners of the Radical party both in the North and South. He detests slavery but says that it must be allowed to die out gradually and would have done so without violent means. With it the war will be continued till one or the other give it up from total exhaustion. In the afternoon I visited Jebb who is come to our hotel his party having gone off to Syria. He looked very ill, having just had an attack of gastric fever. It must be very lonely for him out here by himself.'

Away this morning from filthy, dusty Cairo by train to Alexandria. The train kept its time with unusual punctuality, so that we had very good reason to be satisfied, seeing that there have been sixteen collisions in the twenty-eight days ending 14th March. On getting to Alexandria after six hours journey, I was agreeably surprised to find our heavy baggage arrived. We found the P & O Hotel very full, but we have good rooms on the second floor. I went to the P & O offices where I found that we are to go in the *Syria*, a fine paddle steamer on her first trip.[179] The day of starting is of course uncertain, depending on the arrival of the mail from India. The shops look wonderfully bright and showy after the Egyptian bazaars. My missing box from London of which I had given up all hope after the failure of my enquiries of the P & O people, turned up this afternoon in the hands of one Amin, being a shipping agent. The contents in the shape of clothes and papers were very acceptable.

CHAPTER TWELVE

Spain and France

A month after Chafyn's diary ends in Alexandria on 24th March, Julia's begins on 24th April. The siblings began their journey home through Spain and France, looking forward to seeing Devey's work on the finished Zeals House. Aiming to see as much of Spain as possible, they travelled by hired dilly carriage or by train, where the rail was in place. Spain was in the process of extending the railway lines, but in 1864 this was far from being fully operational and the services were lacking in organisation and punctuality. The process of travelling from one town to another was scenic but disruptive and tiring.

Julia's diary starts in Seville. With her fascination for faith, she visited the cathedral and the University Gallery to see the religious art of Murillo and Morales, along with Moorish works, but during the short stay in the town she had time to shop. Meanwhile, Chafyn had purchased a ticket for a bull fight but on arrival found his place taken by lawless ruffians.[180] Troops with bayonets were sent to haul them out but he decided to abandon the chaos.

> Out after breakfast to buy a Spanish fan – an implement which scarcely a woman of any class is seen without, and they work them incessantly, even on their knees in the Cathedral. I have in vain tried the magic Spanish flick in and out of the fan. It must be born with them – little girls of six years of age flirt them with a gravity and elegance that must be innate. The black silk spangled are most elegant. I bought one for one dollar ten reals and two common ones for four quartos each. At the bull fights they are sold for one quarto each – and bonfires made of them after the show is over![181]

Zeals House from the south-west.

They left in the afternoon for the station to catch the 2.15 p.m. train. The line ran through 'mops of purple thistle and red poppies and the wheat and barley high and thick' to Cordova (Cordoba). Arriving at 7.30 p.m. they were met by an omnibus pulled by three large mules through very narrow streets to the Hotel Luisse and had an early night.

Julia was enthralled by the exquisite Mesquita Mosque. 'The Cathedral is a marvel. The interior contains 850 columns of different marbles – many from France – and taken from temples there and in other parts of Spain. The arches are double, small ones spring over the pillars and are interlaced with ribbons. The mosaics in the Zancaron, the holiest part in the Mosque turned to Mecca and the "Ceca" pilgrimage was held to be equal to that of Mecca, which the Spanish Moors could not always accomplish, are superb, the roof of the Chapel is in the form of a shell and wrought out of a single piece of marble.'

Wandering on to the hotel where Julia met her friends the 'Irish potatoes', the Murphy trio, they visited the Spanish Churches which 'disgust the protestant mind. To my ideas blasphemous representations of our Lord, of indecent figures of the Virgin Mary or the Holy Apostles. I never saw anything as repulsive as the dolls, the Virgin in a mantilla and clasping her hands with a lace handkerchief between her fingers, small and large editions of our blessed Lord in velvet and silk, frippery and tinsel of the commonest order. When I look at a noble work of art, in painting, a sculpture or architecture, or listen to it in music, my thoughts always turn in worship to that Divine Giver of all good things. This frippery is not anything approaching to a noble work of high intellect, but 3rd-rate millinery.'

There is no mention of Chafyn joining the group, as he had no inclination to visit churches – and none to spend time with the Murphys. He wrote letters and went to the library to see if he could find some recent newspapers. International and domestic affairs were more interesting for him than visiting Catholic churches with the Catholic trio.

From Cordoba, Julia, Chafyn and the trio, Mr, Mrs and Miss Murphy, went by train to Cadiz to catch a steamer for Malaga. It was a fourteen-hour trip on a 'comfortable boat'. May Day was spent in Church at the Consulate and strolling along the Avenida with the Murphys before commencing a trip in a hired dilly called 'Diligence' to Granada. They were seated omnibus fashion, 'with ten mules and horses to their equipage, the leaders conducted by a ragged lad about the vehicle, jumping up and down when going a good pace, and belabouring the miserable (for skin and bone they were) animals with sticks about their heels, which they flung up and then broke into a gallop for a few yards – the first stage lasted four hours, and the poor brutes were bathed in moisture and showing frightful galls from ill-adjusted harnesses when relived from the traces.' Changing horses, they soon left behind the views of the hills. 'The country now became wilder and more barren, the less cultivated, the soil poor and stony, with thin crops of wheat which looked like reaping about June. In the <u>lovely hills</u> around Malaga, the corn was rich and strong, the vines stumpy, the olives large and nutty. Near Malaga the hedges of the pink geranium were already in masses of silk blooms. All of a sudden "halt" was cried.' There was a clatter as the fore wheel buckled.

'We all bungled out of the interieur and passed two hours strolling about the road bemoaning our hard fate and the prospect of not reaching our gite until midnight in lieu of 10 p.m. Picked quantities of wild flowers. At last, we go off and rattled merrily along, then in less than a mile we came suddenly to a stop, and looking out I saw the wheel on a slant a half turn more and an upset would have been the consequence.' Looking for a shop or café where they could source some refreshments, in the next village they found 'cold chicken which we ate with our <u>fingers</u>, no water at hand, so we quenched our thirst with mangoes and bought some oranges and bread'.

The wheel having been repaired, at 11 p.m., 'a rudder grating was heard in the other front wheel and again a <u>cancellation</u> was held, which resulted in our all turning out again, another high road in the cold, and the dilly being guarded by two men, we walked to a beuta, or more a stable with a place outside through which the horses and mules were led into their shade. Here we established ourselves as well as we could, Ms Murphys extended themselves on a corn rack, Chafyn on a stool in the chimney corner on a rickety chair, Mr Murphy burnt his boots, and <u>slept</u> all night, as his snoring testified, close to the fire. At dawn we all shook ourselves and went out to see the sun rise, which over the Sierra Nevada was gorgeous. We found a better looking beuta where we obtained coffee, chocolate, and some ham and eggs.'

After a row over the bill, Chafyn and Mr Murphy were taken away by the Guardia to the Consul. The matter was settled in favour of the landlady who became abusive when she was not awarded costs. The dilly being repaired again, they proceeded on their journey arriving in Grenada to their hotel in the Alhambra grounds. 'It is very hot, but the shade of the elms given by the Duke of Wellington is delicious.' Julia accompanied the Murphys to Mass at the Cathedral and while the service was taking place visited the tombs of Ferdinand and Isabella 'of beautiful alabaster. Near them lie Philip and Juana, the carvings on the tombs are very rich and well executed.' They strolled about the streets, walking back via the Avenida de Darra by a ravine, a mill and the remains of a picturesque aqueduct. In the evening it was the Alhambra, 'which is lovely, an exquisite creation of Moorish taste. Here we watched the sun set.'

Julia's friend Mr Murphy, 'also an invalid in delicate health like Chafyn' was musical and liked to whistle along to the spinet which was being played in the dining room of the hotel. 'He is a complete fanatic in music, having an excellent ear and great love for melody.' Whilst out sightseeing he purchased a guitar which he played while walking along and was asked to perform. Julia decided to make a purchase of a guitar too, so Murphy helped her choose one in a pretty inlaid case. 'The Murphys will take it to Gibraltar for me and from thence send it per P & O to Southampton.' Chafyn was also shopping. At a model man's house, he 'fell in love with a lovely model of the Kiosk in the Court of Sious for which the Don wanted forty dollars'. 'In the evening we had the "gypsy king" to play the guitar to us. The fandangoes were very pretty, but some of his music was very uninteresting and devoid of melody.[...] I wanted Chafyn to give up Madrid and be contented with returning to Malaga and Gibraltar and going quietly home. I am afraid the long journey will tire him too much, and after Madrid we shall have four long days before Paris.'

Chafyn would not be contented with returning to Malaga and Gibraltar and did not see that route as going quietly home. The Murphy trio were returning to Gibraltar and Chafyn was not tired, just tired of the Murphys.

On their final evening in Granada, Julia went to the Alhambra again, for the fourth time, with renewed pleasure. She was drawn to the romance of its history, the ethereal Nasrid buildings, the four-hundred-year-old cypresses and the English style parterres. The spiritual connection she felt there would stay with her, helping her to experience serenity after her constant anxiety over Chafyn's health.

The Alhambra is lovely – no feeling of disappointment can be felt in seeing this exquisite creation of Moorish taste. The colouring is fading, the Alberea has a fish pond in it. Then on to the Court of Lions, with its fountain in the centre. The Moors in Spain abound themselves to represent human life, but sparingly, the honeycombed roofs are exquisite, and the many varieties of interlacement too exquisite. Strolled about the gardens and looked at the lovely views from various points. When I went forth, I stumbled on and ascended by the fast path and was amply rewarded at the top by a noble view, a panorama – a large college is a conspicuous object below the hill on the N where tradition says some Christians suffered martyrdom under the Moors. In the setting sun, the Generalife was below me, with its rows of cypresses.

The Court of the Lions at the Alhambra.

Julia left the Alhambra 'with regret and a fervent hope that I may be able some day in my life, if it is spared, to come here again'. They packed and prepared to leave.

'Left Granada for Madrid 8 p.m. for the last time – many donkeys and mules bearing coal, metal water jars passed us, after having filled at the fountain. The Murphys accompanied us to the Victoria and there we dined at 6.30 – and with regret bade them adieu, with our mutual and sincere, on my side, promises of letters and visits someday. We started with ten mild mules at 10 p.m. - a lovely moon light night, and galloped and trotted merrily up and down hill to Jaen, where we arrived at 5 a.m. to a gorgeous sunrise. Chafyn slept during the night, not I, I wanted to see as much as the moon allowed of the country.'

Having been given chocolate, Julia and Chafyn washed their faces in the Rosada, and were taken to a tidy room on the first floor. It was clean with a brick floor rug, and red calico curtains. 'The stolid German in the interieur gazed at my face washing with astonishment.' After breakfast of hard eggs and bread they resumed their journey to Bailen, 'the scene of the solitary and much boasted Spanish victory over the French under Dupont – a miserable, badly paved town, and our dilly reduced to a post's pace in managing the streets full of holes and awful ruts.'

On leaving Bailen, the road descended in a gradual series of windings, where the dilly went full tilt around the bends. The hills were shrouded in wildflowers and mauve rhododendrons.

The horses, although no bigger than mules, work better – pull more pleasantly. The beater, when he sees instances of lagging jumps down and belabours the horses until they scramble off in a wild gallop. We had two mules sprawling in the road down a hill, but they picked themselves up. Water is much wanted in La Mancha – and trees. The plains produce corn and wine and saffron.

We did not reach the station until 5.p.m. (twenty-two hours from Granada instead of seventeen), and when arrived at that wretched place, we found no waiting room, only the one place at the station where luggage is heaped up, tickets given where to eat our late dinner! At last, we spied a table which in spite of a grumpy official we carried into a corner and there we consumed the rest of our chicken, managing with our pocket knives, and fingers. I felt very tired with sitting up so long and wanted to lie down, and we besieged the director for leave to pass the rest of the time in the carriages, which were waiting for the hour of departure, but he was inexorable, and Chafyn doubled himself up on some things in a corner, and I established myself on the hard bench, with my feet up, to pass the dreary hours till 9.30.p.m., when we were to start. I now began to feel very anxious at the prospect before us of a second night on Chafyn's account. We ought to have been in Madrid at midnight, as promised, and did not arrive there until 7 a.m., a trial for strong people, but enough to make one very anxious where an invalid is concerned. At Alcazar we were turned out of the train at 1.a.m. to wait for the Alicante train at three, which ought to have been in at 1.45! Such was our ill luck!

Brother and sister drove along the acacia-planted Puerta del Sol, with a large fountain which cooled the air: 'The Prado is handsome, but the town is a second-rate French city, broad streets, with houses of five storeys, with large windows and no irregular projections to break the monotony of the long façades.' They had a substantial meal and rested for the remainder of the day, and very early to bed. Julia had four letters, from Uncle H (Harry), Emily (Grove), Aunt Anna (Michell) and Susan Blake. She read *Galignani* and the *Times* – 'no news'. Julia was in a reflective mood, being overtired from the journey and anxiety over Chafyn's health had made her morose. For a brief moment, the beauty and serenity of the Alhambra had touched her heart and her emotions were at peace. Her worry was driven by her love and duty of care for Chafyn, and concern that he was in denial about his health. Chafyn, as a former army officer, would not have baulked about having a sleepless night on a bench at a railway station. He was well aware of his health problem and took the doctor's advice seriously, but aside from that he carried on with his enjoyment of life. His health was not something he wanted to be defined by, his sister's constant reminders and introducing him as 'in delicate health' being an irritation. But like Julia, he was brought up in a family that loved travelling and having been bitterly disappointed that he had to forgo his army career, he was determined to experience the world.

Julia was missing her jolly Murphy friends. The trio made her stay in Grenada more interesting as she could share her joys of discovery, Chafyn being uninterested in visiting and analysing religious establishments.

I miss the tinkling guitar and the sweet shades of the Alhambra. This dusty noisy town is a poor exchange. I never liked any place as the Alhambra, it grew upon me, and has fastened itself into my heart. The quiet repose of it delighted me, constant anxiety has made me dislike bustle and the great animation of existence, and noise now bewilders me. I don't like dullness but the delight I used to have in excitement is gone. Is it that I am getting so much older? Care and anxiety do age people greatly through time. It is now just two years since anxiety began its work amongst us, and in one form or another its claws have been upon me.

Well rested, the following day, a Sunday, Julia found there was no chaplain at the Embassy and blamed it on the Spanish, 'who have a low opinion of English religious feeling', so she set off for the Prado. 'My thoughts and mind are more elevated and spiritualized by the superb works of God's richly endowed creatures, than I have by many museums at home. The Velasquez are unrivalled portraits, so alive and noble.' Having seen the Murillos, Julia left to go to the Church of the Atocha, a poor place near the Alicante railway station. In a side chapel, 'I was horrified by a disgusting sight, to me as a protestant. There was a full-size figure of our Lord with a tulle veil and the Virgin robed in a crinoline satin tulle ball dress with gilt crown ornamented with coloured glass, her head reposing on satin pillows. I never saw such votice offerings, all dirty and dusty and falling to pieces, wax arms, legs and eyes and numerous plaits and tails of long hair!'

After church, Julia accompanied Chafyn to the Armoria where there was a superb collection of armour and weapons from very early times. In the heat of the day, they visited the Royal Stables where Chafyn waited in the shade. The stables were 'dirty and unswept from a hundred fine mules in one, and about fifty horses in another, but they seem well treated. The civil, dirty groom unclothed some for me, and I went to their pretty high-bred heads, but I shouldn't think them fast as they are short from mid to tail, and cover little ground.'

While Julia went back to the Prado to see her favourite pieces again, Chafyn went to a bull fight in Mandez at the Plaza del Toros. He felt he could not return from Spain without having seen a bull fight, rather like returning from Egypt without seeing the Pyramids.[182] He was disgusted – 'the horror of it in the treatment of the horses, who after being horribly gored were beaten with sticks to make them stand and continue the battering scene. He says he will never visit another, being horrified by young girls of twelve or thirteen who stood up, clapped their hands and <u>laughed</u> when the horses were mangled by a bull.'

A trip to Toledo was followed by a visit to Escorial, but Chafyn did not go, Julia being accompanied by a young German whom they had met in Toledo. They left Madrid to travel by train to Burgos,

then on to Alazoquitia where they disembarked and loaded the
dillys. Tightly packed with four others, they passed Vitoria, 'of great
interest to English people' and arrived at Besrain. 'The journey was
lovely through the Spanish Pyrenees, first ascended through chestnut
woods and well cultivated fields where in the Basque country one
sees one man to every two women in the field, and the men have
exchanged the conical cap for the beret.' Arriving at the top of the
pass then descended for five or seven miles, frequently at a gallop
along a fine tourniquet road. 'Nervous people would be greatly
alarmed at the rapidity of the pace and the wild equipage, ten
mules, harnessed and driven in the usual Spanish mode, i.e. a bag
on the leader, a rein to each wheeler, the intermediate taking care
of themselves. Scenery lovely, fine mountains and verdant hill sides
carved with the fresh green of the bilberry and wild flowers, but not
in the lovely variety of South Spain. The dust is overwhelming.'

The siblings were on their way to San Sebastian where their
father had fought in the Peninsular War. After a half-hour stop at
Besrain they reached their destination and arrived at the 'Tranda di
Beraza – a nice French feeling Hotel with polished oak floors, and
a very good supper for three francs vin compris. We here see the
last of Spain and bid adieu to the patient bullocks merrily dragging
carts slowly along. I like them – I am glad to have seen Spain, and
in a few years, if I am alive, and railroads have progressed and
introduced a little gleam of civilization amongst the people I should
like to take the south-east coast and Granada again – but now there
are many drawbacks to comfort in Spanish travelling, the food is
undeniably bad.' San Sebastian

...is beautifully situated at the foot of a rock called Argella, which
rises four hundred feet above the sea, and the hills rise all round
covered in vegetation. Walked out early and around the rocky
hill on which the castle, so spoiled in the Peninsular War stands,
but had not time to ascend to the top. Found slabs let into the
wall recording the deaths of several English officers, 'her brother'
Fletcher, Capt. Collier and Lt. Mackel altogether – all in 1813.
I would have liked a day here, and to explore the hills around
which must offer lovely walks. We go to Juan de Suz the first and
last town of Spain. Juan was for a long time the headquarters of
the Duke of Wellington, and I have so often heard my father speak
of all this country and these places that I have a great interest in
them, and the gallant deeds of our noble army half a century ago
must have an attraction for us – fast even as the world goes now.

The train journey to Bayonne through a succession of tunnels, cuttings and embankments had only been open one week. On arrival at the hotel, they found it very clean and fresh after Spain and had an excellent dinner at the table d'hôte. 'The public walk by the river is pretty, and the place has an air of intense civilization after Spain, but of great formality and un-picturesque.' Julia and Chafyn went to Biarritz in a hourly dilly that runs backwards and forwards along a straight Roman road between rows of poplars and planes. 'The bay of Biarritz itself is very small and devoid of verdure and attractions, but the views of the Spanish coast and the Pyrenees are very lovely. The shops are not open, and the place is redolent of paint and preparation for the season.' After dining at the Hotel de France, a poor and scanty dinner, Julia bought a straw hat for the garden at home and filled the crown with a pound of cherries from the market, before returning in the dilly.

One reason Chafyn wanted to travel home via Madrid was to go to Bordeaux to taste and buy some wines. The train left Bayonne at 1 p.m. and reached Bordeaux at 5.30 p.m., 'where we saw some men on stilts supporting themselves against their staff in the flat deary brushwood. They reached up to mark stragglers. Put up at the Hotel de France where the rooms are fitted up with beds in alcoves and velvet chairs. The table d'hôte does not supply much in this wine country!' Having allowed a day in the schedule for wine tasting, the following day they set off to Barton Guestier's wine vaults, 'immense places, where we tasted some excellent Sauternes, Leoville and Meschawell wines and some first rate cognac. The Sauterne was positive nectar! Chafyn wanted to buy some wine but B & G only sell to the trade. The vaults are very cold and much damper than I would have expected to have seen them, the mildew had gathered like cotton wool on some of the wines. Walked about this fine town which is much adorned by boulevards and trees. [...] To bed at my usual virtuous hour about 9 p.m., as we make an early start tomorrow.'

Leaving the station at 7 a.m. they arrived in Paris on the Grande Vitesse train at 6.30 p.m. 'We put up at the Grand Hotel. There is a handsome salon with plenty of papers, the *Quarterly*, etc., with the restaurant apart from the hotel. The people are chiefly Americans I think and almost all vulgarians.'

Familiar with Paris, Julia and Chafyn visited their favourite restaurants and bistros. Julia went to church, having to wear a hat as she had no bonnet. There she met the Beaumonts who were also on the Nile, but was not impressed with the service, there being no litany and a very poor sermon. But of the utmost importance for Julia was shopping for clothes. She headed for the 'grand shops she knew well.

I chose a bonnet at Euphrosine's and then went off for some plates of fashion, in order that I might have an idea of what I should invest in. Passementerie trims everything and ladies all have a basquine either all round, or behind only. Bands <u>may</u> be worn with plain bands, but there are very few of them and sleeves are all very small. My room is full of parcels, and I must leave some old worn-out things here to make room for the new, but I like to take my old home when I can for the dear old souls at Zeals, to whom all old gown or ribbon is a boon, much greater than any new thing they can buy.

The siblings arrived at Havre at 7.30 p.m. 'A tossing about the first few hours and then subsided. I passed the night dozing on a sofa until daylight. It rained all the way on board, and a miserable wet morning dawned on the 1ˢᵗ June.'

Having arrived in Southampton in a fog, stopping at Halley's for breakfast of coffee, ham and eggs, Julia and Chafyn caught a train to Gillingham, changing carriages at Salisbury on the way. The phaeton was as the station to greet them and as the weather had improved, they rode home to Zeals House in it. Farmers and labourers working in the fields doffed their caps on seeing their landlord and his sister return and as always, Chafyn would have acknowledged them.

CHAPTER THIRTEEN

Coming Home

Arriving at noon, everything was ready for them. Kerten, Julia's dog, and Tip, Chafyn's dog, came bounding out of the house to greet them in great excitement. The Mere and Silton church

Zeals House from the south-east.

bells rang out all day, and then the ringers paid a visit, 'and did not go away empty handed of course'.[183] Chafyn and Julia were excited to look around their new house both inside and out and were delighted with it. The builders had finished at the end of the previous year, but there was still some work to be completed inside. Julia wrote, 'The carpenters are in full possession of my side of the house and I occupy "King Charles" room.'

Although Chafyn had signed the papers for the purchase of the Silton Estate before he left the previous autumn, completion only took place in the New Year, so he would have visited the farmers in Silton, checking on the progress of setting up the partridge and pheasant shoot there. He met Squarey who was given a Cairo dagger, and he also had to catch up with 'S'. The mysterious S in Julia's diary is not given a name at this time. If it was one of Chafyn's male friends, they were always referred to by their surname, which indicates a girlfriend. In the discretion and morality of the Victorian period, it is feasible that strict rules on declaring romantic relationships until an engagement was announced would have precluded revealing the woman's name to save her reputation. Being and appearing respectable was essential. Later in Julia's diary, S is revealed as Sue.

Julia's first preoccupation was to secure two servants from Sedgehill. The village being next to East Knoyle where Julia was born was often a source of servants for Julia, and she frequently went there to see her Grove cousins, on this occasion with Chafyn and S. The Revd Charles-Henry Grove was Charlotte Downes's youngest brother. He lived in the rectory, happy to secure a living close to his Ferne family, with his wife Eliza and six daughters.[184] All the daughters feature regularly in Julia's diary. On her return she drove to Witham to interview a footman, 'who is young but promises satisfactorily'. Bath was her next destination to look for a housemaid. 'Bath looked dreary and deserted. The agricultural show in Bristol delayed the trains much. Found Daniels tuning p.f. [pianoforte] on my return.' Having put the house in order, the enlarged house needing more servants, Julia went to see her aunt Fanny and uncle Harry in Salisbury before returning to her daily routine of going to Zeals village to teach the children in the school room next to the church. She was training them to sing hymns as a choir for the church. The school was flourishing and Julia was delighted to see thirty-eight children present, so she asked for a holiday for the rest of the day. 'Called on some poor women all very smiling at our return and full of enquiries for Chafyn.' The school may well have been thriving but the church was undergoing an extraordinary upset. Revd Dalby had gone mad and was in an asylum and a curate filled his place.

As delighted as Julia was when she first returned to see her part of the house, less than two weeks later, 'the new building to this house certainly has not progressed as we expected – it will be very nice when finished, but although the masons are gone the carpenters make a great deal of dust and noise.'

Sunday was a busy day for Julia as she often went to church at both Mere and Zeals and oversaw the Sunday school. If the weather was too wet, then prayers for the servants would be read in the Zeals House dining room. Although Chafyn did go to Mere Church occasionally for a service, most Sundays Julia found it hard to persuade Chafyn to join her. He was either too hot or too cold or he was too tired. When he did go to church, he preferred Mere to Zeals. However, neither the weather nor his tiredness stopped him from going to London regularly. On his first trip to town soon after his return to Zeals he lost his portmanteau containing photographs, probably the ones taken in Egypt, to show to Myers and other friends.

The gentle pace of the countryside life continues through Julia's diary, a way of life drifting through the seasons with visits to and from neighbours, family and friends. There were more people to visit with the addition of the Silton Estate, Mr Benjafield, Chafyn's great farmer, and Mrs Shorland, the Rector's wife who became a good friend. Tenants were visited when they had a new baby or when they were sick. 'Drove out in pony gig. Mrs Pearce's son will not be long in this world – poor woman, he will be the fourth she has followed to the grave, taken away by consumption; little Harcourt is better but his cheeks are very pink.'

The Troyte-Bullock family at North Coker near Yeovil across the border in Somerset were regularly visited. Aunt Maria had married George Bullock and their son George Troyte-Bullock was Chafyn's heir. On a visit in July to see the hunt, Julia found 'Aunt Maria has had a slight paralytic attack – son George [Troyte-Bullock] and Alice [his wife] there and the two children. Mabel is a love.'

During the summer the Chafyn-Groves liked to be outdoors as much as possible. They liked to sit by the pond, the small lake filled with trout, on the west side of the house to enjoy the afternoon sun and the sunset. Croquet parties were fashionable and these were regularly held at Zeals; invitations to tea and croquet were the order of the day, but it was not always gentile. 'A croquet party at the Cardews – Miss Morgill distinguished herself by quarrelling over the game with Ella Locke who then refused to let her play.' Summer was also the time for festivals. 'Choral Festival at Mere – 120 singers who did very well, but the clergy sneaked in shabbily instead of marching in a processional way, and Mr Morrice appeared carrying a large black leather bag with his surplice in it. Our Vicar has no organ of order – the want of which was signally displayed at the evening Amateur Concert, when all was dire confusion and disorder, and mob law reigned.'

The day after Tom Grove of Ferne and his family visited Zeals, Chafyn and Julia went to London. Julia 'stayed at Suffolk Street, had luncheon and went out shopping in a brougham, dined at 8 and to bed early'. As with other visits to London, Chafyn stayed separately and they met up during the day. After breakfast Julia went to the Royal Academy. 'Landseer is a great force this year, portraits very numerous.'[185]

'As usual – Chafyn called for me and we went to Manchester Road where I dropped him at the Doctor's and on to Druce's Furniture Bazaar [in Baker Street] where I passed nearly three hours choosing beds and tables etc. Chafyn joined me there: the doctor thinks he is better, he looks better certainly than he did a month ago. In the afternoon I drove alone and shopped and then round the Park but did not see the princess.'[186] And on the following day: 'Passed the day as we did yesterday, ordering the painted [stained glass] windows at Powell's in Whitefriars, and dined with the Jeffreys.'

On her way home, instead of the route to Gillingham, she decided to take the Reading train and visit her Aunt Anna, her mother's Michell sister, but Anna was not at home, having decamped to the Isle of Wight. Not having time to wait for the carriage, she took a fly to Bruton, but when she arrived at Zeals she found that Chafyn had departed for Ferne without her knowledge. Julia felt entitled to know her brother's movements. With sisterly concern for his health, she had a fire lit in his bedroom at night – in summer – if the weather turned chilly. Watching over him and praying for him, she rarely accepted invitations to stay overnight. It was her duty to be at Zeals to care for Chafyn.

Finding it difficult to cope on her own when he was away, Julia filled her diary with daily tasks, 'to school and then called on Roberts, a farmer at Silton and on Mrs Maggs, a nice old woman who lives in a neat little place on Furze Hill. Called on the Newalls.' But it was not fulfilling. She had to return to an empty house and have dinner alone. She would invite friends for tea and croquet, especially Charles-Henry Grove's daughters who were her regular companions. Her concern for Chafyn's health was mixed with her need for his companionship. She was unhappy that he was staying so long at Ferne and was jealous of her Grove cousins' fondness for Chafyn but coldness towards her.

On her third day alone, Chafyn had not returned, so lonely, unhappy and angry at his preference to be with the Groves than with her, she whisked her wagonette to Ferne House before breakfast, after only a cup of coffee, to bring him home. She had been a regular visitor with her mother to her Grove cousins at Ferne since she was seven years old.[187] After the drive across the downs, and always preferring to eat before starting her day, she arrived at Ferne where she was put into a room alone and given breakfast. Julia was annoyed that Mrs John Grove, Tom Grove's widowed mother, was not there to greet her: 'She had not descended from her room, and did not appear for ten minutes or so.' The families had intermarried on several occasions, but when the dowager did appear, Julia received a frosty reception. Considering this a snub, Julia promptly left, taking Chafyn with her.

Caught up in her own feelings, Julia was unaware of the embarrassment the incident caused for Chafyn. She had grown used to having her brother by her side for eight months when they were on their Egyptian travels and had not adapted to the separate lives they would inevitably have to lead. This was aggravated by Julia's unfriendliness towards her Grove cousins at Ferne. She did not want Chafyn to be too close with them. Her high-spirited brother was not about to be treated like a disobedient schoolboy by his big sister, but he held back from confronting her. His usual way of dealing with problems, nurtured by his army training, was to move on and move swiftly. He was well aware he was living with a life-threatening disease without Julia treating him as an invalid. It was not pity he needed, but the freedom to enjoy the life he had left. He found the care Julia was giving him suffocating, but also knew she was doing it out of love. He would try to please her by going to church at Zeals with her on Sunday.

The country landscape continued to dominate the Chafyn-Groves' lives. The following day Julia writes: 'There was a violent thunderstorm in the afternoon which caused serious damage in many places. It refreshed the gardens, much in want of rain. The spring was dry and there has not been much rain since we returned to England, and the cattle are being fed on hay in dry counties – all abouts the soil is damper, and although turnips, etc. want drink sorely, there is no lack of grass.'

When Sunday arrived, there was turmoil at Zeals Church. It looked as if there was no hope of Revd Dalby recovering, and the Ecclesiastical Commissioners had improved the living to £300 per annum after a request from Mrs Deane, the Church Warden, and the building of a rectory had been agreed. Revd Spencer Fellowes had been offered the position. Chafyn was asked to donate the land for the rectory to which he agreed, but Julia was not happy. She complained that Chafyn should have been asked if there was any friend of his who would like the living, as happened previously when Revd Sweeting resigned – or she could have offered it to a Michell relative. She was suspicious that everything had been agreed as soon as they left England, and no doubt reminded Mrs Deane that Chafyn was the benefactor of the church. It was in this sour atmosphere that Chafyn accompanied Julia to Zeals Church.

Neither Julia nor Chafyn were yet to meet Mr Fellowes, but Julia, as she often did, had already decided that she would not like him. She had just arrived back from Wincanton having 'brought back Chafyn's hose – his machinery for watering the house in case of fire, with which we now get the garden nicely watered' when 'Miss Mary Turton arrived, dined and slept here. She was Revd Fellowes' fiancée. 'A nice girl, but not much to say for herself'.

At Fellowes' first service at Zeals Church Julia declared, 'He seems a cheery sort of man,' but on another occasion when he went to dine at Zeals, 'He is shy and appears dull.'

In August, Chafyn went to London for a few days and returned for the cricket party just as the Murphy trio arrived at Zeals.

> A cricket party of farmers, with a very small sprinkling of gentlemen. Mr de St. Croix from Longbridge Deverill brought a party – and Mere was the winner. A croquet party was appended to the cricket – and we had tea for 27 in the dining room – but I now find that these things have expanded, and that the proper thing is tea handed at 5 o'clock in the afternoon, and a cold collation with mine at 7. Everyone is croquet mad. We had the Hoares, Bicknells, Deans, Turtons, and Charles Phelips over and Shorlands. Our party grew in size insensibly, as I did not intend so many at first, not to tire Chafyn. A little music ended the day.

There was another croquet party the following day at Sedgehill Rectory with Charles-Henry Grove's family. '4 sets playing and a very smart cold collation at 7. The black mare Nightshade felt limpy coming home and has been unfit for use ever since, luckily Chafyn bought a horse last week, and we have Capt. Phelips' pony here during his absence.'

The entertainment for the Murphys continued with a visit to Wilton where they called on Lady Herbert 'who with her children showed us the house and her Syrian tents – she had eight of them, making quite an encampment, and the Murphys were charmed by all they saw.' Onwards in a trap to Salisbury, they had lunch at Browns, followed by a quick visit to Aunt Fanny and the Cathedral and Chapter House. 'The Murphys are Roman Catholic and are much surprised by our churches, as in Ireland Protestantism takes a very cold, uninviting aspect.' Chafyn did not go to another croquet party at Gillingham, but 'the guitar went and we had good music of all sorts. In the evening the vicar dined and we had a musical performance in the dining room, guitar, voices, castanets and tambourine and a ringing of bells! which made a fine row altogether.'

By invitation, Lady Hoare invited Julia and her guests for a row on the lake, and to stay for dinner. 'Lady Hoare was as pleasant as she can be, when dull at home. The guitar and castanets went in company with the Christy Minstrels on the water, which had a very nice effect. Chafyn did not go.'

The Murphy trio then went to Chapel, taking with them Julia's dog Kerten, who 'remained during mass under the slat'. Afterwards, Julia, Chafyn and the Murphy women drove to Fonthill 'to see Mr. Morrison's wonderful china'. Lady Hoare's daughter Gussy went with them. They saw the rows of lovely caskets set with jewels on the chimney piece in the drawing room and under glass and lock and key. Mr Morrison went with Chafyn to the Beckford Arms, which Julia thought was just as well as 'he would have been frightened by four women on their own. The house is studded everywhere with pictures, likewise huddled away in corners, from want of space.' When Alfred and Chafyn returned, the group was inspecting the horses in the stables. Further trips to Wardour and Longleat are described in Julia's diary and on both occasions 'Chafyn did not go.' The Murphys for him had not 'grown on acquaintance'. Out of politeness, Chafyn remained at Zeals until the Murphys left at the end of August, then he immediately departed for London. He was making plans, and they involved leaving Zeals House for some considerable time.

CHAPTER FOURTEEN

Going Away

Julia often went out riding on the downs with Henry Ainslie and Augusta Hoare's daughter Gussy (Augusta).[188] 'She improves on acquaintance.'[189] Gussy was a nervous rider but they both enjoyed the outings in their own way, with Gussy pleased to have a riding companion. The Hoare family were at Stourhead in the summer months and Gussy was an only child, her brother having died at the age of seven. Her mother Augusta was an unhappy woman, her husband being a compulsive gambler and spending most of his time in London and Paris. His addiction would later result in the sale of

Zeals House from the lake.

all of Richard Colt Hoare's topographical library and many works of art including a Turner and a Poussin.[190]

One day, a thunderstorm started as Julia rode to Stourhead with Gussy and she was driven back by the rain. When she returned to Zeals, Alfred Morrison was waiting for her.

'He called for the second time this summer, and stayed two and a half hours, which shows he has conquered his shyness of ladies, as I was alone to entertain him. The rain partly detained him, but it cleared up long before he went away. I always rather liked him for he has conversation and nice tastes in art etc.' It was unusual for a visitor to arrive without any notice, but Julia has no complaints at his unexpected arrival, nor was she in any hurry to see him leave. She regularly took various guests to Fonthill to view his china, but perhaps it is Mr Morrison she hoped to see. Gussy Hoare, aged 18, would be unlikely to enjoy viewing a collection of china. After another ride with Gussy which was called off by rain at White Cross, Julia went home to see that Chafyn had returned, his friend Mr Hoffman with him. The following day was a Sunday and 'Chafyn came to Holy Communion only, the whole service tires him, having the will to go to church also.' George and Alice Troyte-Bullock arrived. 'Rain again, too catching for riding or driving, so walked a little with Alice, George and Hoffy'. When the weather improved, they rode to the Tower, Alice and George climbing it.[191] 'Pony has a pinched shoulder. It is Gussy's saddle, made by Standerwick – I must provide myself with another.'

Henry Hoffman was a friend of Chafyn's from Trinity College. Although five years older than Chafyn, they were at Cambridge at the same time, as Hoffman was taking a further degree. He qualified as a medical physician but his later chosen career was as a medical inspector. As Hoffman liked shooting, 'Capt. Phelips and Col. Henry were invited to shoot and dined here on Tuesday.' Capt. Phelips lived at Bayford, a neighbouring estate just across the border into Somerset and was a close friend of Chafyn's. 'The small Colonel has shrunk into minutest proportions, what can he look like in regimentals?'

Devey came and Alfred Morrison drove him over, changing horses at Willoughby hedge gate! Mr. Hoffman is very sociable now. [...] Chafyn, George and Alice went to Salisbury.' George Troyte-Bullock must have assumed that he would be Chafyn's heir, trawling through family pedigrees was not an unusual pastime for landed families to check their houses were safe for future generations. Passing on the house securely was their biggest responsibility, but it is likely that Chafyn confirmed to George that he would inherit Zeals House and the estate in the event of anything happening to him; planning a long journey could be hazardous and his illness would have hampered marriage and a family of his own. Also, that Julia would stay at Zeals House for life, and he asked both George and Alice to visit her regularly in his proposed long absence.

Chafyn and George and Alice came back in the afternoon. I warned the kitchen maid today, as she is so inveterately dirty and careless, and does smash crockery wonderfully. I had an inspection of washed dishes and plates, which were covered with dirty thumb marks, and uncleaned grease. She smashed two cups, two tart dishes and a vegetable dish in one week, having been here three months now she ought to have learnt the carefulness and neatness of a gentleman's house.

It was Harvest Home Day, Zeals Church beautifully done up with wheatsheafs and flowers.

A dull sermon, then Phelips, White, Rose, Parfitt, Mitchell and Baker joined, the Jupes kept away and the other small holders. Non-conformists were not welcomed. The procession with flags and band was wending its way up here, where they marched around the house, then proceeded to games, running for prizes etc. in the park. Dinner was very good and well arranged by Goldsborough in the school room, about two hundred and ninety sat down, besides a few at the high table. Chafyn was chairman, and got through the speeches well, but was very tired the next day. All went off well.

Another festive day followed, 'Tea in the coach house, followed by races and prizes. Two hundred and sixty tea'd and the remnants went to old women and men who gathered at the gates.'[192]

The following day, Julia drove Alice Troyte-Bullock to Fonthill House to see the china and engravings. Alfred Morrison was four years Julia's senior and unmarried. As Julia reveals, he had a shyness with women which could be the reason for his single status, but he seemed to enjoy being with Julia. He appeared to appreciate her enthusiasm for his exquisite collections, her knowledge of art and literature, her superb horsemanship and her stoic character.

To our dismay Mr Morrison was out shooting, after a short consultation we sent for him, as the servant said he was not far away, the man sent a horse for him, and in about half an hour in he came in great haste, received our apologies for bringing him away with the greatest good humour, in fact he begged us to come someday this week not giving any time, and said he should like to show his valuables himself so our visit was somewhat by appointment. After a while, when we had given it up in despair, he bethought him of lunch and ordered some for us, and after that we again went to work and were 3 hours looking over his china and old engravings which are sumptuous and evidently his delight, he was very pleasant and went on bringing out one portfolio of engravings after another with the keenest relish and was pleased at our admiration of the things – lots of the china came from the Summer Palace at Peking. We felt quite bewildered by what we saw. Mr Morrison asked me if I would like to take a book home which I jumped at.

Alfred Morrison was not looked upon kindly by his Fonthill neighbour Hugh Grosvenor, the Duke of Westminster, who referred to him as having 'amassed a fortune from trade'. In a letter to Mary Wyndham at Clouds, he wrote: Mr Alfred is an eccentric individual with peculiar views on most things – having thirty-three hunters valued at three-hundred-a-piece and never to ride one of them, and rearing a thousand pheasants and to shoot them all himself.[193]

He denounces all art and artists except those of which he himself approves (and they are a queer lot).'[194]

Returning home, Julia giving nothing away about her thoughts of the day, wrote: 'In the afternoon Alice and I went nutting and blackberrying in the wood and brought back baskets full.'

On 20th September Alice and George went home and Chafyn and Julia went to London. 'Messrs. Myers and Hoffman dined with us. Mr Chafyn and Mr Hoffman have had their thing,' wrote Julia, resigned to the plans for the long trip the two young men planned to take for the winter and maybe for longer. Chafyn would have discussed his need to get away for the winter months for his health with Myers, his best friend. Myers told Chafyn that his friends Dr and Mrs Chisholm and Mr Attwood had booked a passage on the *Vimeira* to Australia. The ship would arrive at the end of the year in mid-summer.

The next day Julia accompanied Chafyn and Hoffman to Silver's Cornhill, the outfitters. 'The ship's cabins are not fitted up or furnished, so the occupiers have to do that at their own expense. Very warm day and the city very crowded as we had to go through narrow streets, in consequence of Cheapside being in course of partial repairing. Came back, lunched and drove out in the brougham to Marshall and Snelgrove's etc. Chafyn doing chores and house commissions.'

After breakfast the following day, 'Little Hoff came and we drove down to Blackwall to see the *Vimeira*, went through some of the worst purlieus of London, Poplar, Limehouse, to the East India Docks. The ship was in the hands of the carpenters and Silver's man was unable to fall on to Chafyn's cabin fittings as we expected he would have done. The *Vimeira* is a fine large ship, but not fast they say, broad in the beam, which adds to the comfort of the passengers.'[195]

It was the end of September 1864, and last-minute arrangements were being made before Chafyn's departure. 'Devey came, and Mons. Vaillant from Paris about the tapestry for the new drawing room and we consulted over it from 2.30 p.m. until 6 o'clock. It will be lovely, I think.' Chafyn was making final arrangements and signing off the plans for Devey to build the row of almshouses which Chafyn had commissioned from him for Zeals village.

The final day of September saw rifle shooting for prizes. 'Mine is a fish knife and fork, Chafyn gives the other two prizes. Barnes took 3rd prize, John Coward won the cup and Roberts of Silton, Chafyn's new farmer, 2nd prize.'

On 1ˢᵗ October. Mr Messiter of Wincanton, Chafyn's solicitor, came to see Chafyn to get his signature for the purchase of the Silton Estate and for his new will. There were legacies for various friends, godchildren and his uncles, but the change was that all of Julia's religious requests in the former will were taken out. Although the legacies for the vicars of Zeals and Mere remained, instead of providing funds for items like the coal club and the clothing club there was a codicil to explain that instead of these items he would provide funds for a row of almshouses to be built in Zeals village in memory of his dear mother, Eleanor. Julia requested a legacy for her closest companion, Emily-Charlotte Grove, the eldest of Charles-Henry's six daughters, as she was past thirty and unlikely to marry.

'Uncle Harry came yesterday. I fetched him from the station in the phaeton. Plymouth Royal Hotel - arrived per Express at 6.10. Met Mr Hoffman at Exeter, also spoke to Bobby Mayne there, now a cadet on board the *Britannia*, going down in charge of his uncle "My Lord Mayne". Uncle Harry fell in with Mrs Knatchbull of Babington.[196] The sea was rough on the Dawlish coast. The Hotel is comfortable enough for an English Hotel.'

[2ⁿᵈ October.] Sunday. Out early and up on the Hoe, the lookout place over the Sound and from thence came the *Vimeira* at Anchor. She arrived yesterday at 4.p.m. having passed the downs at 5 a.m. on Friday morning. 36 hours – a very quick passage. The wind is blowing furiously from the south-east and it is bitterly cold. To Church at 11, good sermon and bad singing. Dined at 2 and ¼ to 5 went in the fly with Chafyn and Mr Hoffman to see them off in the boat to the ship, as she was to sail at 10 next day, it was thought advisable to go on board overnight so as to get into place in quiet water. It was to me a miserable parting from the only family tie I have now in this world. God grant we may all meet next year and that this separation so bitter, may be rewarded by my seeing Chafyn in better health then. Uncle Harry and I went up on the Hoe to watch the boat to the ship, where we learned from Mr Hoffman they arrived without getting wet as we expected they must. After watching the ship for some time, returned and went to evening Church. To bed early but not to sleep, the howling wind made me think all night of my dear traveller's voyage down Channel in this fierce, though favourable gale.

[3ʳᵈ October.] At 10, Mr Hoffman came in and reported going out of the Sound at noon. Saw Mrs Chisholm who seems a nice little woman, and promised to take care of Chafyn. She spoke and looked so kindly and kissed me at parting. Out at 8 a.m. up on the Hoe, very cold and so blowing. I could hardly stand. Bought the last *All the Year Round* for Chafyn and gave it to Mr Hoffman, left by Express at 10.40, ran up to the Hoe and took a last look at the ship, may God be favourable to her and those on board her! No one knows but He who sees all hearts and minds how mine follow her. The cold wind has given me a very bad cold. Home at 3.20, how solitary it does feel here now. My daily, hourly care is gone and I feel a complete blank as if I had nothing to think of. Winter is sticking his fangs in betimes, how I dread this winter, solitude and cold and anxiety will be mostly my share in it.

[4th October.] 'Uncle Harry left. A letter from Chafyn dated Sound, still at anchorage, the pilot refused to take them past the Breakwater with 2 tug steamers, but if the wind lulls, they will leave next morning at 5 a.m. The wind is excellent for them in the Channel, and will waft them in four days into mild breezes, how I wish I was there, much as I hate the sea.[197]

This would be the last letter Julia would receive from her beloved brother until he arrived in Sydney, New South Wales.

CHAPTER FIFTEEN

Vimeira

'The *Vimeira* looks very different to what she did in the docks. Her decks are filled up with pens of sheep and pigs, flocks of poultry and casks of water. At tea at 6 we saw some of the passengers, save myself, Hoffman and the first mate, no one spoke. After tea, set to work unpacking and after some time made the cabin really comfortable. How long it will remain so is another matter. I made acquaintance this morning at the hotel with Dr and Mrs Chisholm and Mr Attwood, all friends of Myers. Attwood is an invalid and going like me in search of health. Dr and Mrs Chisholm are going out for good, the gentleman to practise as a doctor. They seemed very pleasant people, and both Chisholm and Attwood having been out before can and will put one up to many a good wrinkle. Grog time (9 p.m.) has struck.[198]

Sea sickness also struck as they eventually got underway and went through the Bay of Biscay. When the wind moderated Chafyn and Chisholm made their first appearance on deck, and Mr Chisholm tried his ice-making machine. 'I had no idea that the process was so simple, for at our first attempt two moulds of good water ice were turned out in about twenty-five minutes. It will be a boon in the Tropics. Whist in the evening with Chisholm and Attwood and the Skipper, Capt. Green, a pleasant unassuming sort of man, and lost two points.'

Pistol practice by shooting floating bottles kept Chafyn and Hoffman amused, until a large bird was spotted close to the ship, which Hoffman despatched with a bullet. There was a general meeting in the saloon to discuss the possibility of creating a magazine. 'The chairman opened the proceedings in the style of Mr Skimpkin at Pickwick's trial, keeping all he knew carefully to himself, and leaving the audience much in the same state as when

Frigate ship *Vimeira*.

he began. However, after the meeting warmed up and after some talk, it was decided that a magazine should be established to be called the *Vimeira Magazine*, and that I should fill the onerous and "oner-able" position of editor, a piece of uncalled for greatness thrust upon me.' The first edition of the magazine was produced at breakfast a few days later 'much enhanced by Hoffman's frontispiece'. James, Chafyn's bright young steward, formerly a cabman in Sydney, 'was sent to pour water into Chisholm's filter, and poured it all into the ice machine!'

The wind and sea soon sent all the passengers to the cuddy, except Mrs Chisholm who was in a delicate state and rarely went on deck, being carried back and forth to her cabin. She had not fulfilled her promise to Julia to look after Chafyn, she could barely look after herself.

Our party is as follows: Mrs Robey, widow of a Sydney ironmonger lately deceased in England with her nine children, Miss Robey, my neighbour at dinner, the best and quietest of her family, Miss Louisa Robey, loud voiced and forward, Miss Clara R, poetical and voluptuous, Master R, a hobbledehoy of sixteen or so, two little boys about eleven or twelve, unobjectionable, a little girl with a gigantic crinoline, and finally two small boys most objectionably noisy and generally in the way. The three young ladies affect considerable airs of young ladyism, and talk much about the poets on the strength of an acquaintance probably derived from collections of elegant extracts. They anticipate much more pleasure on their voyage than when they came to England two years ago as there are so many 'single young men on board'. Then we have what I call our own party, whom I fear the R clan look upon either as exclusive or stuck up, because forsooth we are not sufficiently appreciative of their society. We consist of Chisholm, 'the many dodging' Mrs C., Attwood, Hoffman and myself, besides Attwood's dog Moses – then Bayldon the ship's doctor, going out for his health, very argumentative and sometimes intrusive – under his charge is a youth called Robinson subject to epileptic fits and quite half witted, and who furnishes a berth for the juveniles – next come the two Hills, the younger going out for his health, the elder plays in the Covent Garden Orchestra – decidedly second rate. Robertson, a long quiet fellow, who shares Hoffman's cabin. He is going out for his health broken by work in the Indian Civil Service. Pizzala, a decent sort of boy, going out for his health.

<u>Christie</u>, a sturdy little fellow going out to farm, and making much in the evening with the R girls on whom he is in constant attendance, and finally <u>Smith</u> who left London in perfect health, and has been laid up in his cabin ever since, occasionally being carried on deck, by an attack of rheumatism in his feet which he doesn't seem able to shake off.

By mid-October, the *Vimeira* was heading straight for the Canary Islands and had to change course to avoid running into Tenerife. The weekly magazine day was the highlight of Chafyn's week. Each passenger would write articles to be included for the amusement of all, Chafyn writing a four-page article about the bull fight. The committee included a sports editor, reporting on deck games, shooting birds, fishing and general exercise, and an illustration editor with sketches by the artistic Hoffman; short jokes (excluded if not original) were edited by Chafyn. There were card games in the evening, and also many birds and fish to examine. Chisholm liked to haul small fish and jellyfish on to the ship and put them under his microscope. They spotted dolphin, with their attendant pilot fish, some of which were caught. The black spots on their bellies were, Chisholm declared, parasites. Once the Tropic of Cancer had been passed there was claret and champagne at dinner, then the Trade Winds returned.

> Chisholm and Bayldon are at issue over the dolphin question. The latter appealed to me on the matter in the most solemn manner in my cabin, declaring that I had behaved in a sarcastic and ungentlemanly manner to him. I declined to interfere and advised him to let the matter drop. Thanks to Robinson and the Hills who are awful jam sharks the jam at breakfast has been stopped, as it could not stand the present rapid rate of consumption.

The heat increasing by four degrees. All lounged about the deck, collars and waistcoats being discarded. 'The sea was magnificently phosphorescent tonight; the top of the waves being lit up as far as the eye could reach. Had some conversation on deck in the evening with the fantastic Fanny who reads novels of the present day at the rate of four a week, when she can get them. Walter Scott, she thinks is dark and cowardly.'

At the end of the first month at sea, it was the custom to have a celebration called 'throwing overboard the dead horse'. 'At 6.30 p.m. a solemn dirge sung by the crew in the forecastle announced the commencement and slowly they advanced aft dragging along the 'dead horse', a very doubtful imitation of the noble quadruped. Looking in front of the poop the procession halted at the lanyard up to which the animal was hauled and then cast off into the sea amidst much cheering. The sunset as usual magnificent, the clouds piling themselves into the most extraordinary forms.'

The Doctor [Bayldon] who reads prayers on deck, in future, wants to be referred to in the magazine as 'the Shepherd', as he thinks Doctor is too personal. He had a long conflab in the morning about an advertisement in the mag which he considers personal. Smoothed him down as far as possible and then he said that the little boy's letter in last week's volume was excellent and amused him much, rather a different tune to what he said in the early part of the week when he abused it as bad taste and personal but that is his way. He generally comes round and not only recants his old opinion but denies having asserted it, e. g. the Dolphin issue, where by the by he was originally right.

On 9th November the *Vimeira* was not quite at the line but the passengers were sensing it. There was sport on deck in the moonlight of cockfighting in which the skipper, Hoffman, Hill and others 'distinguished themselves'. The following morning at 7 a.m. they crossed the equator. The crew, who had been sulky having had their grog stopped because one of the crew was complaining about rations,

...were now allowed an extra tot of grog at eight bells. [...] After dinner Chisholm proposed the Captain's health on the strength of having crossed the line today. As however, we have been three days about it (from unlucky winds) and no fault of the ship or Captain, it was a rather sore subject with him. Attwood then proposed 'the Ladies' and called on Christie to return the thanks which he did in a faint ramble after we had vainly attempted 'here's a health' in which oddly enough hardly anyone could or would join at the other end of the table. More speechifying had been intended but it was cut short by the sudden disappearance of Mamma Roby and the girls, so sudden as to suggest the idea that something had offended them, not certainly our riotous proceedings, for we had only as yet partaken of two glasses of the small claret supplied by Dewitt and Moore. I expect the abortive 'here's a health' scandalised them.

The wind was less strong now as the *Vimeira* was only a hundred and twenty miles from the American coast. A booby was caught in the rigging, which was killed and dissected. A nine-inch flying fish was found inside. In the evenings Chafyn was kept amused with whist, but when Attwood went down with pleurisy, Smith, who was out of practice, was brought in to play along with Chisholm and the Skipper.

'On Sunday the doctor read service in his usual <u>excellent</u> manner on deck. Lovely evening, the moon being nearly at its full and shining as only a tropical moon can. I had the satisfaction of frightening fantastic Fanny into a maiden blushings this evening on deck by recounting what she and her sisters evidently thought a naughty story to Mrs Chisholm who was sitting near them. I need scarcely say that it was really a relation of the trivialist nature. I fear that I have shocked them more than once.'

The South-east Trades blew up fresh with the stern sails set. Attwood was better and came on deck but Chafyn was 'not quite the thing in the afternoon having taken in a draught'. A barracuda thirty-six inches long was caught and cooked for luncheon, Mrs Chisholm declaring it was too bitter, but Hoffman approved of the flavour and likened it to trout. They were now almost directly under the sun 'and at midday a man's shadow is quite under his feet.'

Christie and the fantastic one had a tiff tonight – cause unknown. 'amantium irae'. [lovers' quarrels]. The parted lovers made it up again this evening and played an amicable game of whist. [...] A rough night and a rougher day with a headwind and sea producing a most unpleasant motion. Having narrowly escaped destruction last night by a tin of biscuits which bounced off a shelf and fell on the floor close to my head, I passed the remainder of an uncomfortable night, and woke very sleepy and seedy. Saw an Albatross today. They are rarely seen this far north. Also saw a brig homeward bound. Several of the passengers more or less bilious today. The butcher had a close shave of being swept overboard by the sea as he plucked a goose in the forecastle. The steward's state of mind was great, his anxiety being for the safety of the goose, not the butcher.

The strong winds pushed the *Vimeira* in a southerly direction: 'At this rate we should find ourselves at Cape Horn instead of Good Hope.' They were proceeding at an average of two hundred and forty miles a day. It was not only the weather that kept most of the passengers in their cabins, many became unwell. With no refrigeration, keeping food fresh was more or less impossible – unless it was alive, like a pig or a chicken. The cure prescribed was 'bad brandy'. Chafyn stayed in his large stern cabin, which the other passengers thought was the best on the ship. He felt lucky and relieved that his furniture was safely secured. When he was not 'between the sheets' he worked on the magazine, 'a very heavy day's work, seven pages of Naval pages by the Doctor'. Because of his spacious cabin, there was space for passengers' visits for a levee, which kept Chafyn up-to-date with proceedings. 'Tonight, I presided over a considerable levee by the ever voluble and argumentative doctor, who laid down the law on every subject, moral, social or spiritual.'

Feeling better, and hungry, Chafyn was up for dinner, which he enjoyed, but he felt weak about the legs and he had lost his voice. The weather was calmer and there were 'sumptuous birds hanging about, an Albatross, Kittihawks, Cape Pigeons and Cape Hens. A whale had also been spotted. 'Hoffman shot and bagged a large brown bird called a "frigate bird" which he subsequently skinned in my cabin creating thereby a not very fragrant atmosphere.' Being couped up in their cabins had brought on a surge in writing for the magazine and the next edition was a bumper twenty-six pages, which Chafyn managed to edit and produced it at dinner, which gave much satisfaction. Afterwards there was a levee in Chafyn's cabin at 10 p.m., where he and others were 'favoured with a dissertation on rifle shooting by Robinson, being a subject on which he does not know much. Voice getting better.' He went to bed with his hot water bottle but there was much heavy rolling in the night, a hen coup had come loose and was crashing above his head and getting caught in one loose roll he fell amongst some boxes: 'All property save books kept their equilibrium, though once I and my chair and table broke loose and took a little journey together to leeward.'

On Friday 23rd December Chafyn put together a 'quite Bibliographical' issue of the magazine for Christmas. On Christmas Eve 'the minstrels gave a tremendous concert in their national costume, black faces and hands, white skirts and so on, thanks to Hills' capital leading it went off most successfully. After it was all over, they all came and exhibited themselves to myself in my cabin as I had not ventured out to see them owing to the cold of the cuddy.'

Xmas Day. A fine calm day made about as merry as mince pies and champagne could make it, considering that it was Sunday. I dined in the cuddy, the first time for about three weeks. After dinner the skipper proposed 'friends at home' in a very real and feeling speech, which he brought out with unusual fluency, probably because he has read it several times before on similar occasions. I sat in the Chisholm's cabin in the evening while Hill and the doctor at the piano immediately outside bawled 'Jerusalem the Golden' and other hymns at the tops of their voices for about the space of two hours.

Christmas celebrations continued with 'much speechifying and drinking of everybody's health, accompanied with much smashing of glass caused by the increasing liveliness of the ship at untoward moments.' The play 'Whitebait at Greenwich' rehearsed in Chafyn's cabin during his illness, starred Attwood, Chisholm, Christie, Jonny Hill and Pizzala.

All went off very well, all pieces were well played, especially seeing that some of the actors were rather ignorant of stage business. Chisholm heads up very well but was imperfect in his part and often succumbed so as to be inaudible. Hill and Pizzala as the lady characters were splendidly made up thanks to Mrs Chisholm who not only contributed her wardrobe but got up and dressed to assist in making up the heads, etc. The Roby girls lent crinolines and dresses but were rather shocked at the (look) of the men not wearing their trousers! They went a week before to Mrs Chisholm and asked her about the propriety of lending their crinolines and did not think they could do so unless the gentlemen wore trousers but finding that Mrs C had promised the things unconditionally their scruples were overcome.

1st January 1865. Sunday. 'The greater part of the passengers sat up to drink the old year out and at midnight made a hideous hubbub, as did also the crew, who however hadn't much to be jolly upon. The New Year has brought us a promise of stronger winds and we seem likely to get in soon for which I shall not be sorry, as I am beginning to long for the shore luxuries of fresh eggs and butter and meat, roast not baked etc.'

Eight days later Chafyn went on deck at 9 a.m. and land was sighted, Queensland appearing in the distance.

The first view of land for three months was very refreshing. It is to be hoped that the wind will keep its present quarter, as our last pig was killed this morning, the last goose yesterday, and no fresh provisions remain save one sheep and a few fowls. We passed between Redondo and Curtis Island, both high rocky land. [...] At 2 p.m., I was summoned mysteriously from the deck by the steward. 'The Capt. wishes to see you in the cuddy, Sir,' down I went wondering what was up and found the Magazine Committee sitting up solemnly, each with a glass of champagne before them, with which, after a laudatory speech by the skipper, they proceeded to drink my health. I was much pleased of course, but could not help being a little amused at the solemn and formal nature of the proceedings. After a little talk about the printing of the V.M. the meeting adjourned until the second day after our arrival at Sydney.

After sheltering in Quarantine Cove and having a close shave with the Quarantine Ship,

With our jib boom the *Vimeira* progressed to Manley Beach – a sort of Sydney Richmond where a good many men of business live.' Some of the passengers left on a steamer. For dinner there was only 'Hoffman, Robertson, Smith and myself. We got a taste of Sydney beef, and oysters which Robertson and the second mate had got off the rocks. The latter small and sweet and unlike ours, in season all the year round. [...] It was a showery day but I saw enough to convince me that it well merits the character it bears, as the most beautiful harbour in the world. Between the beauties of nature and the many ships in harbour together with the ferry steamers continually plying from shore to shore, the first approach to Sydney is a sight to be remembered. We anchored in the vicinity of Pinchgut Island which we soon reached in a boat, glad to get our ten toes once more on firm ground. First, before we landed, a boatman appeared with a note for me from Griffiths who was at Trinity with me and having seen our names in the papers as passengers by the *Vimeira* had very good naturedly got us made courtesy members of the Australian Club where it seems there are beds and to which he advised us to come in preference to a hotel. Of course, we did so and after a short walk up a hill, Sydney is up and down hill (which is tiring for my weak bellows) soon found ourselves ensconced at a well-appointed table with bright silver spoons and forks and a good breakfast with nice butter, all of which luxuries, especially the latter, met with due appreciation after three months at sea.

CHAPTER SIXTEEN

Home Alone

While Chafyn was crossing the line on 10th November, Julia was returning to Zeals from a visit to Yorkshire. She wanted to have a break before the weather became bleak with impassable roads and uncertain rail. She set off in mid-October with the cook Mrs Breaks who was leaving Zeals of her own volition, although Julia was not sad to lose her. Boarding the train at Witham she arrived at Paddington and took the Metropolitan Line to King's Cross where she was greeted by a porter who was a Zeals man, George Dove: 'None of his family now live there. He saw my name on my trunks. Arrived at Harrogate at 4.40 and then on in a fly to Midd four miles off.' Julia was well looked after and went to Ripley, Harrogate several times, and Knaresborough, visiting people she had met before, although she had not been to Yorkshire for some years.

Returning to Zeals via Bath she arrived at Witham. 'Sir Henry Hoare and Gussy at the station with a marvellous lot of luggage. The bright sun accompanied me to Zeals, therefore I did not feel too gloomy at my return to my more solitary home as I think I could have felt. The kindness I received at Midd and my pleasant visit there have braced me up, and I am at least contented with my solitude.'[199] The ongoing finishing touches to the interior of the house were causing Julia annoyance: 'I am still condemned to the study, the work people not being yet out of the hall.' A day later, she seemed to be far from braced and contented in her solitude. 'Quiet day, this year's left me alone in the world, except with Chafyn – he is now all I have, he is a good brother, and I have much to be thankful for – a comfortable home, confidence placed in me, kindness I expect from him and from neighbours. I should be cruelly ungrateful did I not weigh things in the balance against my solitude, and anxiety for my nearest and dearest absent.'

Because she had been away, Julia was devoid of social plans and was alone for ten days, 'passing my time in school, visits to the poor, riding most days, the much exercise keeps my spirits up when alone.'

George Troyte-Bullock went to Zeals to see her and to attend the hounds meeting at Zeals Green. 'He rode out with me. Dear old horse was wild with excitement and pulled like a three-year-old. They found in Magmore and ran into Norwood and back to Silton. They ran to St. Mead and killed there late in the day. A large field was out, several scarlets from the Bart's, and a carriage full of ladies, with one on horseback, Lady Keave. I left them as I was obliged to return to meet Devey.'

Later in the sporting month, 'Squarey and young Rawlence came to shoot but had a poorish day, owing to the cold hail storms which crept over us, with a strong foretaste of winter. All went away after dinner – shot forty-eight rabbits and only seven pheasants.'

After being alone for another five days, she invited Bella and H to stay. The former she had not seen for six years, 'and she seems improved, more variety of manner, and less quietly self-affecting and opinionated that she was in former days – much altered in looks and dresses horribly, not smart, but shabbily and unfashionably.' The girls did not stay very long.

'Miss Mary Turton, the vicar of Zeals' fiancée, came to help me out in the music for the first reading in Mere, we were provided with a little upright p.f. [piano forte]. To Sarum, leaving Miss Turton at home en route, and brought back H [Henrietta] and Grace Hussey with me. They are very nice girls, companionable and happy without excitement to keep them up.' But after two days, to Julia's regret, the girls left. 'I could not try to keep them longer, as it is a dull house, and I don't wish to be the hostess of a prison which Zeals to girls would be after a while.'

By mid-December, Julia had moved into the new drawing room, which kept her busy. 'When Miss Mayne came, we sat to admire the room: it looks lovely and so cheerful after the "Tank" – the polisher and his assistant only left the house yesterday.'

She always took great care of her horses:

On driving home in the phaeton from Stourhead 'Ginger' had blisters and seemed a bit shaky on one leg. So I can do without her but the sooner the remedy is applied the better. [...] The Vicar and his curate dined here. Frank and Georgina Michell [cousins] ought to have arrived from Speen, but the train would not take them further than Devizes and they arrived at 11.30 p.m. Frank Michell is very dull and appears to have nothing to say. He left the next day as he had a shooting engagement. [...] Bobby Mayne came on his way from the *Britannia*, the training ship at Dartmouth on his way to Brighton for Xmas. He's a nice little boy, but awkward on shore like a sailor, upset his wine and removed the glass after dinner, and threatened a variety of mishaps with the china and glass, so I was glad he left the table.

As Julia prepared to spend Christmas at North Coker with her aunt Maria and George Bullock, on 24th December she made her way to Gillingham Station where she met George and Alice Troyte-Bullock to go to Sherborne station. 'We took a fly to Frome, ten miles west. It was bitterly cold. England [Julia's lady's maid] and the traps met us having come by rail, at the gate. It was dry, and Sunday gloomy and wretched – not a very happy day for me now' –

25th December, Xmas Day, 1864.

'All Saints Church in Dorchester, beautifully decorated and a good choral service. Dined early and went again in the evening. Most wretched and un-Xmas like weather, which is perhaps partly the cause of my constant depression, if the sun would but shine, I would feel it in my inmost heart and soul, now the gloomy side of the picture will show itself and I am always pounding upon the traveller by sea, who now ought to be within sight of land, and full of hope and joy.'

There was a children's party at Frampton attended by 'the celebrated Mrs Norton, who is now sixty and more lovely and so fascinating in manner. The tree was lovely. Mabel [Troyte-Bullock] was the prettiest girl there, she is a sweet darling – her brother Eddie is red-cheeked and jolly'.

'The last day of the year. Would I were with those I love basking in the sun on the old Nile beast – happy existence – I <u>did</u> enjoy it then, and look back to it as mighty pleasant from the gloom and melancholy of dear old England and my solitude and anxiety.'

[1st January, 1865.] The bells are ringing in the New Year, why so much pleasure in welcoming it, and why such ungrateful forgetfulness of the old departing and now departed period of time. I feel thankful for blessings etc. at its hands and niceties spared me much and these have endured that it has been happiness strictly speaking to me I cannot say, but content with growing hope for the future that Chafyn may enjoy not life but a health as he had. I know only a miracle could affect that happiness, brought his kin and friends high and low. As for myself, for years I did duly live for myself, now I have been drawn out of that forcibly, and I must think of others, although the old temptation to fret and make much of No. 1 is certainly recurring, yet the before has been one of mercy, and my life is more wholesomely happy for it. Very cold today, to Church.

Julia relied heavily on the friendship and support of her cousin Charles-Henry Grove and his wife Eliza, the latter now appearing to be ill. Revd Charles-Henry was the youngest son and ninth of the ten children of her father's great friend Thomas Grove Snr of Ferne. In his young days, out of all the siblings, Charles-Henry was the confidant and closest friend of their cousin Percy Bysshe Shelley. He and Harriet were the only remaining siblings of their generation. He had met his wife Eliza when he was a Rector in Arlesford in Hampshire, before taking up the living at Sedgehill. Julia relied on the friendship of the whole family, but especially the first three of their six daughters. The eldest Emily (b. 1832) was seven years younger than Julia and a constant companion, Agnes (b. 1841) a year after Chafyn, and Alice (b. 1843). The girls feature regularly in Julia's diary.

6th January. 'Gale last night, I dreamt of falling chimney pots and prostrate trees. Rode to Sedgehill to Church – being Epiphany Sunday and found no service in the morning. I found sadness and anxiety for the mother [Eliza] who is in London for advice.'

On Monday, Julia was not feeling well, she had a 'hideous swelled face and stayed in all day, poulticing it with bread and milk – a most marvellous mixture, and hot fermentations applied externally, it ached most disagreeably all day, and England made several appearances with applications to cure' – but there was something to please her. 'Today at last the workmen have vacated the new bedroom and descended to the drawing room – leaving me in peace and comfort. The furniture for the bed and dressing room is come and coming and until the rooms are painted and papered, I cannot unpack it, and have no place to store it. The grate is not in order, or the tiles yet placed, but they are all ordered.'

My life now is decided – visiting the poor, school and riding, and paying bills, the two first useful in one way and the third necessary to enable me to keep up my spirits to do them for my life is very <u>lonely</u>, when I am alone in the house, and were it not for the feeling that it is useful in a measure, and as it well marked out for me, I could not support the solitariness <u>of it</u>. A glimmering comes over me sometimes that in one's duty lies one's happiness, it may not be of a brilliant, exciting, passionate nature but it is therefore the better where trial and trouble and anxiety have shown me this. I did think solo happiness but a name for misery of a wearing falling nature.

The cold, damp weather had made many of Julia's acquaintances ill, so invitations for dinner at Zeals were often with either a husband on his own with a sick wife at home or vice versa. George Troyte-Bullock went to stay with Julia in mid-January, but Alice was not well enough to go. The Bailwards went too, as well as Emily and Agnes Grove.

'I cannot have more than ten now, on account of the little drawing room, it gets so stuffy with a larger party. Mr Bailward is a dull man. I like Mrs B and she has improved immensely. Walked to Mere and showed the Church to the Bailwards. The Bartons dined, the daughter they brought is a poor miserably shy thing and was cruelly dressed in scarcely presentable style and Mrs B. was magnificent for her and really well dressed, with good diamond earrings and locket.'

Julia did not have sufficient self-awareness to realise that guests she considered either dull or having nothing to say for themselves were intimidated by her. Lacking warmth, Julia's disdain for her guests may well have been apparent, as she looked haughtily at people's clothing and appearance with few examples of any compliments.

'Snow storms. Mr Jordan came to shoot and the gents went to Silton but being the first year they did not shoot much. Mrs Jordan was home and could not come. She had nine excuses, illness and Lord Ilchester's death.'

When the visitors left Julia took Emily and Agnes Grove to Gillingham where they took the train to Semley. 'Agnes too unwell to dine'.

Hard frost. Tom Grove dined and slept here. His speech at the Gillingham Agricultural dinner where he launched forth into politics has made a most unfavourable impression and had the election taken place soon after were it now impending, it would go hard with him, even at home several think so, he has no tact or discretion and totally wanting in knowledge of the world, there's the air of a neglected education, no public school or university with only a few years in a heavy Dragoon regiment in the times of peace.[200] Fifteen years ago, it must be when he quit the service and in previous years the army, especially the heavy cavalry was considered the asylum poor of the family. [...] At the Cathedral yesterday and home in bitter cold, I could have cried I was so chilled. I could not stir myself to walk up Harnham Hill. Mrs Goddard came to Zeals with me. This house is much warmer and although [the servants] keep fires, they don't close the doors, or shut up early in cold weather, the cold is much repelled by such measures. Snow last night and all the afternoon which stopped me from going to Horsington to the Bailwards, which I regretted.

Owing to the wind, the path through the fields was impassable and I had difficulty in making my way through the land from Zeals to Woolverton. There was a little path trodden down, but for wheels there was no passage. Having runners made for the pony gig, if they were ready today it would be tidy sledging as the snow is well trodden down and thick. The runners finished, sat in the pony gig and out sallied Mrs Goddard and I and riding down to the lodge, but the soft snow prevented any sledging, and we made an inglorious re-entry to the stable yard. [...] Rode to Sedgehill, being sick of the wretched weather and my solitude. I have every comfort and many luxuries and blessings, thank God for them, but I do long for that one comfort which would give a zest to all my other comforts, one to speak to at home, especially in evenings.

By February Julia's spirits were lifting. 'Went to Salisbury for a concert'. She had been attending the practice and had reservations about the delivery of the Bach. 'It will be hard wrestling with the notes.'

'The concert went off fairly well, the Bach was as I foretold and was described to me by a listener as 'wrestling with the notes! Mrs Osan's "Rest in the Lord" was a failure, her voice is so very uneven, she has a si-do-re, but it is wooden below.'

The daily routine continued. 'Walked to Zeals school. In for a friend to talk to! A howling wind and with a good fire and my double windows my room is not above fifty degrees at 11 p.m. The drawing room has not been above fifty-eight today and I am always at the fire. How happy it was that two years ago in my great anxiety for Chafyn we were spared such weather as this, it was a very mild open winter'. The snow showers continued. 'Tom Grove called and lunched' and 'Emily and Alice came and we rode to Gillingham,' followed by their mother Eliza.

At the beginning of March, 'Coakley and Devey came, and my two new housemaids, who promise very well. The hounds met at

Zeals Green on Friday and as we have now Silton services there, I did not go out. The hyacinths are lovely in the new bay window, which seems made for flowers.'

On 16th March, Julia had her first letter from Chafyn 'with as good a report as I dared hope for. They were 101 days going out and 104 before the weather allowed up to the landing, and were very comfortably treated all the time, and had very little rough weather other than the first night out.'

CHAPTER SEVENTEEN

Sydney

January, 1865. 'I bought a very pretty brooch today, which I have sent home to Julia, at a shop in Hunter Street, kept by a working jeweller, a German of great taste and skill. The papers today

The Australian Club, Sydney, *c.* 1879.

contain a full telegraphic summary of European News, forwarded from Adelaide. The mail will be here on Friday.'[201]

Chafyn's friend Powell, who had visited him frequently at Zeals House, had gone to New Zealand having been unable to wait for the late arriving *Vimeira*, but Griffiths joined them at the Australian Club for a table d'hôte menu and introduced Chafyn and Hoffman to many of the guests. Then the new arrivals, after strolling around George Street, had their hair cut.

'Set off in a good Hansom cab to search for a printer for the magazine. I found that Reading and Wellbank will do it best and cheapest so to them it will go. Strolled along George Street, the chief thoroughfare, the lower end assumes a Tottenham Court Road character being one storied. There followed a meeting of the *Vimeira Magazine* committee at Cohen's Hotel for a progress report.'

The printing of the magazine into a book was agreed and signed off by the passengers, Mrs Louisa Robey, for Clara, Fanny, and William Robey, Dr Henry Hoffman, James Attwood, George Robertson, Pizzala, Dr John Bayldon, Johnny and Julias Hill, Dr Edwin Chisholm, Emily Chisholm, Christie, Smith, Robinson and W. Chafyn-Grove.[202]

From the *Vimeira Magazine* book printed in Sydney, it is possible to glimpse how Chafyn was perceived by the other guests. The words affable and big-hearted were applied to him along with references to his breezy jokes, although some were hardly worthy of a Christmas cracker. He flirted cheekily with the Robey girls and on one occasion the whole Roby family ignored him at dinner, possibly he had overstepped the mark. The ship's doctor, Bayldon, also the lay preacher of the Sunday services, often went to Chafyn's cabin to complain of his immoral behaviour, his lack of interest in spiritual matters and to make hurtful, sarcastic remarks which he took personally. Chafyn listened to these outpourings, then advised him to go away and forget about it. There were also rowdy nights with the Dewitt and Moore claret while the young men took part in saucy bar room banter and played whist. Chafyn wrote extensive articles on the horrors of bull fighting, the experience of seeing a Dewlish religious ceremony in Cairo, and one on the holiday he took with Julia to Heligoland. The magazine included an article written to tease Chafyn by Attwood's dog, Moses:

17th December, 1864.
To the proprietors of Private Lunatic Asylums: Missing, from the breakfast table, a gentleman of about 23 or 24 years of age.

Had on, when last seen, a long and rather shabby frock coat, a dark blue waistcoat, and loose fancy trousers. Wore a slight moustache, but is supposed to have shaved since then. Although the peculiar circumstances of the case prevent a reward being offered, any tidings of him will be thankfully received by his disconsolate friends. Address: Moses, No. 4, Port side.[203]

Chafyn had taken on trial the second mate George Robertson, 'a man of wars man who worked his way out on board. He was nine years a seaman, school master and very handy and willing and I think will make a good slave.' In the afternoon the three of them went on board the *Vimeira* which was still out in the stream, had some luncheon and did some packing up – 'i.e. Hoffman and Robertson worked and I lent my assistance with my powerful mind. From here we went for a cruise up the harbour, which looked to perfection, after a slow and lazy sail round Goat Island, where the powder magazines are. We sailed close by the HMS *Brisk*, a corvette of sixteen guns and the only man of war at present in the harbour. We got back to a late dinner, well pleased with what we had seen.'

The exploring continued the next day, after visiting the fruit market where they sat at a table eating grapes, they visited the Chisholms, in order for Hoffman to draw Mr Chisholm, but he had gone fishing.

'Mrs Chisholm looked much improved and no wonder as on the whole voyage she only had three days free of sickness and was for about six weeks in bed in her cabin.'[204] Instead, they went to a park.

'I saw gum trees close for the first time, in the domain are the Botanic Gardens, which run down to the water's edge. The collection of plants and flowers is very good, the latter in particular being most grateful to the eye, after the long spells of greys and neutral tints we have had. We stopped sometime by the water as Hoffman sketched, and were joined by Griffiths, with whom we walked home. Everything here is intensely English, looks, photographs, conversation.'

On Sunday, Chafyn went to church at St. James's, not so much for religious observance, but curiosity. He dozed in the long sermon, 'a monotonous oration delivered by a Titus Oates like parson. The church is a model of the old-fashioned London one, with high pews and insufficient ventilation. The ladies were well dressed but they all looked washed out and also very burnt. The men are brown

The Botanical Gardens, Sydney, 1884.

and indulge in a certain latitude of dress in the consequence of the hot climate but otherwise looked much like an average London congregation.' After church, with his love of botany, Chafyn could not resist another trip to the Botanical Gardens, to take in all the trees, shrubs and flowers, some familiar, some new to him. He was still disorientated after three months at sea and absorbing his new surroundings.

During the last trip to the *Vimeira* to take the remainder of their items, Chafyn and Hoffman went for a champagne luncheon on the *Duncan Dunbar* in the harbour, which had taken the same route from Plymouth a month earlier. She was a larger ship than the *Vimeira*, and due to sail in a fortnight. 'A magnificent ship'.[205] When the sun was shining, they sailed around the harbour, went fishing with Pizzala, unsuccessfully, and out with Panbury in *Xarifa*, the winning sailing boat of the Regatta.

In the evening, they were at the Chisholms for dinner where they were given suggestions for excursions, Hoffman and Chisholm planning to go wallaby shooting. While Chafyn liked to look at buildings, plants and armour, Hoffman's main interests were shooting and sketching, he was proficient at both. Although Chafyn and Hoffman had different interests, Hoffman proved to be a good-natured companion. When unpacking his saddle, Chafyn realised that some riding clothing had somehow not been brought. As the weather was wet and windy Hoffman went back on board the *Vimeira* to retrieve them for him, while Chafyn went to Government House to leave their names and Lady Herbert's letters.

The *Vimeira* made another voyage at almost exactly the same time of year in 1865, leaving Portland, England, at the end of September arriving in Western Australia on 22nd December 1865. But instead of a first-class passenger list of fourteen adults and nine children, it was commissioned as a convict ship. Captain Malcolm Green had 280 convicts on board, thirty of them being former army soldiers who had been court-martialled for various charges. Also on board were ninety-nine passengers, forty-seven crew, four wardens, a ship's doctor and a religious instructor. One convict died on the journey.[206]

Invitations were arriving, there were three for the following Monday. They were continually introduced to more and more people by Griffiths so dinners at the Club were large parties, 'NB Australian wild ducks particularly fine'. Griffiths also took the two young men to inspect buggies and horses. The buggies with their small bodies and huge wheels looked 'anything but strong'.

'To a tea fight at the Government House. He, the Governor, [Sir John Young] is a pleasant gentlemanly man, his wife is less popular and I thought her manner a little brusque, but what little I saw of her niece, Miss Dalton, who is supposed to be rather "swell", I liked. There was good music in a good large room, then came tea and ices and then croquet and lounging in their very pretty garden.' With Hoffman away shooting wallaby for a few days, Chafyn accepted an invitation to dinner at 7.45 p.m. at Government House. 'I had a long chat after dinner with Miss Dalton, whom I found very agreeable. She goes out riding at six or seven in the morning, and Sir John Young being an early man, everybody went away at 10 p.m.[207] The party included the Lord Bishop of Sydney, who is a fine specimen of the muscular Christian order and would proof a tough 'un for the bush rangers. Met Speirs, late of Trinity College Cambridge, who has been travelling about out here and talks of going home by the April mail, and Powell returned from New Zealand early and was rather disappointed by it.'

They arranged to go with Powell to Melbourne and take a run in Tasmania for a few days. Chafyn, at this stage, contemplated returning to England via Panama, as the weather on the Red Sea route would be unbearably hot for him in May.

Invitations from the Governor continued. A picnic on his barge in the harbour was followed by croquet at his house, 'handsome castellated and standing well on a point overlooking the harbour'. Chafyn was substitute for croquet, but his services were called upon and he distinguished himself.

I like Miss Dalton very much. Later, dined with Powell at the Royal Hotel, and on my return home I was horrified by the sight of a strange pair of boots and portmanteau in my bedroom. Happily, the owner was not in the bed, but had been accommodated elsewhere, so that I did not find myself adrift. In the afternoon went to a cricket match, Melbourne v Sydney. The tart ensemble came up to Lords on the Eton and Harrow matchday but there was a fair array of ladies in a grandstand in the centre of which was a pen for the Governors' party, who were present all the afternoon. Accompanied Powell to Government House where he was exhibiting his New Zealand and Queensland sketches, of which, it is needless to say, he has a capital collection, and in the evening went with Lord John Taylor [A.D.C.], to a lodge of the freemasons. The brethren were no great shakes being mostly shop keepers.

On Saturday 11th February, Chafyn, Hoffman and Powell boarded the S.S. *Adelaide* bound for Melbourne. 'We were much annoyed by the hawks which fell in crisp black showers all over the poop, and the dense masses of smoke, the colonial coal being much smokier than the English.' On arrival they took a cab called a 'Single' to Scott's Hotel.

Holding three passengers, it is something like an Irish car, but with the seats facing the same way as a dog cart. They have two wheels and one horse and trot at the rate of about twelve miles an hour. After breakfast, we walked and visited Bright Brothers where Powell had letters. While there we faced one of the officers of the C.S.S. *Shenandoah*.[208] The uniform is smart, grey and gold. The streets are broad and regular and superior to Sydney. Hoffman and I went to the Club, which is a fine building arranged in the style of a good London Club. Thanks to Griffiths we have been made honorary members and got a good read of the English papers.

CSS *Shenandoah* in Victoria, 1865.

The three men then went to the Public Library, the small picture gallery where there were some horses and poultry of Herring's'.[209]

> In the afternoon we took the train to Williamstown (about 20 minutes from Melbourne) to see the *Shenandoah*, which is still on the slips there. We were unlucky in being unable to get on board, as no one is admitted. She is a fine full rigged steamer, and pierced with eight gun ports. Her lines show her to be a fast one. Workmen were engaged fitting her screw, and she is expected to be ready in three or four days. Just as we were coming away about eighty policemen arrived, together with some artillery, come down to detain her. What was the real matter no one seems clearly to know, but as far as I could make out they refused to let the inspector of police execute a warrant on someone on board, and so she was to be stopped until she did. Another account was that they were keeping some English people prisoners on board. At all events it seemed pretty clear from what I heard afterwards at dinner at the hotel, that they have been smuggling on board lots of contraband stores, and taking every advantage of the liberality of the Govt. lending them the slip for <u>necessary</u> repairs. In the evening I removed to the Club, as on my return to the Hotel this afternoon, I found another individual in my room which is a double bedded one. He had been using my brushes and otherwise making himself objectionable. This, putting strangers

together without saying a word about it, is rather too much in the Yankie line for me.

This morning, met Capt. Standish to whom I had a letter from Griffiths. He is the head of the police, and from him I heard the reason for the seizure of the *Shenandoah* yesterday. It seems that they have been infringing the Foreign Settlement Act, by getting men on board concealed as stowaways. An inspector of police having been twice refused admission on board with a search warrant the only step open to Govt. was to detain the ship. It was reported that the Capt. has said he would give up the ship and return to America; at all events he gave his word that there were no stowaways on board, and during the night four men were caught by the police coming over the side who acknowledged themselves as such.

After the short stay in Williamstown, the three men boarded the S.S. *Black Swan* for Launceston, Tasmania, at 10 a.m. arriving at their destination in the afternoon ('the first colonists here, I suppose, Cornishmen'). It was race week, all business being suspended and they were lucky to get rooms in the Club Hotel. The coaches were booked in advance and there being no way of getting to Hobart by this method, they hired a coach and horses for the two-day journey, changing horses on the way. 'The scenery is especially good, being very English and the red soil further on reminds one of Devonshire, but the numerous parti-coloured parrots, which sometimes fly across in convoys rather dispel the illusion.' Staying overnight at Campbelltown, they changed horses and went on to 'a strange jumble of places, Jerusalem, Jericho, the river Jordan, Bagdad, Melton Mowbray, Bayford, Shepton Montacute, and a public house with the sign of Wardour Castle. There must be some colonist about here who hails from my part of the world.'

'We came on the remains of the coach which left Launceston on Friday morning, and upset with thirty-eight passengers from sheer top heaviness near Melton Mowbray. It was an American coach put on instead of the ordinary one in consequence of the number of people returning from Launceston races, and drawn by six horses, to the management of which the driver was unequal. Five people had bones broken, besides blood, which we afterwards found out had come out of one Mr Davis, the editor of a paper here.'

A friend of Christie's made them honorary members of the Club, luckily, as it was the only place to eat after 1 p.m. 'We put up the horses and while Hoffman and Powell sketched, I wandered about on the chance of finding some of the fern trees for which this part of Tasmania is famous but owing to lack of energy to penetrate deep enough into the bush I did not find any. Thanks to one of the horses having the migraines we reached the Club very late for dinner, the affable waiter, however, bustled about and got us some food.' The following morning Chafyn took a drive by Government House and the Botanical Gardens, 'which are smaller and less well kept than those at Sydney but the flowers are very brilliant. The beauty of Tasmania makes one regret that we cannot spare more time here. Dined at the Club.'

On horseback the three men rode off, Chafyn in search of tree ferns in the gullies on the sides of Mount Wellington, the others sketching. They followed the trunk of the Hobart town waterworks, then leaving the animals at a small public house, Chafyn found a beautiful gully full of fern trees. 'These fern trees will only grow in wet dark places, and are particular to the South of Tasmania and part of N.S.W. The fronds grow out of a brown mossy stem up to fifteen feet, the taller ones not unlike palms.' From their different directions they met up 'where we left our nags, and had a most capital luncheon of roast lamb, exceptionably fresh peas and first rate beer. At 5 p.m. we bid farewell to Tasmania from the deck of the screw steamer *Derwent*,' bound for Melbourne.

At Melbourne, Chafyn and Hoffman bade farewell to Powell who went off on the mail steamer *Madras* to Hong Kong. 'Every green thing all over is parched up owing to the hot winds they have had this summer' and bush fires were expected. In the afternoon the two men hired a Single and explored the outskirts of Melbourne, including the bathing resort of St Kilda, where the sands and several large sea baths were enclosed for fear of sharks. They also visited Ballarat, an old gold mining town, and a penal colony.

Leaving on the *City of Melbourne* with strong headwinds made the journey a slow one. 'Arrived at Sydney at 5.30 a.m. where Robertson had been waiting for us all night.' They happily went back to their old quarters at the Club, but most of their friends had gone away for a time.

Chisholm is also gone up to his brother's, and has left the magazine affairs which he undertook in my absence in a confused state which it took me the morning to rectify. It is now completed and makes a very good book. Went boating to Garden Island, the views of the harbour very picturesque. Everything looks very green and refreshing here after the parched up-state of Melbourne. In the afternoon, went to the nursery garden at

Double Bay. It has a magnificent collection of ferns and exotics from every part of the Southern Hemisphere. I saw some most gigantic Begonias and Camellia trees. I ordered a small selection of seeds to go home by the *Kimsara*.

CHAPTER EIGHTEEN

Zeals – Spring

The sounds coming from the fields surrounding Zeals House were the bleating of lambs and the view from Julia's south-facing bedroom window was of neat lawns and daffodils swaying in the gentle breeze. With sunshine, the joy of spring and the return

Zeals House from the top field.

of green leaves on the trees, Julia was in happier spirits. She could ride for miles on the downs taking in the views during the busy ploughing and sowing season. 23rd March: 'Small dish of strawberries – French beans about this time'.

> Aunt Fanny died. We shall miss her terribly, although she had been declining for some time and was becoming quite infirm in body and mind. She was my father's favourite sister, and in her days of strength who could be nicer and kinder – she was a true English <u>gentle woman</u>, for she was patience itself and good to all. May my love be like hers, and if I had half the hopes of heaven for myself which I have for her, I should rest and be thankful. My uncles [Revd Charles and Harry] are overcome, and they did not see her <u>failing</u> as we all did.

By the end of March it was milder and the winter gloom had lifted. 'Rode for the first time these three weeks – Daniels tuned grand piano forte – Agnes Grove went home and her mother Eliza came with Emily.'

Coakley and his builders had still not finished the interior fittings. 'Masons picking at the house again – new windows in hall, study and King Charles bedroom, new Garden Entrance step raised – pink room thoroughly repaired and Chafyn's room also to be done – my windows were glazed and leaded, staircase casements now to open.'

Julia went to Brighton for Easter, to 5B Regency Square on a lovely spring day on 5th April, then left to go to London 'to buy my mourning as I have no clothes fit to wear. Provided myself at that good but expensive shop Jay's with a prim hairnet, paletot and head-drop, and ordered the whole to be sent to Mrs Phelips in Lowndes Square. Chose a hat at Heath's to be made from a pattern from France, lunched with Mrs Phelips.' On Palm Sunday Julia headed for St Paul's in Brighton, 'which has advanced a few steps since I was last here'.[210] Julia headed for another service on this important day in the church calendar to St Michael's, served by Mr Wagner's curate. No litany at St. Paul's but it was said at St. Michael's, the church decorated with palms.[211] Everything is blossoming'.

'Easter Day. To St. Michael's by myself and later to the poor people's church in Bread Street, a modern and neat little edifice, and built for five hundred. I was much gratified by the congregation which although not filling the Church seemed to consist chiefly of mechanics and their wives and women looking like needle women respectably but plainly draped.'

The streets were full of people for the Volunteer Review: 'About six thousand arrived, but all orderly, although merry. The place is crammed. Not a ticket left on the cliff and the hotels turning away multitudes.' There was an 'amusing variety of uniforms, we all saw them marching past well – the Artists, Victoria, Sertern and Trish looked splendidly, the real soldiers considered the marching to be very creditable to volunteers on the whole, in some cases quite smart. The bands in the enclosure played in turn, and those not singled out to perform, marched past mute. It was a delightful day.'

A week later Julia reached Gillingham station and was soon at Zeals House. 'Everything looking fresh and lovely. The windows are not as far advanced as I hoped, the pink dressing room garland open. [...] The plastering on the ceiling has only been one coat.' Mrs Eliza Grove and Emily came to luncheon. 'Strolled about with them. Very hot day, then went to Sedgehill where the girls played croquet, much amused by Charles-Henry's curate Mr Johnson, his eccentricities much the force.'

On May Day there was a croquet party at Zeals House. 'Although there was a high wind pitching the hoops upon the lawn near the ha-ha there was play without the players being quite dishevelled by the wind. I had thirty guests and at 7 p.m. a supper, cold things on the table, with hot cutlets handed about, and dancing in the new hall ended the evening well.'

Margaret Hussey and Agnes Grove were staying with Julia. Rain forced them to resort to Battledore as exercise, but later they rode ponies through Stourhead woods, after which they rode to Sedgehill where very heavy rain came whilst they were in church, which drenched them on their return. 'I was very angry with King for not taking the wagonette down for us, as he was at home.'[212]

After spending a lovely afternoon in the wood and Castle Hill where the children rode 'Nelly' alternately, the Husseys left. Julia was alone again, 'which is much more dreary in summer than in winter weather. Parished in the pony gig.'

15th May. 'My letter from Chafyn put me in good spirits. It was from Wollongong, a place forty miles south of Sydney – dated 15th March. His return this year seems doubtful, and I shall write and beg him to remain another season, as the climate suits him, and let me go out to him in October. None of the papers I sent him have come to hand, so I shall make a formal complaint to the Post Office since I have sent them regularly, until the end of February, and by the March mail, [...] in April forwarded four to Ceylon and Suez.'

CHAPTER NINETEEN

New South Wales

It is clear from Chafyn's letter to Julia that his plans had changed and both he and Hoffman had decided to stay longer in Australia than originally planned. From another letter to Julia, it appears the original route home was to be via Ceylon and Suez. Chafyn regularly changed his plans, sometimes at short notice, not wishing to be tied to a rigid schedule, but mostly in response to his health needs. The climate in Australia suited him, he liked the friendly and welcoming people and there was much to explore.

[Sydney, 7th March.] Started soon after nine with a buggy and a pair of horses to drive to Appin but unluckily as we were slowly ascending the William George Street near the railway station, a bus came down on the wrong side about ten miles an hour, and ran into us, breaking the splinter bar and springing one of the wheels. It was lucky that it was no worse as the man's horses were entirely beyond his control. He was very penitent after the accident but we shall probably summons him on our return.

After having the damage repaired, they boarded a train to Campbelltown, and from there to Appin in the buggy by moonlight. 'It was an adventurous proceeding.' They arrived at the Burke Inn at Appin and started early for Wollongong in the afternoon. The road ascended through the bush for several miles until they began to turn downwards.

The descent is a series of sharp steps, and lying at an angle which no English horse master would think of attempting with wheels. Thanks to the lightness of the carriage, the strength of the horses, and to Hoffman and Robertson hanging on behind, we got safely down to the great satisfaction of all parties, for, I confess, I much disliked the look of some of the places down which I had to pilot the trap, some of them being so steep that I would scarcely <u>ride</u> an English horse down them'. We got good accommodation at the Queen's Hotel, although troubled by mosquitoes, and in the afternoon walked along the shore where a magnificent surf was breaking. There is a small harbour where colliers were shipping coal which is brought down by tramways from the mines in the mountain side.

The journey continued to Kiama 'like Wollongong but smaller', stopping from time to time for Hoffman to sketch and for Chafyn to explore the vegetation. 'Magnificent cabbage trees, and fern trees inferior to the ones in Tasmania'. They also visited a dairy farm where two good 'tan-faced' Irish women were milking about forty cows, and they tasted the luxury of cream, unavailable elsewhere, as it was mostly made into butter to supply Sydney. They stayed overnight in Wollongong at a public house run by a Cornish family called Laing. At dinner they had a new bird called a 'sea beak'. 'Its flesh is brown and is about the size of a duck but substantially a land bird. In answer to a complaint we made of queer taste in mine hosts' brandy, which tasted like spirits of wine, Mrs. Laing naively remarked that she didn't know what it would be, as they never <u>adulterated</u> it with anything but water!!'

Hoffman went out shooting birds, 'a Jackass, like a large kingfisher, an overshot Crane and a Satin bird'. Meanwhile, Chafyn drove into Kiama to look at the telegraphic summary of the English news. On the American Civil War, there were negotiations between North and South. 'Unless both parties make some concession there is not much chance of their coming to terms.' When he returned, he walked down a gully to the sea and some way along under the cliffs into a pretty little bay. The tide was out exposing a plateau of rocks. 'It is a very humble township, the settlers nice hospitable people, offering one cream or wobblers *salon le gout*. This is such a pleasant domestic place that we don't seem at all inclined to move from it.'

On 17th March, St Patrick's day, several Irishmen spent the day in the bar here celebrating the occasion in wobblers. Right glad was I when in the course of the evening they became too drunk to make any more noise, and were accordingly turned out, and the doors locked on them by Mrs. Laing, who in this, as in many instances, is the better half. Hoffman has been very seedy today with a bilious headache, which has not been improved by the noise in the bar made by the roisterers.

On Sunday, 'there was a congregation of about forty-five including a small dog and a sheep in the church which also served as a schoolroom. Compelling Irish clergyman from Kiama who illustrated his oration with many pointless anecdotes. In the paddock outside the horses of the congregation were hitched up or left to wander about ad lib with their saddles and bridles on, a proceeding to which bush horses are well accustomed.'

Sorry to leave the Laings, they made their way 'dowsed by the most enormous mosquitos' and having to 'axe our way' through the sandy bush track to catch the steamer *Illalong*. They shipped the horses and trap and the steward made up some beds for them in the saloon as they progressed along the Shoalhaven River into a smooth sea. On board was a 'miscellaneous cargo of butter, corn, potatoes, etc. and the deceased wife (No. 3) of a squatter being taken to Sydney for internment in a large black box which directed like a seat was placed with the disconsolate widower and his son's luggage on the poop! At Kiama we stayed about two hours shipping more tubs of butter which, considering the heat of the day, must have been in a state fit only for fish sauce, and again at Wollongong a large shipment of butter, coal and livestock, finally reaching Sydney about 10 p.m. and went to the Club.'

CHAPTER TWENTY

Zeals – Summer

An important part of the Zeals Estate management was the connection to the South West Wilts Hunt. It was the responsibility of Mere to host the annual 'Friendly' for the members at Zeals House, and in 1865, with Chafyn away, Julia was hosting the event.

[7th June.] There are 80 benefit members. Afterwards, Lord Harry Tregonwell in the chair, and Col. Bathurst and Tom Grove came to Zeals and we all dined after the service. Mrs White, Hoare, etc.

South West Wilts Hunt at Zeals House.

dined too. Goldsborough really provided a capital dinner, jellies, creams, and lobster salad for 31, including a fair share of wine. The speeches were enlivened by a 'passage' between Lord Harry and T.G. [Tom Grove] in which the latter showed some irritation and the former kept his temper, but was rather sarcastic. The members, proceeded by their band, came up here, and played cricket, and we had a large set to tea in the evening, but all were gone by 6.30. Very hot day.[213]

The house with some items left unfinished was still causing irritation for Julia. 'Coakley and Devey came, and we consulted over the hall shutters and various other matters. Devey slept here, it was rather heavy work talking to him all evening so I went early to bed. Rode to Salisbury. Brought back some paper for the pink room, Druce having lost the measurements and written again for them, and Coakley, and his man arrived by early train this morning.'[214]

In mid-June, Julia went to London with her friend Susan Blake and stayed in lodgings at 8 Hanover Square. Clothes shopping was, as ever, her first priority. After ordering a bonnet at Sevilly she drove about and called on George and Alice Troyte-Bullock who were staying at Jennings' Hotel in Albemarle Street. She went to the Opera to see *The Huguenots*, and when Susan Blake left Henrietta Hussey arrived, 'she is very kind and agreeable.' St James's was the Church she attended and when George and Alice called on her and lunched, they all went to Westminster Abbey, then walked back by Warwick Square and then the park. As was Julia's routine in London, she went to the Royal Academy for the watercolours and French exhibition – 'it seemed average.' She liked Landseer's portrait of himself and his dogs best. Henrietta accompanied Julia to lunch at the Phelipses in Lowndes Square. 'He is changed. Did not offer to go anywhere with us, and was stiffish.'

When Henrietta left, to Julia's regret, she concentrated on house commissions, ordering Chafyn's stair and passage carpets at Lapworth's, going to Hoare's bank and to the stained-glass window makers, Powell's in Whitechapel. After having a tooth 'stopped' at Cartwrights, she drove a little in the park. Quickly changing her dress after being caught in pouring rain, she drove out to Hampstead to see the Powells. Mrs Powell, 'with the remains of great beauty', was at home. A lawyer brother of David Powell was there, 'a good-looking lad, who showed me his mother's Australian and New Zealand sketches'.

After another Sunday service at St James's Church, Julia visited the Rose Show at the Horticultural Gardens. 'The roses are <u>gorgeous</u> but coarse to my mind from the great size and overflow of bloom.' Julia returned to Zeals on 4th July. 'Very hot, and having rubbed off the dust I shall gladly leave London.'

Charles-Henry and Agnes arrived at Zeals for lunch and as they left Emily arrived at Zeals to stay. Emily, the eldest daughter, was now thirty-two years old and still unmarried, having avoided an offer from a Mr Hall the previous year. Hall had written Emily 'a nasty letter'. 'He wanted her to ask her father to give her 300 per annum, which, as he had 2500 for all would leave him penniless if all his 6 daughters were to marry, which was unlikely to happen.' When Lady Hoare brought Hall to Zeals on a rainy afternoon the previous summer Julia was unflattering about her guest. 'He deserves to be ducked in a muddy pond for his conduct, silly hypocritical old flirt.' Emily was now being courted by the Vicar of Mere, Charles Townsend, who had arrived as Rector of Mere Church four years previously after graduating from Brasenose College, Oxford, and being a Perpetual Curate at Laverstock near Salisbury.[215]

When Julia went to Salisbury to look for flunkies and found two tidy ones, she returned to find that Emily had sat on the lawn all day swooning. Ascension Day – 'to church at Mere at 11. Mr Townsend and his curate Howley came up after church and the former proposed to Emily Grove and was accepted.'

Mrs Charles-Henry and Alice called to luncheon – full of the marriage – but not approving more than they did at first. Truly, Emily deserves someone more paternal and the speeches he makes are not of a nice nature for a man-in-law elect. However, if he makes her happy her friends must overlook his want of refinement. I don't want him brought nearer to us, although as my clergyman both like and respect him. I think my liking for his society has not increased with my reacquaintance, for he has no conversation, only an occasional outburst of schoolboy behaviour, as for an opinion, he hasn't got one, on any subject I have ever heard broached.

On a lovely hot day, Julia and Emily rode to Chicklade and met Tom Grove canvassing with Mr de Boulay.[216] 'The pony "Nelly" carried Emily well.' Tom Grove was aiming for the second time to become a Member of Parliament, spending £5,000 on his campaign.

Nominations of MPs for South Wiltshire at Sarum. Alice and George [Troyte-Bullock] and I went by the 10.20 train and arrived at the station, where joined by Tom's sisters Louisa Selwyn and Emma-Philippa Grove, who came up from near Crewkerne to hear and see their brother nominated. The market place near full of men making a noise close to the hustings in front of which were the anxious expectants of electoral favour. Tom Grove looked black as night and dreadfully anxious. At our arrival the nomination was proceeding, several carriages were drawn up. Mrs de Boulay arrived just as we did and was taken up into the Ferne carriage, and without the least apology we were left to manage as we could. We met Mr James Hussey.[217] He took care of the other ladies whilst we retreated from the heat of the sun into the shelter of the pavement, but close to public houses where I had my nose for some time well filled with beer and tobacco. When Tom Grove began to speak some roughs had come to make a disturbance, by the acquits of the other party kicked up such a row under the hustings that not a word could be heard and the police succeeded in taking some prize fighters into custody, who were engaged by Mr William Day, the trainer of bloodstock. The townspeople got hold of three of them, and ducked them in the river, and they were finally captured by the police and lodged in the lock up. We lunched at the James Hussey's and returned by the 3.10 at Gillingham. A lovely day.

Three days later Tom Grove was elected as a Member of Parliament but was ousted at the following election. He later returned as MP for Wilton.

[12ᵗʰ July.] Letter from Chafyn yesterday by the missing Australian mail, and being 'insufficiently paid', and I did not receive it via Marseilles. He will not return this year, and I must make up my mind to remain here another winter alone. I wish I might go out to him, but I feel I am more necessary here than there, as he has a nice and careful companion in Mr Hoffman. He leaves the decision entirely to me, and says he shall acquiesce in whatever I may elect to do, and I must stay, but would it could be otherwise! The ties given by Providence to him here, call for consideration at my hands, as he cannot care for them personally, and there will be a comfortable house for him when he can come, so I must be contented – many are much worse off.

CHAPTER TWENTY-ONE

Llangollen, N.S.W.

'A piping hot day. Went out in the morning and got some letters and papers at last, from home.'[218] Still open to ideas for changing plans, Chafyn inspected a barque advertised to sail for San Francisco, but found her to be 'an unlikely craft to suit me being deficient in accommodation and smelling most ancient and fish like'. Keeping to their plans, they boarded a train to Penrith en route to Bathurst 'and were decently put up, with many mosquitoes, at a public house near the station'.

The following day they progressed to the Blue Mountains, halting for breakfast in a 'very nice-looking public house, The Pilgrim's Inn by Varcoe. When staying here about three weeks ago and returning from the garden full of unripe peaches, which Sir F Pottinger had been picking, he was shot by a pistol going off in his pocket as he remounted the coach.[219] From here the road continues along the top of the Blue Mountains. It was severe for the horses the way being deep in sand, like a sea beach, and barely being hard enough for a trot where we stayed at the Weatherboard Inn. We could not wait to get away from the bugs and the dirty navvies, who had been spending their day singing (and spending their week's wages) in the bar.'

Chafyn appeared to be tired as there were several instances when Hoffman rode off to sketch and visit places of interest like Govett's Leap, while Chafyn stayed at the lodgings.[220] He either took a short walk in the bush to look at the vegetation, making acquaintance with 'the Bathurst briar, a prickly weed of such a noxious and rapidly increasing nature as to call for figurative interference for its suppression', or skinned a bird if Hoffman brought one back.

With a boiling hot sun, and no breeze to blow away the dust, the view was 'very extensive, but like most of the views in these parts, monotonous from the endless ranges of fern clad mountains, rising like waves one behind the other'. At Bowenfells, Chafyn had an introductory card from Graham of the Australian Club to the Brown family, where the group had dinner. 'Their house and garden is quite in the English style, indeed sitting in their drawing room one might have been in a country house at home; books, piano, flowers, everything suggestive of the old country. It was the first good country house I had been into in this colony, and I was much surprised to find everything so comfortable, the Sydneyites rather trying to make out that the up-country life is not so refined and civilized as their own.'

After ascending for several miles, the road began to descend into Bathurst with Chafyn driving the horses and Hoffman and Robertson behind. They left the bush and came out in 'an open undulating plain, covered in short turf like the downs'. They then ascended a small hill outside the town, to the Royal Hotel, and 'got an extensive but dreary view over the surrounding plains which seem much burnt out. It was staggeringly unpicturesque.'

'Roll up, my lads, roll up; now's the time or never etc. etc. roll up!' was the dawn greeting from outside Chafyn's bedroom window, where an old man was auctioning horses. There was much shouting and ringing of a bell to sell his wares, 'but the purchasers did not roll up with the alacrity desired at all,'

'The high land along which the road to Sopola runs for some miles is honeycombed with diggings mostly worked out. At one place we stopped and talked to a digger at work. He was an old hand and had worked at most of the diggings here and in Victoria, had made a lot of money and had spent it in failing speculations. He washed out a very pretty nugget in a piece of quartz while we were there, of which Hoffman became the purchaser.'

On reaching Sopola, while Hoffman went off to hunt kangaroos, Chafyn went to the races, 'there being only three events run in heats to prolong the sport, and generally as far as I could make out arranged beforehand. A mare belonging to a black won a race, and a row ensued, not very creditable to the spirit of fair play of the English rules, who set on the unfortunate man and thrashed him.' Chafyn left after 'a thorough baking and dusting' and Hoffman had 'a blank day, the dogs being out of condition'. From Mudgee to Cassilis they had a hot drive over good road in open bush and after concluding the day with ten miles of rough and sandy track they stopped at a bush public house in Greenhill Creek, 'with accommodation unsuited to fastidious minds. The landlord, whose wife appeared recently to have bolted and left him all the household work to do, did his best for us, with many apologies. However, there are worse things than beef and damper to be got.'

Having been moving through the bush for over a month via roadside inns, the young men were ready to settle and have a rest. They drove through Cassilis and with difficulty found Llangollen, Mr Lambe's station.

> Lambe had met us at Sydney two months ago and had asked me
> if we came round this way to look him up. Unfortunately, on our
> arrival [...] we found him away, at Collaroy, Dr Trait's station
> fifteen miles off, but as his return in the afternoon was stated to
> be certain, and as we were very hot and hungry, and unwilling
> again to face the creek, we determined to wait his arrival,
> which up to this hour (10.30.p.m.) has not taken place. His
> housekeeper has however, fed us most hospitably, and the quiet
> and cleanliness of a private house after the long spell of public
> house we have had is certainly refreshing. The house is the usual
> one-storied bungalow, standing on nicely sloping parkish ground,
> grass land and clumps of trees, and in rear are the cattle sheds,
> men's huts and other farming offices of the station. In the distance
> the mountains rise forming a good background to the pleasant
> homelike view, very refreshing after the shrub and wildness of
> the Blue Mountains and gold districts. [The following day was]
> mostly spent in the pleasing novelty of reading in an easy chair

under the verandah. About 1p.m. Lambe returned and gave us a hospitable welcome. Our party was increased in the evening by Mr Wilson, the incumbent of these parts, who is living here until his own house is completed. He is a nice fellow but unfortunately quite deaf from an attack of diphtheria about three years ago. Parsons at home grumble about overwork, but what would they think of doing more than two hundred and fifty services annually in about twelve different places, scattered over about twenty miles square of country!

After breakfast, Chafyn and Hoffman rode to the Busby family who lived two miles away on a neighbouring station. 'Mr Busby is a very gentlemanlike man, and has lived here for thirty years. His house is very comfortable and fitted up with every English comfort including a very good grand piano. He is a great horse breeder, and goes in for it with greater care than the generality of colonists, who seem to aim more at quantity than quality both in horses and cattle. This is very much, I am told, owing to the expense of fencing and so keeping the stock separate. Therefore allowed to run wild in herds, they multiply *salon le gout*. After a very pleasant afternoon and evening, we rode home in the moonlight.'

But worryingly for Chafyn, he was not feeling well. 'I remained all day on the premises having a bad cold in my head which renders me very stupid and uncomfortable, the result of the cold night at Greenhill Creek where it blew hard in the night and the house was anything but airtight, indeed decidedly overventilated.' He slept badly that night, 'disturbed by a dry cough and by an opossum which ran about at intervals overhead'.

'Did not go much beyond the homestead. Wilson came home in the evening having ridden thirty miles and done three services. His regular parochial rounds of which these are two involve such a ride of about one hundred and eighty miles!'

Having recovered from his cold, Chafyn, Hoffman, and Robertson, who experimented with cooking and became their chef, stayed at Llangollen with Mr Lambe for four months with regular visits to the Busbys. Winter was coming, although not as fierce or cold as in England, Chafyn had no wish to move too far and they were all enjoying the hospitality of Lambe and the Busby family nearby. Decisions, out of necessity, revolved around Chafyn's health, and Hoffman was compliant. Having decided to stay with Lambe for a few months, their hired buggy was languishing unused and was expensive. It was decided that Hoffman and Lambe would return the buggy to Sydney while Chafyn stayed at Llangollen. During this time he spent many hours with the Busby family, although Mr Busby was away. The family persuaded him to stay there until Hoffman's return. 'Between the piano and books and conversation I got through the days very pleasantly, but as is often the case when the master is away the wine did not flow so freely as it might have done, the ladies being in the water drinking line. Read for the first time Dickens' *American Notes*, very amusing. Some parts of it might stand verbatim for descriptions of Australian scenes, viz: the journey by mail coach in Virginia, and the general appearance of things in the back woods.'

When Hoffman and Lambe returned, the Busby party was to come to luncheon and much preparation was going on in the morning for the unusual event of

> ... a reception of ladies. It rained so heavily about 1.30.p.m. that we had given them up when suddenly an alarm was given and then, sure enough, they were driving up in the rain, three ladies and Mr Busby in a dog cart with a landau. The ladies were for the first few minutes decidedly slow, being more or less damp and having had to get out and walk part of the way from the leader jibbing. But a little of our affable conversation soon smoothed them down, especially when they were disabused of the idea which they at first took into their heads that we had lunched without them before their arrival, and the entertainment passed off with great Eclat, including pistol practice by the ladies, in which they behaved much in the way usual of the sex on those occasions, shutting their eyes and complaining of the 'nasty noise', save Mr Busby's elderly mother-in-law who displayed more pluck in the matter.

Towards the end of June, the weather was warm and mild. 'One of the finest days I have seen for a long time. Spent much of the morning inspecting the process of classing a flock of sheep, and marking the superior ones. Some of the ewes had already magnificent fleeces. Hoffman was out with his rifle, 'the last two nights shooting opossums in the trees in the paddock. I was at work all day skinning them for a rug.' During the day, when he was not away working, Lambe took Hoffman bull hunting, while neighbouring Mr Busby chatted with Chafyn about farming and horse breeding. He had forty thousand sheep. Chafyn was interested in visiting the stock arrangements as farming was his family business, too. But mostly Chafyn stayed indoors at Llangollen, keeping himself amused by playing the piano and reading., He regularly went into Cassilis to receive the English mail and telegraphic news. 'Letters on the whole satisfactory. Amused myself reading the *Spectator* wherein I found some articles of no great merit by one Henry Grove a clergyman. Our chef, Robertson, tried his hand at a curry, but produced a rather curious compound. He is getting ambitious for success.'

The damp weather had brought out a swarm of pestering flies, 'very objectionable and almost reminding one of the Delta, and an unusual number of ants' nests or mounds, sometimes three or four feet high. The ants are large red and black fellows.'

A visitor arrived. Jack Fletcher had been to visit the Busbys as he was 'out here looking for a sheep station. My old friend, whom I had not seen since I left Cambridge. When he heard I was here he came up. We prevailed on him to dine and sleep and had a great talk over old times. He showed me a letter from Henniker giving a detailed account of sundry Cambridge men of whom I had lost sight. All the most unlikely subjects seem to have taken to the Church.'

One day, when it blew and rained most violently, 'the mail brought the English papers to console my solitude, and by way of excitement, though not of the most pleasant sort, I had to adjudicate in a case of wife beating. Wilkinson returning from Cassilis sulky drunk, proceeded to thrash his wife, the housekeeper, who rushed into me in tears for protection. It is not pleasant to have to interfere with other people's servants, but in a case of this sort I had no alternative, and I wish that my strength would have allowed me to repay the gentleman in kind, physical lecturing being more suited for such cases than moral.' This was followed by another incident involving Mrs Wilkinson. Chafyn and Lambe were returning from Cassilis where the latter was seeking to engage some extra help for the lambing season. 'Mrs Wilkinson in great trouble having as she thinks knocked one of her eyes out with a stick. Hoffman examined it on his return, and is evidently doubtful about it.' Dr Morris was sanguine about her injury. He came from Cassilis for lunch, 'yarning about the Messiters, Surrage and other Wincantonians whom he knows'.

At the end of the month of June,

The English mail arrived at last. It is too bad of the P.O. and they are under no penalty to the colonial Governments, so that of course they do not put themselves out. They have been about forty-six days late in the last six months. The *Bombay* that took the April mail from this has not been heard of. It is supposed that she has broken down and gone under sail to Mauritius. It is peculiarly annoying as by that mail I sent an account of my change of plans, and the non-arrival of either myself or any letters will cause much anxiety.

The Federals seem to have really given their opponents the coup de grace this time, but should Lincoln's assassination turn out to be a Southern scheme the conquerors will not be disposed to such leniency, especially with such a man at their head as Johnson, who succeeds to the Presidency by virtue of his office of V.P. and is such a rowdy as to disgust the Yankees themselves.

[20ᵗʰ July.] The English mail arrived, and I had the quite unexpected pleasure of a letter from home, together with a duplicate of the deed of conveyance of the land for the parsonage house at Zeals, which I signed in January and sent off, but appears somehow to have miscarried, and as the Land Commission won't give any money for the house until this is executed, and Fellowes can't marry until he has a house, I feel that I am interrupting the course of true love in an unfortunate manner.

CHAPTER TWENTY-TWO

Zeals – Late Summer

18ᵗʰ July. 'Letter from Chafyn today – with a good account. A parcel of Ferne deeds and others arrived via Valencia today.[221] I went to school at three and when I was deep in a hymn with the children they stopped and gaped at the door, when I reached round and there was Mr Morrison, who Mrs Huntley told, would find me there, a conclusion she justified from my having a book in my hand as I spoke to her at the Lodge.'

Alfred Morrison, in the habit of arriving unannounced, wanted to see Julia, but when she was not at home he decided to go and find her, so she closed the school for the day. 'I had to walk back with him, Charletto leading his horse, a superb chestnut – and he stayed till 6 o'clock.'

Zeals House from the south with hay.

In August, Julia had various visitors to stay at Zeals including aunt Anna, whom she took to visit Charles-Henry's family, his wife Eliza 'looking very unwell', and the Troyte-Bullocks continued to go to Zeals regularly. When aunt Anna departed for Weymouth, more guests arrived.

'Nelson Goddards and their daughter Fanny came to stay. They are looking very well and Fanny grown a monster, her hands and feet are hugely disproportionate to her figure now, which is a common fault at twelve years of age. She is a beautiful and well-mannered child, and in her way naturally beyond her years, from being an only child. Mr Morrison dined and slept, and Mr Fellowes dined.'

The following day Julia and her Goddard guests started for Fonthill.

Our host gave us a good luncheon, with such lovely glass and appointments, that hungry as the drive over the downs had made me, my attention was more than divided from my luncheon by admiration for what it was served upon, and the tapestry and china that surrounded us. We stayed until 5 p.m. lively all the time looking over the curiosities which now include a score or more of lovely snuff boxes, and we finished up with a hurried look at the horses, which charmed Fanny who is a true country girl. Mr Goddard delights in china, and was quite happy all the time, so I was delighted that I had arranged so nice a plan for my guests. We had a thunderous storm coming home, but with waterproofs we escaped tolerably.

Julia took her guests to a croquet party where there was 'tea, coffee and champagne cups on the table with sandwiches etc. at ½ past 5 and we came home to dinner at 7.30.' When the Goddards left David Powell came.

'I was curious to see him, as he was with Chafyn in Tasmania and at Melbourne. He brought his Australian and New Zealand sketches with him, which were beautiful, especially the latter, the Island boasting such fine scenery. New South Wales is not generally pretty – about Wollongong it is so – and Sydney is lovely.'

George and Alice Troyte-Bullock were staying at Zeals while they were waiting to move into a house in Sedgehill which was not nearly ready, as 'the Seftleys left it like a piggery'. Julia rode to Sedgehill, which she so often liked to do, enjoying the surroundings and absorbing the seasonal changes. 'Out for three and a half hours. The wind on the downs was very high. The harvest is in full swing, but the wheat is a good deal blighted, on the downs especially. Home via Knoyle, a delightful long ride.'

Devey arrived and went away the following day. He would have been at Zeals to oversee the building of the almshouses as his work at Zeals House had finished some time previously, leaving Coakley in charge of the remaining decorative elements. When he left, Julia went out in the gig with Alice to church. After the service they drove to Sedgehill, returning with George. The next day she rode to Stourhead with George, and the three of them walked to Mere in the rain, returning in the wagonette. During this period, Julia was contented. 'I rode on the downs alone, whilst my guests went to Sedgehill again to rub up the workmen,' and later took the pony about Silton, visiting some of the cottages.

Returning from a drive to Wincanton, Emily arrived to stay, 'in tip-top spirits, and joked about her engagement to Charlie. I wish it was anyone else – I think Mr Townsend more common minded and unrefined. Free him – he has no courtesy whatsoever, and no conversation.' Emily thought herself lucky, she was the daughter of a clergyman and was marrying the clergyman of Mere Church, so close to her Sedgehill home, and she was, after all, thirty-two. Although Julia did not want her clergyman to be a member of her family, she would also have been dismayed to lose her closest companion. 'Practice at school. Rode the pony and called at Stourton to enquire for Mr Bicknell who is in a declining state.[222] Lovely afternoon. Rode across the downs to Pertwood with George – the Church is a neat little place to hold about twenty people – the farm belongs to Mr Seymour – the farmer and his spouse are civil people, the wife a Yeovil woman, and fraternized with George for a long time.'

20th August. 'Letter from Chafyn on the 10th all well, still with Mr Lambe at Cassilis'.

'Wrote to Chafyn as usual – four sheets of foreign papers – and told him everything I could think of to secure and interest him in his present place far from home and all he cares for.'

At the end of the month, 'the cousins are gone.' George and Alice moved into their house at Sedgehill and Julia was alone again, 'which is worse in the long days than in the winter. Coakley today – and scolded him well for the slowness of his men in the hall work.'

Julia spent her days riding and driving. 'Ginger' had been retired, her shoes taken off and put out to grass. 'There was Chafyn's grey pony which was put to use and Capt. Phelips horse in the stables too. Rode to Sedgehill and home by Knoyle, a pleasant ride, which would have been pleasanter with someone to greet me on returning to dinner – however, I must not <u>complain</u>. Mrs Charles-Henry is not too well and has been to see Ferguson.'

On Sunday Julia went to church at Mere and, resigned to Emily's marriage, asked the Revd. Charles Townsend's family to lunch. 'They came after draping themselves in silk gowns for the occasion.'

CHAPTER TWENTY-THREE

Sydney Revisited

[2nd August.] After breakfast took a farewell of Llangollen, where I have spent nearly four months very pleasantly, though latterly rather dully, calling on my way at the Busbys' to wish them goodbye and thank them for their hospitality. I rode for the last time by the mangey township, and so through the bush to Collaroy, where I found that Dr Traill was going to start for Sydney on the morrow in his buggy, so changed my plans, and instead of rattling down in the mail on Tuesday determined to accompany him.[223]

There was another reason why Chafyn was anxious to get to Sydney. He was suffering from toothache. Dr Rowland Traill, not a medical doctor but a Professor from Edinburgh University and author of two articles in the last edition of the *Encyclopaedia Britannica* on Light and Heat and Medical Jurisprudence, diagnosed Chafyn's plight as indigestion.

They reached the Royal Hotel at Muswellbrook and there parted company, Dr Triall to go on by the mail later that night. Meanwhile, Chafyn waited for Robertson to arrive from Cassilis with the luggage, the latter having travelled *en prince* with the coach all to himself. Chafyn had booked the coach and could not get out of it when he changed his plans. 'Started at nine in a day coach with Robertson in the other coach, both pretty much filled. We started about the same time and we amused ourselves racing

Government House Sydney, *c.*1879.

for the first fifteen miles, which as the great Northern Road on which we were is tolerably well macadamized, got us along at a pleasant speed with no great danger of jolting.' Having stopped for lunch they boarded a train for Newcastle. 'The rail runs to Newcastle along the valley of the Hunter, which is well cultivated, and has several good-sized towns, Maitland, Morpeth, etc. After four months in the bush the sight of an elegant gentleman on the platform at Maitland in a hat and tight frock coat quite staggered me by its novelty. Arrived at the Caledonian Hotel a little before 6 p.m. Good accommodation and the first coal fire I have seen since leaving England, but here we are in the land of smuts and coal dust.'

After a good night's sleep, they started for Sydney and boarded the Australasian Steam Navigation Company paddle steamer *Cawarra*.[224] 'A miller from Morpeth with thirty years' experience of his trade in England, Canada and Australia, said on board the steamer that, having ground wheat from every part of the world, the best he had ever seen was grown near Woolonton in the Hunter Valley – yet all the wheat is imported. Arrived after a good passage of about six hours. Put up at the Australian Club, which is rather empty. Traill, Lambe and Fletcher are here and of course the old standing dishes like Graham, etc. who was prosy as ever. Had a good rubber in the evening, and so to bed, not sorry to be once more among the fleshpots of civilisation'. Unlike the disorientating first experience of Sydney after the long sea voyage, this time Chafyn fell straight into the familiarity of the social system.

Spent an hour kicking my heels in a fireless room, in company with several trembling ladies, at Dr Belisario's the dentists, until I was summoned into 'the presence', and after a short examination was kicked out and told to come again as my case must wait. Went out shopping between showers, and to luncheon at the Chisholms, who gave me a hearty welcome as usual. Robertson was there also. He goes to Melbourne tomorrow en route for England. Attwood is gone to Brisbane, so Sydney society has put up its shutters! [With weather and health concerns uppermost, Chafyn] withstood the temptation of going to the opera owing to the wet evening, and was rewarded by a good rubber.

To church in the morning at St. James' with the beauty and fashion of Sydney including the Governor and Governess. Spent the afternoon with the English papers and inspecting the birds and beasts in the Botanical Gardens. The glass falling (in this Antipodean country a good sign) and a fine day savouring of approaching spring. The trees and plants are beginning to burst, some already in flower, notably a species of magnolia which is in full flower without bearing a single leaf, the effect of which is not a little curious. The ducks, kangaroos and sight scenes were much as usual, particularly the latter who were most orderly.

In the evening spent an hour in polite society at an assembly at Government House. The rooms were not overcrowded and had I been a dancer I should have thought it a good ball. As it was, I contented myself with playing wallflower for a period and then retired after paying my respects to the Governor and Lady Young who were civil as usual.

While Chafyn was awaiting the arrival of Hoffman, he paid a further visit to Dr Belisario for treatment. 'He is far less rough than my old friend Cartwright, and a skilful performer to boot.'

Returning from Brisbane, Attwood took Chafyn for a drive in Botany Bay in his buggy, followed by an invitation to his house in Paddington where they had a good rubber in the evening with a friend of Attwood's, late a Cape mounted rifleman, 'but rather more tobacco smoke than I quite care about'.

Attwood drove Chafyn into town in the morning, and 'in the afternoon Hoffman arrived from up the country very flourishing. In the evening Lambe and Traill departed by steamer. Dined at Government House. Much conversation about Lady Young's fancy ball which is hinted to the XVIII Century. The expense of costume will probably render the ball rather select.'

Now that Hoffman had returned, it was time to go to the harbour to secure a passage. They went to see the P & O steamer *Northam* 'which is to carry us away.[225] She is a fine ship with good cabins but very low in the water. Took our berths by next mail steamer for Suez.'

Until the sailing date, on 22nd September, Chafyn and Hoffman had to keep themselves amused. Chafyn went to Freeman of George Street where he was photographed, sending the photograph to Julia and went to luncheon in the barracks, 'and saw some rackets afterwards at the court there, an indifferent one, but the only one in Sydney.'[226] Hoffman, meanwhile, went to Penrith with Slade on a sketching exhibition. On Sunday, Chafyn went to church at

St James's and heard a sermon from the Bishop of Sydney on behalf of the cathedral fund. 'His delivery is very monotonous. A windy disagreeable day with clouds of dust, the water carts not working on Sundays.' He went to the dentist again for a four-hour session, and started packing, sending sundry packages and several boxes of heavy traps including some colonial wine for *Queen of Nations* bound for London. He dined at Government House. 'There was a very small party, among them the Premier, Mr Cowper, who seemed a pleasant intelligent man'.

Lunched with Hope, 1st Lieutenant of H.M.S. *Falcon*, a screw corvette of seventeen guns, and afterwards went down to Manley Beach in the pinnace. After a short stroll in the cockney paradise of sand and becoming spectators of a shocking accident to a poor child who was knocked down and run over by a run-away horse and cart most carelessly left standing alone close to the steam boat pier. We started to beat up the harbour in company with the cutter. But as it came on to blow hard, and we had no ballast whilst the cutter had, we were soon left behind and moreover shipped such a lot of water from the determination of the 2nd Lieutenant in charge not to give in, and reef, that we became after a time waterlogged, and unmanageable, and in considerable danger of capsizing, as we were constantly gunwales under. At last we anchored at Rushcutter's Bay to bale, and as it was getting late and this proceeding was likely to take some time, the cutter came back, and took me up to the ship which we reached about an hour before the pinnace. The former having prudently reefed and being properly provided with ballast had shipped scarcely any water. After dinner in the Ward Room and a rubber of whist I went on shore and to bed. Hoffman returned from Penrith.

Chafyn was pleased to find that he had not caught a cold from his ducking of the day before. He called on the Chisholms and walked in the Botanical Gardens with Chisholm. The following day he was 'out of sorts with a headache, and stayed in all day till just sunset. The club was very empty in the evening, Hoffman and I being the sole diners. Consequently, no whist!' Travelling may have been losing its appeal, there were signs of home sickness.

On 1st September, Chafyn wrote: 'First day of partridge shooting today.'

CHAPTER TWENTY-FOUR

Zeals – September

'George Troyte-Bullock came and <u>shot</u> and he and Huntley killed twenty-two brace and a half in the watering fields only, so shall distribute game to everyone now. Very hot – partridges half roasted before they arrive in the kitchen. Emma Grove and Emily and Agnes came, and we had croquet. To church at seven.'[227]

The Revd Spencer Fellowes, firmly established as the vicar of Zeals St Martins Church and being assured that his new rectory was at last being built, initiated a power struggle with Julia. 'To my great surprise Mr Fellowes gave out a school sermon yesterday, for Sunday, without any notification to me of his intention! A mark of discourtesy undeserved by me – without us

Zeals Parsonage.

he would have had no school at all, and now he seeks to take the whole management to himself, ignoring any other claims of co-operation.'

Julia then went to Speen, near Chippenham, to visit her mother's Michell relatives, where aunt Anna picked her up at the station. She called on Kate, 'the nicest of the Michell girls, now married to the vicar of Stockcross and living in a pretty little nice house', on Mrs Bert at Donnington Grove and then drove to Standen, 'and have got that over with! Mrs Michell looks as well as ever, she did up grey hair which I have much, my uncle very thin and white. There were plenty of partridges, peaches and nectarines have ripened well, under the hot sun of the cart for thirteen days.' Julia took George Michell home with her.

While at Speen, Julia received an invitation to dinner at Stourhead and went there on her return to Zeals followed by preparations for the harvest celebrations.

Harvest House – and a brilliant day and an ample gathering, the Church well decorated by Mrs Rumsey and her assistants. The vicar preached and the dinner came off in the school room as last year provided by Goldsborough and gave great satisfaction. I gave thanks for Chafyn's health, standing on a chair in the middle of the room, to the astonishment of everyone.

Sermons for Zeals School today – Mr Fellowes, whose manner I thought very odd, and rather rude yesterday has written me such a nasty letter, about the management of the school, which he desires to have entirely left to him, and asks me rather noisily about books and money – the former he has had for several weeks. I shall take no notice of his letter, it is strange that two days only before his marriage he would desire to have school business to settle, when his preparations must take up his time.

Went to Wardour, lunching on the grass with Miss Rawson, greatly enjoyed.

Mere school treat was on the same day and Julia was unable to attend as entertaining her house guests, the Maynes, was her prior duty. So, on their way back they called at the Mere Rectory and had tea and met the George Troyte-Bullocks.

The double wedding at Gillingham came off today. I only went to the breakfast, the bridesmaids were dressed in pink and in blue, five of each colour and the sister in white. There were fifty at breakfast, and I thought the speeches stupid and tedious.

The Groves of Ferne dined here, and Mr Grant Dalton shot and dined and K Michell came to stay. Nine at dinner which is as many as I can manage in the little drawing room. Mrs 'I am' went to Weymouth and family asked to stay another night.[228]

Miss Rawson went away at 6.30. George Troyte-Bullock shot and slept here on Tuesday and shot again on Wednesday, partridges abundant, but very wild. Received a very impertinent letter from Mr Fellowes on Saturday inspecting the school arrangements, which he thrice asked me to leave entirely to him which is an odd request considering that upon Chafyn falls the far largest there of the school expenses. And we have for many years had the whole weight of the school to support, and to try and grab it from us, and constitute himself over the school, he being also beholden to Chafyn largely for the land upon which his house is building. I shall take no notice of this and I will not do so.

With the building of the almshouses in Zeals village proceeding well, Devey's clerk arrived. 'A man I dislike, conceited with his tongue too large for his mouth, and with much more opinion of himself than has "le singe" Devey, who is not conceited or self-sufficient, as are some professional men. Thomas Wyate to wit!'

Julia with her house guest George Michell went to church and 'started for Longleat at a.m. and rode by Sheerwater nine miles, the three and a half of dusty road we walked, slept at Sheerwater, chic sandwiches and sherry, and let the poor hot horses rest a bit and then had the next part or our ride through the woods to the house, where we remained half an hour, shown about by a most obliging housekeeper, did not get home until 7 p.m. and darkness had set in. This and the short evenings, makes one miscalculate the duration of daylight, and night overtakes one as a surprise.'

'To croquet at East Hayes of the Pyt House, three sisters, three Grove girls, Emily – with her "Charley" being round her neck as usual and the "Great Soap" constituted the party. Dined early, had tea, and drove home by the loveliest moonlight.'

CHAPTER TWENTY-FIVE

Northam

On Saturday, 23rd September 1865, Chafyn and Hoffman boarded the P & O *Northam* steamer bound for Point de Galle, Ceylon. They were homeward bound but unlike their three-month long journey out, they were staggering the return.

Farewell to Sydney. A lovely day with a light northeasterly wind. The tardy mail from England arrived this morning and was not delivered before we started, but thanks to the kindness of Major Christie we got our letters out of the post office on the way down to the wharf. Punctually at 2 p.m. the *Northam* started and we had our last view of the harbour as we steamed down. I am sorry to leave Sydney now that it has come to the point having met with so much kindness there and made many pleasant acquaintances. The Chisholms, Slades and Hoffman's friend Frederick Darley came on board to see us off. The old Pacific for once did not belie his name, and was and is still most unusually smooth, and as we have lots of room, and fair feeding (notwithstanding the arrest of the French cook one hour before starting, for debt) we have not much to grumble at. At present we have only seven passengers for Galle, but shall probably pick up some more at Melbourne.[229]

I got five very satisfactory letters (save one – a begging letter from Mr Fellowes) from England. Poor Brand's misfortune I am very sorry to hear of. All well and cheerful at home.

After a good night's sleep, the cabin being forward of the engines, 'the usual matutinal ships' noises began heightened in this case by the hinderance and clatter of the Lascars (who are by the by mostly Africans). At noon we were off Gabo Island, and the weather beautifully calm though rather chilly. Just as I was turning in about 1.15 p.m. a violent gale from the Westward came up with the suddenness of a southerly "buster" and took everything aback, roaring through the rigging at a terrific manner.' The ship rolled a great deal, washing away the port life boat. They were off Wilson's promontory at 10 a.m. but the gale did not subside and there followed an uneasy night with violent lurches. 'I do not think the *Northam* a good sea boat, although we certainly had real heavy weather, as bad probably as any we shall get.'

At Melbourne, Chafyn and Hoffman and a Mr Marsh, returning home after a flying visit to his stations in the north, went ashore where they dined at the Melbourne Club and looked at the English papers, before reboarding, along with 'a not very aristocratic looking addition to our party, among them two very sharp American conjurors, one of whom has been amusing select audiences'.

The *Northam* steamed out of the bay, picking up mail left by the *City of Adelaide*. That night there was more unpleasant rolling, 'shipping continual seas aft which rendered battening down necessary, making things below still more cheerful, darkness and damp prevailing everywhere'. Chafyn slept in his clothes as there was a leak over his bunk, which he had repaired the next day. 'Mr Marsh, who is always prophesying about the weather, foretold a fine passage.' On Sunday, 'Captain Skottowe read service to a rather unsteady audience, the sea much abating in the evening.'

'A sleepless night, anchored in the outer roads of King George's Sound about 1.a.m. with firing of rockets and guns. At daylight went into the inner Sound and commenced coaling, which continued all day, six hundred tons having to be shipped. The harbour is a desolate looking place. Took on board six passengers from Adelaide, including another doctor making up the number of that profession on board to five. Steamed out of the harbour at daylight and were soon tacking about in a heavy sea with head wind making very slow progress and shipping plenty of sea. Saloon battened down, everything tumbling about. Everything below damp dark and wretched.' In this uncomfortable environment Chafyn celebrated his twenty-fifth birthday.

By the following Saturday, the sea was smooth and fine with a pleasant breeze from the south-west.

> We dined today for the first time since leaving the Sound without fiddles and with our complete party. Everybody very perky on the strength of the change and Mr Marsh additionally eloquent on all subjects especially prawn curry and pomfret. The stewards gave a Christy minstrel performance, which was on the whole well done, and was at the worst a break in the unvarying routine

of reading, dozing and playing whist. A fine sea eagle was seen this evening probably from the Keeling Islands which are about a hundred miles off.

A row among the black stokers in the afternoon, the 2nd engineer having knocked one of them down for subordination. The wounded man immediately came on deck bleeding considerably from the mouth and nose, and tried to jump overboard in which proceeding he was stopped, and then sat down on deck and bellowed. About twenty of his fellow stokers then came aft brandishing sticks, but were promptly sent about their business by the officers and the ring leader threatened with irons.

A few days before land was sighted the weather was 'cloudy, but dry on deck until after dinner when it became squally with very heavy rain such as falls only in the tropics. In the morning we sighted a ship standing across our bows. About 1 p.m. we passed within two hundred yards of her and she proved to be the *Victor Albert* from New Zealand, forty-one days out, with troops for Calcutta. The men crowded her decks and gave us three cheers as we steamed by, which we returned.'

The following day was muggy with heavy showers and sea jolting ahead. 'Two services à la Presbyterienne by the skipper, those who tried to stand up being immediately flopped down again by the punkahs.' The black minstrels held a second performance on the Monday on the quarter deck 'to an admiring audience, who organised in return a collection'.

Land was sighted before breakfast the next morning, 'and at 9.30 a.m. it was well in sight, thickly wooded with cocoa nut trees down to the water's edge, with high land in the interior of Port de Galle'. The journey had taken just over three weeks.

Presently the pilot came on board in a catamaran, certainly the most unsafe looking sea boat I ever saw, but really quite the contrary. In Port de Galle harbour, which is only an open roadstead quite unprotected, we found three steamers before us, viz: the *Delhi*, with the home mail, the *Ottowa* for Bombay, and the *Ellora* just come out round the Cape to replace the *Northam* on the Australian line, she going up to Bombay for boiler repairs. The moment we anchored we were surrounded by boats and catamarans, while the swarm of boatmen and pedlars from different hotels boarded the deck and jabbered and gesticulated like an army of lunatic monkeys. After some time, we extricated ourselves from the general confusion and got safely ashore at the wharf which is backed by the wall of the town. Passing through the only gate of Galle and by the barracks of the Ceylon rifles, who looked very warm in their coarse green jackets and very slovenly. A short walk brought us to the Eglinton Hotel, which is immediately on the ramparts and is kept by a very civil Portuguese. We got two decent rooms up a sort of loft stairs in a 'dependence' adjoining, all the rest of the accommodation being taken up by a circus company.

CHAPTER TWENTY-SIX

Ceylon

[17ᵗʰ October.] After tiffin we sallied out on one or two matters of business, and certainly the streets of Galle present the most novel and picturesque scene. The houses are all fronted by a sort of verandah very often supported on pillars, under which in the case of shops, the wares are laid out, while in private houses screens of matting hang down. Passing through the gateway the throng is incessant of carriages (some only to be described as "satchbores in mourning"), narrow two wheeled carts drawn by meek little bulls about as tall as Breton cattle, and foot passengers. The Cingalese are fine handsome men and wear their black hair generally long and clubbed at the back of the head which gives them a rather comical appearance. Everybody wears a sort of bed curtain round the waist and hanging below the knee. The amount of clothing on the upper man appears to vary according to the position of the individual, the lower classes wearing nothing, or at least a film of cocoa nut oil. Before dinner we drove out to the Cinnamon Gardens, about six miles out along a capital road close to the sea and very little above it. The beach is low and sandy, and the cocoa nut trees come down to the very water's edge. There was much traffic on the road, and by the side were plenty of native huts, bamboo and mud, and shoals of naked children. At the Cinnamon gardens is a public house kept by an Englishman where we got shelter from the rain which had come on and rather restricted our operations. We however, took a short stroll and were certainly astonished at the variety and luxuriance of the vegetation, almonds, cinnamon, china mangoes and no end of these. The ripe nutmeg is very pretty, the colour and size of an apricot. The rain not stopping, we were obliged to start home after tasting the milk of a young cocoa nut which, no doubt, is very pleasant if one is very thirsty as a substitute for water, but certainly inferior to that same fluid when of good quality. The rain fell in sheets as we drove home meeting crowds of natives standing under the shelter of a large cocoa leaf. At dinner we made the acquaintance of the celebrated brown curries. They are of very delicate flavour, but <u>awfully</u> hot.[230]

Passed a good night on the bed, not *in* bed, for this country a bed consists of only a sheet spread over a mattress on the top of which you are without any covering. The mosquitoes were rather troublesome but compared with those in Australia their bite is very trifling. Rose at 6 a.m. and had a bath and a light breakfast.

As it was raining Chafyn and Hoffman chartered a carriage and drove out to Wackwalla about five or six miles on a good road bordered by paddy fields. The vegetation on all sides was luxuriant, especially the ferns of which there were a great variety. 'After tiffin (we brought food with us, the rest house supplying only water, easy chairs and a cool verandah) we started home again. About sunset the climate is very delightful, but unfortunately it gets dark so very quickly as to curtail much of the enjoyment of an evening stroll.'

Started at 6 a.m. in the Royal Mail Coach, a very comfortable vehicle carrying five passengers for Colombo (seventy-two miles). The road from Galle to Colombo is very good, and almost on a dead level running often within a few yards of the sea, while villages succeed each other at very short intervals. In several areas we saw schools of orderly boys sitting up with books and slates, and most gentlemanlike looking teachers, for the respectable middle class Cingalese are certainly very well bred for appearance which is enhanced by the scrupulous cleanliness and neatness of their linen clothes.

Unluckily, the approach to Colombo prevented the two young men seeing the town clearly. It was surrounded by a double line of fortifications, and 'contained fine buildings with airy streets and broad open spaces. The garrison consists of the H.2 wing of the 25th Company of Ceylon Rifles, with some artillery, royal and local.' They walked along narrow streets in the Arab quarter,

> ... most of the people bearing that caste of feature, and wearing white turbans and promiscuous rolls of white muslin, quite different to the neat Cingalese dress. [...] We then went along the shores of the lake, very picturesquely among islands and peninsulas covered with cocoa nut trees. A poor fellow, James of the 25th was drowned here last week having jumped out of a boat to save a native who had gone in for his hat. The coolie got him round the legs and pulled him down, but subsequently got above himself and was found insensible on the bank. He died the next morning.
>
> Called on the Governor at tiffin time but he was attending the legislative Council. An invitation which he sent us to dine and sleep we were also obliged to refuse having left our evening clothes at Galle.

The shopping streets were selling stones, especially sapphires, and a variety of jewellery. Chafyn bought a pair of silver bracelets, and there were some 'handsome works in carved ebony, and porcupine quills'.

The next day at 6.30 a.m. they set off for Kandy, the first part of the journey by railway which had opened three weeks previously, the carriages lined with Morocco leather. Having visited the ancient capital Chafyn and Hoffman went on to Ramboda and Nuwara Eliya, and although it had poured with rain, luckily, they had good waterproofs. But Chafyn had not felt very well on starting out, and when he reached the rest house he was 'done up' and glad to lie down for the rest of the afternoon.

> The climate here is supposed to be very healthy, in fact it is a sort of sanatorium, but I can't conceive many sorts of complaints being much benefitted by an atmosphere of perpetual rain. Our company at dinner consisted of two silent men who said not a word, and one Jeebed (?), a surgeon of the

25th, who having seen a good deal of service in three or four different regiments was not bad company. He knows Churchill very well.

As I did not feel well enough to ride down to Rambodale with the chance of another ducking, we got a bandy, a small gig with a hood of takpot leaves which banged against one's head with every jolt. In this machine with the help of a broken-kneed horse, who required much stick to make him go, and much holding up to keep him on his legs when in motion we made a successful descent with the additional luxury of a bright morning, as the rain held off until the middle of the day, when it made up for its forbearance by pouring snakes and lizards, or whatever in these parts answers to the cats and dogs of Europe. A large rat snake about eight feet long fell out of the roof of an outhouse close to my head. At my requisition, four natives appeared armed with large sticks and peered carefully in at the door. All of a sudden there was a shout and a rush, and these heroes scuttled away at top speed, while the snake glided out slowly and went off scot free into the shrubs. The species is not venomous, but nevertheless gives a very severe bite. The rest house is a temple of the winds this evening, and the big wicker cocoa nut oil lamps flare and flicker in a most unpleasant manner.

Before reaching Gampolla, the rain came on in torrents, rushing down the sides of the coffee plantations in a manner which made it surprising that the whole thing was not washed away. Heavy landslips do, however, occur and one planter told me that he had just lost half an acre in this manner, which considering that the net returns are about £15 per acre per annum, is a considerable loss. Being wet I stopped at the Gampolla guest house for the night, Hoffman going on to Kandy. To bed in a room with as usual a large hole in the plaster, through which playful lizards dropped at intervals. Luckily my bed was a 4 poster so that the top kept them off me.

In the morning the coach for Kandy was 'crammed tight with natives. On my remonstrating with the driver, a Tamal, for stuffing in more than the proper number, he excused himself by saying that they were only natives! as if a fat native didn't take up as much room as a European of the same dimensions.' On arrival in Kandy and meeting up with Hoffman, the English mail was in and they got a look at the papers.

'After tiffin drove in the inevitable rain to the Botanical Gardens. They are very extensive, and well situated on the banks of the Mahara Ganga, and contain an immense variety of trees and shrubs, but as it was wet, we could not leave the trap and examine them. For the same reason we missed seeing the cinchona [quinine] plants which grow off the main drives and are very successfully cultivated here. Mem: Neither here – in Kandy – nor among the hills can a cup of coffee be obtained, and I am told that this is also the case even in the planters' bungalows.'

The return journey to Galle was by coach which they reached safely a little before 5 p.m. 'The horses displayed their usual eccentricities, and at one change house the coach was pushed by coolies over a bridge and past a turn in the road before the fresh pair were put in, in order that we might get a fair start. When they did go, they went well and one six-mile stage was accomplished in thirty-three minutes. The country showed signs everywhere of recent heavy rains, but we were lucky to come into Galle dry.'

The next day was remarkable as being the first since their stay on the island without rain between sunrise and sunset. Chafyn took a walk before breakfast and in the afternoon drove along the Mature Road. In the evening the steamer *Baroda* from China appeared outside, but it being after sunset could not come in.

The *S. S. Baroda* came in the morning, and soon after her the *Bengal* from Calcutta. Continually contradictory reports of our hour for starting kept coming in all the morning. So, having previously sent our luggage on board, about noon we tucked our legs into a catamaran, the seats for passengers projecting sideways over the gunwale, and went out to the *Baroda*. She is a fine steamer of eighteen hundred tons, and has besides ourselves only one passenger, so that we have as much accommodation as we like, and in fact are rather lost in the great saloon. It is a fault on the right side in a hot climate. After an unsuccessful attempt to get out past the *Bengal* in which, owing to the engines refusing to work at the right moment, we nearly ran aboard her, we both got out in company about 5 o'clock, and were soon in a good bit of sea with a head wind, but this is a very easy ship, and we felt the motion but little – we found the Eglinton at Galle very fair. Washing is also better done in Galle than anywhere that I have been to of late.

CHAPTER TWENTY-SEVEN

Zeals – October

'George Michell left me to my own society of much slack! I do get tired after many days, for I then sit and think of evenings and make myself miserable with some of the memories of former days and of my wasted life, much I have treated as though it would last for ever and its my carelessness, and I have thrown to the winds opportunities with a lavish hand, much I should have caught as they flew past, never alas! to return again. I hope I am a wiser woman now, but all the wisdom of ages will not bring back past days.'[231]

Julia often became reflective when she was alone and filled with self-pity, but at the same time felt guilty about it, believing she should be grateful for her comfortable life. With the days becoming shorter, she tried to put a brave face on the thought of another winter alone without Chafyn. She wanted him to be safe and content and as much as she would have liked him to be home, his health was more important to her than her own preference. She picked herself up and carried on with her life, which she was facing with increasing anxiety.

'George Troyte-Bullock shot fifteen rare pheasants. Alice and the two children came over and lunched and stayed.'

Julia went to Salisbury to the cathedral with Margaret Hussey, who was at home with Agnes alone. They gave her luncheon and tea and croquet, and she was home at 8 p.m. to a cold evening. The following day, the Charles-Henry Grove girls, Agnes, Alice and Phillis (Philippa) went to Zeals for the same. With Emily now married and, on her honeymoon, she would, by necessity, become closer to the other sisters. Being friendly with all six and a firm friend of both their parents, perhaps Julia hoped that Chafyn might consider one of them as a wife, there were plenty to choose from. It would have suited her, as none of the girls would object to her being in Zeals House if she were Chafyn's wife. But it is more likely that his girlfriend Sue was more worldly and better educated than the Grove Rector's daughters, who lived in a circumscribed rural world.

With Fellowes away on honeymoon, Mr Carswell was affiliated at Zeals Church, so Julia walked round by Woolverton and showed him the way to Gillingham. 'He reads pleasantly. A prayer by the archbishop was said today for the sad plague which has fallen upon the cattle, and is extending to sheep and pigs is grievously dear.' Julia went to the stables and walked around. 'Garden done for, as autumn with a foretaste of winter has pressed upon us suddenly. Practice in the school as usual. Emily home yesterday.'

Mrs Charles-Henry Grove – Eliza – and Alice went to lunch at Zeals and Julia took them to see the building progress of the new vicarage at Zeals. The building work was nearing completion. A rectory was supposed to have been built at the same time as the church, schoolroom and school house to complete the ecclesiastical cluster, but this was delayed through lack of funds. Julia had taken a keen interest in the building of the rectory, which was not

The rectory at Zeals.

welcomed. When the Grove trio and Julia walked across from the church for an inspection they were met with obstacles. 'The men at work there were impertinent and tried to bar our progress by nails and barrels.'

The rectory was being built in the Gothic style by the Church Commissioners using the architect Thomas Richards of Wincanton.[232] Having signed over the land, the Chafyn-Groves had no power over the building, but because of all her work in the parish, Julia felt affronted by the rebuke.

As the October days drew in, Julia rode to Ferne to visit Tom and Kate Grove, but they had gone to town. 'The governess and girls, and Miss Masey pleased me as well as their parents, only if soap and brushes were used in that house it would be better. The anti-moccasins were in rags in the south room. Saw the Sedgehill party for a ten-minute chat and had a glass of orange brandy on horseback, which made me feel up to charging the gates on my way back, but as my horse did not have a share of the stimulus it was lucky for us that I restrained myself.' Her exhilaration when she returned home is a reminder of her usual lack of stimulation, and of a woman bursting for a looser life. 'Home at 5.30 and not a bit tired, that's having a lady horse and not too fast a one.'

17th October. 'Letter from Chafyn from Sydney on account of cholera in Egypt his plans on 22nd August were upset and there is as much uncertainty about them, that I fear to start until I know where I expect to meet him. The cholera is had in Spain, and at Malta, and Gibraltar and invalids will be puzzled in chasing their safe abode. Have written to Sue. Which according to plans in August will be on the 3rd November and begged him to telegraph to me as soon as he lands, and I can go out on the 16th easily.'

Julia's jumbled phrasing reveals her anxiety. It appears that Chafyn changed his travel plans because of the cholera outbreaks that forced him to abandon the route through Suez. But not wanting to linger in Sydney he and Hoffman decided to go to Bombay via Ceylon to get some of the voyage completed and to have interesting countries to explore while waiting for a safe passage. Originally, Julia planned to go out to meet her brother in October, possibly to Marseilles where many steam ships docked.

[19th October.] To lunch at East Hayes. A dull party, and from having been worried and anxious for some days, a reaction came and I am afraid I talked much nonsense. I did not care what I said and at any rate broke the formality of the ceremony took my work which no one else has done. Wet afternoon. George and Alice came.

[28th October.] Alice Grove left me today, after staying since Tuesday. Wrote to Chafyn on the 25th to tell him the amazing fact that England [Julia's maid] told me on the previous day, that she cannot go abroad with me, therefore, Tisnall will have to go if I go to Southampton, as I could not travel through France quite alone, and at this time of year. I hope it will be arranged that Tisnall stay and finish up here and gain him in Sicily or anywhere he likes in the long spring. George Troyte-Bullock and Grant Dalton shot on Wednesday. Ten prize pheasants, two hares and Alice came and spent the day. I do feel so uncomfortable and unsettled, the subjects of my and Chafyn's abode during the coming months, but I can do nothing in the business, am quite powerless, even in a way that so deeply concerns my own future life. Women certainly in the scheme of life have the hardest part to pay, for they have to wait – wait, and eat their own hearts up in so doing, very often.

Meeting in the 'long spring' was suggested, possibly in Sicily. This was likely to have been because of the heat in Suez, which would be intense in the coming months as well as waiting for the cholera to abate. The vagueness is probably caused by missing letters, and Julia's realisation that she would have to spend another winter alone would have been stressful for her.

[31st October.] Cold and miserable, all in unison with my dull feelings. Told Palmerston's death is a loss indeed, at eighty years of age could not look to his career as a statesman being prolonged, he was a truly great and good man, working for his country, and doing his best and with a cheerful spirit, which no doubt was partly constitutional, the counsel alone. The results of his actions when he had well considered them were in the hands of God and if we could all act and think in this way how much happier and better in mind and body we would be.

Do what we will we cannot command results. Uncle Harry came today, tired and rather in a fuss as usual.

Diary ends.

CHAPTER TWENTY-EIGHT

Bombay

Chafyn and Hoffman were very pleased they switched from the *Northam* to *S. S. Baroda* for the four-day voyage to Bombay.[233] 'Our skipper, Harshwood, is a Somersetshire man, and knows all the world in these parts. The purser's clerk is the son of Hollinsworth who was quartermaster of the 20th in the Peninsula and whom when a poor knight at Windsor I remember my father going to see some years ago.'[234] The coast was visible for most of the journey and after the second night on board they passed the revolving light of Goa, the Portuguese settlement, 'which is, as far as I can make out, of little commercial value to them'.

On the fourth day, they knew they were approaching a large port, as crowds of native craft were spotted, 'rigged something like

Bombay, mid-19th century.

those on the Red sea, with a thatched cabin aft. Before long, lines of white buildings became visible, and after some intricate navigation we landed in the suburb of Mazagaon. The ground is low rising slightly to an eminence called Malabar Hill on which a great many bungalows stand.'

After dinner on board, they landed at sunset. A row of about two miles brought them to the jetty, but it was low tide, 'and an expanse of slime and rock had to be traversed before reaching it, while the boat itself grounded some yards from the shore in a sea of liquid stinking mud which was being churned up by a score of boats struggling for a landing'.

At last, we were pushed sufficiently near to be carried perilously ashore, one of Hoffman's bearers coming down and letting him down into the mud. I was more lucky, and gained the top of the jetty pretty safely. And now arose the most awful hubbub and confusion of boatmen and coolies, wanting more money, whilst I was afraid of losing the luggage as it was quite dark, and the men at first refused to bring it ashore. Add to this that I knew no Hindostani, and the coolies a quite unintelligible form of English. So that at last I was compelled to resort to the universal language of the stick which is only too well understood out here, and then at last I got my precious traps gathered safely round me. In the meantime, Hoffman had gone off to get a trap presently returned with two two-wheeled cabriolets, called here buggies, into these we stowed ourselves and baggage and after one final altercation jogged off, Hoffman leading with brilliantly lighted lamps, of which my jehu took advantage to be economical and not light his own. A jog of two or three miles first through small streets of native shops, then through suburban roads like those about Hampstead, lined with hedges, and high walls enclosing bungalows brought us to the end of our troubles at Punkah Club were Colonel Longbeare who came up in the *Northam* has got us made Honorary Members. As good luck would have it, we got bedrooms, so that we were very soon at home.

Here we got confirmation of Lord Palmerston's death, sad news indeed for England and all Europe. He leaves a gap which will not be filled up very soon. The appointment of Lord Russell as his successor surprises me. I doubt his getting the confidence of the nation. Lord Granville would seem to have been a more suitable man for the post.

The two men spent the morning unpacking, Chafyn waiting for a Portuguese servant, or boy, as they were called, as the club, although having fine airy rooms did not supply servants to make beds and take care of laundry. Chafyn's things were 'more or less damp from the climate in Ceylon, especially some of my boots which are in appearance like mouldy cheese'. He was amused by one of the club rules, 'viz: that no club member shall strike or ill-treat any of the club servants – fancy that being required in a London club!' After tiffin, the two hired a close vehicle with four wheels and one horse, called a shiggerum and jogged along the outskirts and 'saw some fine bungalows, many of them two storied, but inferior in picturesqueness to those in Ceylon'.

'We afterwards ascended Malabar Hill, and on the top of this the Parsees seemed to be keeping great junkets. The street was lined with booths selling nauseous looking sweetmeats and toys, while in the road was a close throng of vehicles of every description, from London broughams in which rolled fat Parsees of wealth down to odd little vehicles on two wheels drawn by two oxen. Of course, there were the corresponding crowd of foot people and children, many of the latter most gorgeously dressed, while there were a good many native women liberally adorned with bangles and nose-rings. Altogether it was an amusing sight, but as our coachman knew not a word of English, we could not get any explanation of whether it was a special occasion, or an ordinary sabbatical junket.'

Following breakfast, Chafyn and Hoffman went to the custom house to get the rest of their luggage, and money from the bank, then went exploring the commercial part of the town, which consisted or three or four narrow streets and 'mean houses. In one part some fine new houses are being built, but otherwise Bombay is anything but a city of palaces. Commercially, everything is very brisk, and merchants' offices abound, while speculative Parsees throng the entrances to the banks. There is some good work in the shops of the cabinet makers, in the way of wood furniture in a wood called black wood, and two English general stores.'

In the afternoon, there was an excursion to the muddy Mazagaon landing place with Mr Bellasis, Chief Commissioner at the Custom House, Capt. Barker the harbour master, an engineer and sundry officials in a small government boat. 'What improvements they decided on I know not, but that something ought to be done is very clear, and this is the only landing place for this part of the harbour.'

'Dined at the club public dinner, and sat next to the secretary, Capt. Hawthorn. He belongs to a native regiment, and only puts on uniform once a month for muster, as the regiment is over officered, and there is no place for him on parade. We have at last got a servant, a Portuguese who I think will do, so that we shall now get our boots cleaned and our beds made.'

[Wednesday, 8th November.] Had my hair cut yesterday morning by a native barber who had the impudence to inform me that my hair had been all spoilt by the last cutting, which it had received at the hands of the celebrated Mr Lidger at Sydney, and then proceeded to rectify it by cutting it all round in a straight line, so that a considerable quantity persists in standing on end in the most refractory manner. Drove into the Fort with Hoffman, and inspected the stock of Mr Bhinjee Bysamjee, to whom we had been recommended as one of the most respectable of the cabinet makers here. His carving is certainly the best we have seen of the three or four shops we have been in to. After much inspection and asking of prices we finally made a selection, and offered him a reduction of twenty per cent on his demand. At first, he was virtuous and bland, and declared it could not be, and long did we talk over it, going away, and returning again to clinch the bargain finally at seventeen per cent discount with which I was well satisfied, as I am quite sure that notwithstanding the freight and duty, and expense of polishing and probably of re-joining in England that the things will be well worth the expenditure. For £40 I got two chairs, a small round tea table with very handsome carved border and centre leg, a Davenport, and two pier tables as they are called, or sideboards.[235]

[Thursday, 9th November.] The English mail came in this morning. No letter from home. Was much grieved to see Mr Powell's death in the obituary.[236] In the evening I went on board the *Baroda* to get the last items of our luggage. There was a fresh breeze, and I had a pleasant sail.

[Friday, 10th November.] Off after breakfast to Elephanta distant about four or six miles from the Mazagaon border. By the kindness of Mr Bellaris we got a large boat from the dockyard, with a cabin aft like an Egyptian dahabieh. The morning was dead calm, so the passage across took us more than four hours, and we were therefore well baked by the time we landed. Luckily, he had plenty to eat and drink and a good big lump of ice for our consolation under these difficulties. Elephanta is a small island about a mile long, rising into three small hills thickly wooded, and is one of the lions of Bombay partly because of a curious old rock temple, and partly because of the pretty views of the harbour obtained from thence. After safely passing through the perils of landing in a small canoe, in the bottom of which we had to sit without winking for fear of an upset, and being carried across the muddy beach by coolies we proceeded to ascend to the main temple, which is on the centremost of the three hills, by sundry flights of steps (one hundred and seventy-two in number as a boozy old sergeant of the company's artillery, kept on informing me) and long stone slopes, I being borne in state on coolies' shoulders. The view alone from the plateau in front of the temple is well worth the ascent, while the great lion itself is well equal to the accounts I had heard of it. The temple is hewn out of the solid, and consists of one great hall supported by pillars of a particularly graceful form of capital. Facing the entrance (the façade has all fallen down and disappeared) is a large panel containing the Hindu trinity. Brahman, Vishnu, and Shivah. The latter, the destroyer, is represented holding a cobra as an emblem of spite and malignity. To the right and left on the main hall, the rock is excavated up to the open air above forming as it were two courts with dark cells beyond, like those so frequent in the Egyptian temples. In one of these courts human sacrifices were celebrated, in the others there is a pool of water running away under the rock nobody knows where. Two Englishmen a few years ago got a small canoe and tried to explore it, but one never more heard of it. The sergeant in charge told me that he had waded in about fifty yards, that the water was then up to his neck, and that there were clear traces of suction inwards, into the body of the hill.

Soon after Sunset we set sail with a good breeze though not quite in the right direction, nevertheless we got home to the Club by seven o'clock after a very pleasant excursion.

Lord Edward St. Maur and Brand (the latter has just left the Coldstream) have just come out by the mail, the former to <u>do</u> India for parliamentary purposes.[237]

Chafyn's friend Brand had been mentioned in a letter from Julia.[238] Saturday, 11th November.

'I saw Brand this morning and was glad to meet an old friend in these foreign parts. He tells me that they had it very hot in the Red Sea – the bath water 88 degrees!!'

At this point, Chafyn's diary of the journey comes to an end. Later in the day, on Saturday 11th November, the third anniversary of his mother's death, Chafyn and Hoffman prepared to leave Bombay.

CHAPTER TWENTY-NINE

Poona

Captain Henry Brand was a friend of Chafyn from their Coldstream days, and as Julia mentioned his name in one of the last letters picked up by Chafyn in Sydney, it is assumed that they were close friends and Brand may have visited Zeals. By meeting Brand in Bombay on the morning of Saturday 11th November, Chafyn probably wanted to see his friend before he left for Poona that morning, otherwise he would surely have wanted to arrange a more leisurely lunch or dinner with such an old friend.

Chafyn would have known that the Red Sea area was in sweltering heat before it was confirmed by Brand and having seen as much of Bombay as he wanted, he planned to go to Poona, a recreational army base to enjoy a leisurely time amongst British army officers while he waited for the temperatures to drop in Suez, and for the cholera epidemic to subside. Julia may well have been dismayed by not knowing what movements were expected of her, but Chafyn did not know either. He had already told Julia that he would not be back that year, so Poona may have been chosen as a good base for a few months, rather as Llangollen had been.

Poona was about one hundred miles from Bombay, about the same distance as Zeals to London, so easily reached by coach with a break for lunch. When Chafyn and Hoffman arrived, they would have been confronted by a scene which looked invitingly English. The attraction for Chafyn was the temperate climate, being two thousand feet above sea level on the Deccan plateau. Poona was the headquarters of Southern Army Command. The British Government used Poona as a weekend retreat and to escape the monsoon season and excessive heat. In November, it was out of the social season, which was the summer months, roughly the same as in England. Chafyn could rent a bungalow there securely away from intense heat and cold. The ancient city was bustling with carts, market stalls and shops along narrow streets, selling jewellery, cloth, sweet drinks and fruit, especially mangoes.[239] There was croquet and tennis, a military band, plenty of books to read, riding in the hills, two public gardens and opportunities for whist. There was also a jolly club house, with a lively bar with tables and chairs outside, under an awning in the shade. The scene was as British as India could be. What happened from the time the two men arrived at Poona over the next two days is not known, but there was no sign of serious decline in Chafyn's health when he left Bombay. There were incidents of tiredness in Ceylon, but this appeared to be due to the damp climate, and he was breathless when climbing to the top of the temple in Bombay. Yet he had just bought furniture to be shipped to Zeals before he left, and although he was exposed to the sun on his trip to Elephanta and had to be carried, it does not appear to have raised any alarm. But his health must have deteriorated rapidly, in a place where he would have been well cared for by army doctors, surgeons and a supporting medical team.

On Monday 13th November, at the age of 25, Chafyn died. The health issue he was suffering from is apparent from a memorial later placed in the Guards Chapel in Westminster stating that he died of consumption.[240]

As much as Julia prayed for a miracle, her zealous, sometimes suffocating care of Chafyn was well grounded. Chafyn underplayed his illness and although occasionally in his diaries when feeling unwell he became miserable, for the most part he carried on the life that he loved with energy, infectious enthusiasm and a strength of character to overcome the lingering uncertainty about his future. This affable and big-hearted young man's plan to be in the Coldstream Guards was cut short, his chance of having a wife and a family was cut short, his life was cut short.

Having a country and sporting estate, wealth, a loving family, good friends, good looks, popularity with girls, and a love of adventure and of life – Chafyn had everything – except his health.

The disease killed one in seven of the British population in the nineteenth century and was incurable. Technically called pulmonary tuberculosis, it was transmitted from contaminated surfaces and could have been picked up anywhere. The White family living at Zeals Manor Farm had lost several family members, appearing to be particularly susceptible.[241] Young and old, rich and poor, there was no boundary for this wasting, fatal disease of the lungs. Very few survived, and those who did had recurring problems whereby they could not live a normal life. Life expectancy after diagnosis was between one and five years, and precautions against temperature changes and draughts were recommended, which

Chafyn assiduously followed. It would take another seventy years before penicillin was discovered.

Chafyn was buried amongst the cork and acacia trees in the military cemetery at Poona by his good friend Henry Hoffman and presumably a regimental chaplain.

Coincidentally, Chafyn's friend Brand also had to bury his friend Lord Edward St Maur a month later. The two were hunting bison. They separated, each with a hunter guide, and were fighting their way through thick undergrowth when Edward was confronted by a Deccan bear, and although Edward fired his gun, the bear charged him and he was badly injured. Brand raced towards the sound of the gun anticipating a trophy. Edward's mauled leg was amputated but he died of his injuries. Both he and Brand were 24. The two deaths of young men a few weeks apart are unconnected but as St Maur's tragic death was widely reported it gives a glimpse of the formal process of how the India Office reported a death in India of a British citizen in 1865, and how they informed the next of kin. Julia would have received a telegram from the India Office marked 'immediate to deliver', the message reading 'Death on 13th' with no other details.

1. William Chafyn-Grove by George Romney, 1780. (Alamy Stock Photo)

Left: 2. Elizabeth Chafyn-Grove by George Romney, 1779-1780. (© Sotheby's 2022)

Below: 3. George Troyte-Chafyn-Grove. (Geoffrey Sebag-Montefiore private collection)

4. Alice Troyte-Chafyn-Grove, daughter of Sir Glynne Welby-Gregory Bt. (Geoffrey Sebag-Montefiore private collection)

5. Zeals House – drawing room. (Strutt & Parker)

6. Zeals House – dining room. (Strutt & Parker)

Above: 7. Zeals House – barrel-ceilinged drawing room. (Strutt & Parker)

Right: 8. Zeals House – the hall. (Strutt & Parker)

9. The Orangery. (Strutt & Parker)

10. Manor Farm, Zeals. (Philip Cayford)

11. Zeals House – mezzanine ceiling.
(Philip Cayford)

12. Lt. Col. Edward Troyte-Bullock.
(Bill & Ann Woodhouse, private
collection/Philip Cayford)

Left: 13. Zeals House southerly view of lake and park. (Strutt & Parker)

Below: 14. Almshouses, Zeals Village. (Philip Cayford)

PART IV

JULIA

CHAPTER THIRTY

Zeals – November

For Julia, the third woman to take over the Zeals Estate, there was no funeral. She was unable to send her dear brother to heaven personally. She had a recent paramatta black dress from Aunt Fanny's funeral earlier in the year but she needed to go back to Jay's in Regent Street for more dresses and crepe for the six months' duration of the official mourning period as required for siblings. She would have taken the train with her loyal maid Ann England and returned the same day, the boxes arriving shortly afterwards. Unable to wear jewellery, although she kept wearing her cross, she would have purchased some black jet necklaces, but would have been unable to have them entwined with her dear departed brother's hair. Suitably clothed, she would have expected to visit Chafyn's grave in the Mere churchyard weekly to replace fresh flowers in a purpose-built stone vase. This weekly ritual would be denied her. Julia was left with a void that could not be filled, and although heartbroken, she would have appeared stoic and controlled in public.

Although comfortable in her south-facing triple aspect bedroom on the first floor, with extensive views over the lake, the park, and views beyond, it was a rambling house for a woman alone, full of corridors and staircases. Julia worked through her grief with long rides on the downs, breathing in the misty autumn air, or walked around the park absorbed in her own thoughts. Her parents' joy for the future of Zeals House had been wiped out. She reflected on the life her brother may have had, enjoying his new shoot at Silton and inviting his friends for sporting weekends, a military career, a wife and children of his own.

With Devey long gone from the house, Coakley had recently finalised the internal fittings and the almshouses were nearing

Julia Chafyn-Grove (left) with
Miss Yeatman

completion. The wallpaper for the pink bedroom was at last
in place and the barrel-ceilinged first floor mezzanine drawing
room called 'the peacock room', with lavish peacock-decorated
wallpaper from Druce's in Baker Street, was complete, as was the
library next to it. The strapwork feature on the first-floor ceiling
with the Chafyn-Grove coat of arms complete with the black talbot
dog was a great success, being well lit next to a large west-facing
window. The work at Zeals house that Chafyn had commissioned
was concluded, a beautiful new comfortable gentleman's residence
prepared by Julia for her brother's return.

The new drawing room on the ground floor facing south with its
oak half panelling included button-backed sofas and armchairs in
a dark velvet. To retain the heat in the winter months the curtains
were in a heavy jacquard weave or velvet trimmed with swags
and tails with heavy fringes. There would have been a japanned
worktable for Julia's needlework and a secretaire bookcase,
paintings of landscapes, dogs and horses as well as the tapestry
from Paris which had pleased Julia when it arrived. Small chairs

would be dotted around the room, with a central sofa table and supplementary small tables, some with fringed cloths, all swamped with ornaments and artefacts.

The oak panelled hall with open arched entrances to rooms on all sides to allow light in from the large new windows was a typical Devey device, as also featured at Coombe Warren in Kingston upon Thames (since demolished).

With the Chinese market opening for trade with Britain in 1860, there was a fashion for gigantic oriental porcelain vases on wooden stands filled with pampas grasses.[242] These were likely to have been placed by the Bechstein grand piano in the Zeals House hall where Chafyn used to play classical pieces. The vases were either in blue and white, famille verte, or famille rose designs.

The Great Hall dining room would have had a large mahogany table with balloon back chairs, together with a large sideboard in a dark Cuban mahogany with a mirror at the back and antimacassar draped over the surface. A large Jamaican flamed mahogany bookcase with glass-panelled cupboards above dado height displayed china, with a silver centrepiece and epergnes for fresh flowers on the table alongside the Charles II salt.

Zeals House, the hall in 1994.

The position of the current dining room is where the original Great Hall was situated. It is clear that the lofty height of the medieval hall has been reduced and filled in. The doors and ceiling with inappropriate downlighters reveal modern additions although the chimney piece appears to be original. The oak half panelling has since been covered in white paint. Above this is an eight-bay wooden roof with arch-braced trusses.[243] These trusses are supported by large wooden beams of Spanish chestnut.[244] Originally the ceiling of the great hall, it remains in good condition.

Julia was destined to live alone in the much-enlarged house. Mr Messiter, the family solicitor from Wincanton read Chafyn's Will.

As the family predicted, Julia would stay in the house for life with her own income. George Troyte-Bullock would inherit Zeals House, the estate and Chafyn's pair of guns. Both George and Alice had been supportive of Julia throughout Chafyn's absence, as they spent more and more time with her, George getting involved with the tenants in the same way as Julia's father had when his elderly cousin Chafin was living at Zeals alone, to reassure and provide continuity. But the Troyte-Bullocks would remain at Sedgehill until the death of George Bullock, when they transferred to North Coker House, in East Coker near Yeovil. Mabel Cecily Troyte-Bullock, (godchild, b. 1861) the eldest daughter of George and Alice, Emily Grove, now Townsend, Arthur Myers and David Powell the younger, whose father had recently died, would each receive £1,000.[245] Henry Westwood Hoffman would be left £500. Uncles Revd Charles and Harry would receive an annuity of £700 for life, and there was provision for the running of the almshouses with the vicars of Mere, Zeals and Waddon receiving legacies. There was also a donation to the Consumption Hospital at Brompton, London. Myers visited Julia as soon as he heard of the sad loss of his close friend. He would remain in touch with Julia for the rest of her life, becoming executor of her own will.

Julia continued with regular attendance at Mere and Zeals Churches. The two vicars were supportive and read prayers for their dear departed landlord, but she had been unwelcoming to Charles Townsend as a member of the family and fought with Spencer Fellowes over the proprietary of the Zeals church school, which left her somewhat isolated. She had asked Chafyn to leave an amount at his discretion to Emily Grove thinking she would remain a spinster. Now married to the Mere vicar Charles Townsend, Julia was annoyed that the £1,000 would now go to him. However, she did become a godmother to the first-born child of both clergy families, as well as to George and Alice's only son, Edward George Troyte-Bullock, known as Eddie.

Before the year was out, Julia had one duty to perform. She had been in meetings with a stone mason. When his work was completed, the almshouses were opened. The inhabitants, chosen by a church committee, were four of the local 'deserving poor', regular (temperate) church goers, two men and two women. These almshouses were built in a typical Devey style, in red brick with diapered patterning, a decorative device favoured in Victorian Gothic buildings, stone window mouldings, steep gables and tall brick diagonal chimney stacks in clusters with stone dressings. Above the oak front entrance is a stone cartouche with the Chafyn-Grove coat of arms as a reminder for the occupants of their late landlord and benefactor. The terrace is now known as Chafyn Grove Cottages. Inset into the wall, another stone tablet was placed with the inscription:

To the dear Memory of His Mother
These Alms Houses were Erected and Endowed by
William Chafyn Grove
D. 1865.
Blessed is the man that considereth the poor
The Lord will deliver him in time of trouble.
Psalm XLI.

The following year, Julia worked through her grief by making sure Chafyn would be remembered. In Zeals Church she endowed a new organ: 'To the dear memory of William Chafyn Grove this organ is erected by his sister 1866.' A window dedication by the tenantry reads: 'To the glorious God and in memory of their esteemed landlord William Chafyn Grove. May 1866', revealing that Chafyn's easy charm and his early death had touched the heart of the village.

There was a lasting memorial in the Guards Chapel, adjacent to Buckingham Palace. On the east face of the west gallery there was a relief in marble designed and executed by H. H. Armstead, RA., representing Obedience, from an episode in the life of Joshua.[246] The inscription read: 'To the Glory of God and in loving Remembrance of William Chafyn Grove, of Zeals House, Wiltshire, Born 1840. Ensign and Lieutenant Coldstream Guards 1861 to 1863. Died of Consumption at Poonah, India, 13th November, 1865'. A flying bomb destroyed the Guards Chapel in 1944, together with Chafyn's memorial, but the details are preserved in the Imperial War Museum.[247]

The largest and most personal memorial donated by Julia was a new window on the east of the tower in Mere Church. This lofty, densely detailed stained-glass window was executed by Powells of Whitechapel having been chosen because she was delighted with the window they had made for Zeals House, which featured the name of the house in old England script.[248] The new allegorical stained-glass window was executed by Powells' chief designer Henry Holiday and is considered one of his most noteworthy early career pieces of fine Victorian art, with hints of the influence of Edward Burne-Jones. Holiday was also Julia and Chafyn's choice for the earlier window on the west side of the tower to honour the death of their mother, Eleanor.

The overall frame of the composition is classical instead of the usual ogee gothic arches, as a nod to Chafyn's classics education and love of architecture. At the top of the window celestial angels sing over the holy City of Jerusalem and a central figure of a woman playing the mandolin is reminiscent of an oil on board painting at Zeals House thought to be of Eleanor. The predominately red glass represents love and divinity and the music theme suggests Chafyn's love of music was accompanying him to heaven.

Below, the panels edged in lead hold images and inscriptions which are heavily symbolic. Biblical stories had been selected by Julia referring to different aspects of the Resurrection and the Ascension. From left to right Mary Magdalene is telling the disciples that Jesus' tomb is empty. The inscription below from Mark 16:6 also relates to Chafyn: 'He is risen. He is not here. Behold the place where they laid him.' The scene in the centre is from John 20: 17 portraying the Ascension: 'Touch me not for I am not yet risen to my Father.' In the right-hand scene from Luke 24:9, the words 'they told all these things to the eleven' refers to Jesus appearing to Mary Magdalene and asking her why she is crying and he tells her that he has seen the Lord. She then, wearing green representing life, tells the disciples that Jesus has gone to heaven.

This holy scene reveals Julia's deep sense of loss expressed in the faith, culture and intense glorification of death widespread in the Victorian period. The disciples' panels and the inscriptions beneath were chosen with great care. Mark has been chosen with a winged lion representing strength, power, leadership and courage. Chafyn's image from his last photograph taken in Sydney with long hair and beard from being four months in the bush appears to be superimposed on this window with his name beneath, in the same way as Eleanor's image was superimposed on a stained-glass window for her deceased children in the south chapel.

The centre window of John is depicted by an eagle symbolising writing and scholarship and on the right the image of Luke with an oxen stands for faithfulness, strength and stability. The window reflects Chafyn's life and death. The east tower window is elaborate and of a large scale filled with colour, there being no restriction on budget for such an important memorial for the last in the line of the Chafyn-Groves. But there was another dedication in Mere Church which has inadvertently caused some confusion. A tablet reads:

> In memory of William Chafyn Grove of Zeals House. Late of the Coldstream Guards who died Poonah in India on the 13th November 1865. Aged 25 years. This tablet was erected in affectionate remembrance of him by the members of the 8th Company of Wilts Rifle Volunteers of which he was Captain.

Little has been written about Chafyn because of his short life as a landlord, but the wording of this tablet has been understandably misinterpreted as Chafyn dying on active service, when in reality he had left the Coldstreamers in 1863.

Later in the decade, Julia had a more positive attitude to life. She had a genuine wish to help the poor, realising that education would give young girls more choices in life and aimed to use the considerable funds available to her for charitable causes.

She also decided to extend Zeals House and brought back George Devey.

Eleanor Chafyn-Grove in Mere church.

CHAPTER THIRTY-ONE

Zeals – At Home

'Amongst Mr. Devey's clients, he found many warm friends.'[249]

Julia Chafyn-Grove was High Victorian, High Church and High Tory. George Devey had 'a keen sense of humour, and the sparkling sallies of wit, cheery banter, and quiet sarcasm. He always turned business into pleasure.'[250]

Julia was serious in her nature, as befitted the pious Victorian era in which she lived. She valued her Church of England religion above all else and was dismissive of dissenters. Devey supported the Theistic Church, unrecognised by mainstream Christianity, run by the Revd Charles Voysey, the father of Devey's future pupil, C. F. A. Voysey.[251] His wealthy clients were aristocrats and supporters of the Liberal Party and of Gladstone.[252] Julia was a staunch Tory supporter, as was the majority of the gentry. Julia was also known to have an authoritarian outlook.[253]

From what is known of Devey's personality, he was charming and liked to be surrounded by a small group of like-minded friends who were artists or of an artistic nature.[254] In his brightly coloured shirts he was once asked at the Foreign Office if he was a waiter.[255] In contrast, Julia was formal. When her carriage was seen in Mere, local people especially children, bowed as she passed.[256] Julia was a forty-one-year-old spinster in no need of a substantially larger house but planned to extend Zeals House to suit her needs. Although she was now alone, she lived in comfort with a cook, kitchen maid, two house maids, a lady's maid, butler, footman, coachman and groom.[257] In later years the household included a spinster companion, Miss Caroline Bazeley.[258]

When Devey had stayed overnight at Zeals during the time Chafyn's house was being rebuilt, Julia found the conversation at dinner rather stilted. There is much they could have discussed. Julia, with her love of art could have discussed the pictures she had recently seen at the Royal Academy and drawn him into neutral subjects. They had none of the enjoyment of conversation that they both shared with Alfred Morrison, where Devey would probably have preferred to stay and make day trips to Zeals when Morrison was in residence at Fonthill. The awkwardness of their relationship was partly because Julia saw Devey as a man from the professional class who was a gentleman and needed to be treated as one – but was not to be drawn into her life. On his part, Devey would have been aware of Julia's judgemental nature and thought the less he said the less he could be criticised. She certainly would not have approved of his religion, but it was not her inclination to discuss such matters. Nevertheless, they worked well together to provide Julia with a schoolroom so that she could have her own school at Zeals. It was not to replace her work at the Zeals church schoolroom, where she trained the children to sing for the choir, but to teach girls subjects that would help them with skills for life. She also wanted extra space for servants and a cottage.[259] Another request was for a small courtyard with a fishpond, reminiscent of the small courtyards at Alhambra in Granada, but without the cypress trees. Instead, there would be climbing roses.

In a secure financial position, Julia was able to undertake more extensions to Zeals House. The yield from agriculture was strong in the 1860s and the income from nearly all the land, houses and cottages in Zeals village, Queen Oak, Wolverton, Bourton and Silton, as well as tenanted property in Mere, enriched her.[260] Most people of the village were employed to some extent by the house either as servants, for maintenance, or for agriculture.

Devey set to work devising a sympathetic extension to the clock tower with its ogee-topped wooden lantern surmounted on a cross gable, which completed the Tudor Gothic skyline and was visible from various angles of the house at a distance. He built in local materials and wanted his houses to fit naturally into the surrounding landscape.[261] The clock tower was not dissimilar to a lanterned tower Devey built at Betteshanger where he was still visiting socially and for further work. Next to the tower, Devey's extension balanced the pitch of the gothic gable to match the existing angles. The tower had a heavy arched oak door, looking remarkably like a medieval gate house. It resembles the medieval gatehouse with a service range attached at Great Chalfield Manor in Wiltshire, twenty-two miles away.[262] A window above the door was added to bring light into the knocked-through passage. The flanking service buildings next to the clock tower incorporated 'a dairy, a pig-salting room, game larders and additional servants' rooms, which connected to the old kitchens on the east side by a covered passage'.[263]

Zeals House, clock tower, granary and dovecote.

The dividing wall closed off the nunnery walled garden as a kitchen entrance, separating the access to the school room. The small courtyard complete with fishpond lies behind, benefitting from afternoon sunlight from the west. The ancient dovecote a few metres away is in the style of William Arnold. Although most were built in a circular format, the square shape of the dovecote is not uncommon for pigeon houses in Wiltshire. 635 birds were housed in the Zeals dovecote and were eaten as a delicacy.[264] When completed, on the northern facade of the wing a stonemason placed a shield with the initials J.E.C.G, for Julia Elizabeth Chafyn Grove, and on the rear another shield holds the date 1869.

Next to the kitchen courtyard a pair of Victorian stable buildings face each other in a spacious yard which previously had a fountain feature at the centre, resembling the Court of Lions at the Alhambra in Granada. The stables are of the eighteenth century. The architect for these estate buildings has not been established. Built in red brick with triple-arched entrances, the centre arch on the coach house range was higher than the ones either side to receive a tall carriage. Twelve hunters and ancillary trap horses were kept in the opposite range, with loose and foaling boxes and a tack room.[265] With Julia's love of horses, they were well indulged with an abundance of comforts. The stalls had double ceilings for the comfort of the horses long before any form of thermal insulation was introduced into the house.[266]

Bearing in mind Julia's religious devotion, it is likely that she built a small chapel into the new plan of the house, especially as the servants previously congregated in the dining room for prayers on a Sunday if weather prevented a walk to Church.[267] There is evidence of 'books and papers from recess in the Oratory' in the house when these items were removed from Zeals House to Silton Lodge in 1905.[268] The stained-glass windows with the words 'Zeals House' engraved into them by Powells of Whitechapel may have been in this room or area before they were removed to Waddon House.

The stonemason also made a tablet with the entwined Victorian style letters of W C G and the Chafyn and Grove shields in a cartouche to fit between the two windows of Julia's new bedroom on the south side of Zeals House. There is no evidence of it on the finished photograph that Devey took when completing the first phase of Zeals House for Chafyn, so it may have been placed there by Devey in 1869, as it is a device that the architect often used to create a 'Tudor' atmosphere.[269] On a newly built house this may have looked pretentious but for Julia it was poignant. It was her tribute to her dear late brother as a reminder for future generations of the young man who extended the house and who was the last in the line of owners to hold that surname. Facing south, it overlooks the park, extensive lawns broken by clumps of trees with enhanced views of the lake and the beech wood beyond.

At a later date, the local historian, T. H. Baker, who lived at Mere Down Farm, was invited to Zeals House with his wife, where they took tea and had a social chat on the lawn.

The lawn in front of the house was ornamented with two cypress trees and a flower pot at each corner. After tea Miss Grove conducted us over the house pointing out every object of interest. We first inspected the room where Charles II is reported to have slept after the Battle of Worcester. This room is situated in the north-east wing on the second storey and tradition says it is in the same state now as when the king slept in it.[270] The bedstead is a half-tester with a blue coverlet in silk. On the walls are two portraits of a lady – a Chafyn, also an unknown gentleman probably a Chafyn too, and a view painted of the house before alterations.[271]

In Baker's recollection of the visit as he refers to the half-tester bed which King Charles II slept in, the portraits are likely to be those of Bullen Reymes and Anne Coker removed from Waddon House by Chafyn, and the picture of the house before alterations from Hoare's 1822 engraving.

Baker and his wife continued their tour.

> We walked through to another bedroom the furniture on the bedstead was adorned with needlework executed by Miss Grove.[272] We then descended through the billiard room which has been recently turned to its present use, and the front staircase to the hall where we were shown many antiquities. Some old curiosities we were permitted to examine, including a Breeches Bible, an old Almanack 1503, The Golden Legend, some ancient manuscripts 13th or 14th century, the Diary of Bullen Reymes, Rules of Household Management of the Duke of Buckingham – 17th century, an early edition of Chaucer, a scotch translation of the Aeneid of Virgil with 13th century book added and old French printed books, etc. After again looking round we parted having spent a very pleasant time.[273]

In another account of Charles II's stay at Zeals, Arthur Mee wrote: 'Zeals House is the home of an ancient Wiltshire family. Here hid Charles the Second one day when flying from Cromwell's men.'[274]

Items relating to Charles II's stay at Zeals were lent by Julia's father, Major William Chafyn-Grove, to an exhibition at Salisbury Museum in 1855. These included bands worn by Hugh Grove at his execution (spotted with blood) and a portion of his hair, the richly carved wooden comb and pincushion given by Charles II to Mary, wife of John Grove, son of Hugh Grove. From the flight to the coast were the King's blue silk cloak embroidered in silver and a pair of gloves. Also included were a cap, stocking and handkerchief left at Mere when he escaped.[275]

Now that Julia's infrastructure was in place, she found her vocation and embarked on a voyage of philanthropy. Secondary schooling for girls was gaining in importance revealing that Julia was in tune with society's observations when she started her schoolroom. By the end of the decade the Married Woman's Property Act came into force freeing married women who had their own money from bondage.[276] Although this did not affect the unmarried Julia, there was a slow cultural shift towards empowering women and Julia had the power of money, which she would put to good use.

CHAPTER THIRTY-TWO

Charity

The Victorian boom decade of the 1860s gave way to a collapse in farming prosperity in the 1870s. Cheap American corn and wheat were being imported, having been processed by a quicker method than the traditional way. Because of free trade government rules, there were no tariffs, which forced agricultural communities and landed estates and their tenants into financial difficulties, and in some cases disaster. The rural poor went to towns to gain employment and left landlords short of labour. The power of the rural landlord was also threatened by the 1867 Reform Act, which gave some tenant farmers the vote, and a licence to have opinions. Living in a house of fourteen thousand square feet on her own, Julia was well aware of her moral duty to help those in the village who were suffering.

Zeals house ivy-clad.

Zeals and the South West were badly affected, as were all agricultural communities. Like other villages, they shifted from wheat to meat. The estate ran a good business in dairy and sheep, but former wheat fields would have been put to pasture. It was the poor who suffered, and they appreciated Julia's genuine wish to help them. She had the reliable Squarey to audit the ledgers, but she also benefitted from Chafyn's forward thinking to prepare for rainy days. Being a naturally thrifty family also helped the estate to survive. Julia was assiduous in her care of the estate, cottages being repaired when needed, the tenants having an umbrella of protection over them, as long as they attended church regularly. Her work could not be faulted, she knew every parishioner well and was very visible in the community. She wanted Zeals to be a model village and did her very best, but in spite of all her good work she was not well liked. 'There was a sort of disagreeable briskness about her that was not always pleasant.'[277]

When Julia was leaving the house one day in 1873, her horses following their normal course along the lime avenue to Black Dog gates, one ran away with her carriage, knocking down and killing the gatehouse keeper's wife.[278] After this awful accident the north drive was permanently closed and Julia instead used the parallel service drive and the scenic south drive. In the same year, Julia visited the Holy Land to see the place where Jesus was born, and to explore the other religions in the area. She returned with a certificate of her visit.[279] When younger, Julia's devotion extended to hand-copying from volumes of theological and moral works.[280] A few years later, Julia planned to give a major donation to Salisbury Cathedral which had given her so much comfort over many, sometimes tragic, years.

At Ferne, cousin Tom Grove received his coveted baronetcy after pressure on Gladstone from his aristocratic hunting friends.[281] The Earl of Pembroke at Wilton House, as the Monarch's steward for the Wiltshire Militia, could vouch for his pedigree as the Herbert family had known the Groves – and the Chafyn-Groves – as supporters through their local volunteer militia organisations for many centuries. Although Tom Grove was in demand as a speaker and for the laying of foundation stones in non-conformist chapels, he lost his liberal parliamentary seat in 1874. But that was not his only worry. Having huge loans on the land he purchased to help him get into parliament, and spending without thought on his new mansion and his London lifestyle, he was suffering financially. The family's Norfolk estates were sold to reduce debts and other perimeter land sales followed.

With agriculture in crisis, it was inevitable that rumours would circulate in the village about the amount of money Julia was spending on worthy projects at a time when estate income must have been significantly reduced. Revd Tambling who was the vicar of Zeals Church in the 1970s had heard unsubstantiated village stories that Julia did not like George Troyte-Bullock, so although he would inherit the estate, she wanted to spend as much money as she could. This is far from the truth. Julia was very fond of George and his wife Alice, and she was delighted that they regularly went to Zeals and would meet each other if both were in London at the same time. Julia would also drop in to see them if she was in Sedgehill while visiting Charles-Henry Grove's family. The money she was spending on good causes was from the considerable fund put into a joint charity trust with Chafyn in more prosperous times.

To enhance the facilities of George Gilbert Scott's Zeals Church a new schoolhouse was added and endowed by Julia. Both the schoolroom and the schoolhouse are now a private dwelling, but above the front entrance is a shield with the letters J.E.C.G. inserted, an exact replica of the shield on the Zeals House schoolroom, but with the date 1874. A Mrs Senior's memory was of being taught needlework in the schoolroom by Julia. 'She was always very generous at Christmas time when she gave the choir girls she had trained herself a rabbit pie tea and red flannel petticoats.'[282]

In a busy decade of building, Julia donated money for a public fountain to be installed in Zeals village, a ward in Salisbury Infirmary in her will, and realising that non-conformist chapels were gaining round, she set about finishing Zeals Church with the spire designed by George Gilbert Scott but not installed through lack of funds. With the Church Commissioners' approval and Julia's generosity, the missing spire was erected to Scott's original design in 1876. Richard White, a Zeals tenant farmer wrote: 'When the spire was added to the tower, Miss Grove proposed giving *five* out of the *six* bells that are now there, the parishioners giving the sixth. I suggested the parishioners should provide a *clock* instead but that did not meet with her approval. She was the presiding genius. In the church she reigned supreme.'[283]

Not all of Julia's projects were for the local villages of Zeals, Mere and Silton. She also turned her attention to the approach to Zeals House from the south. No longer using the Black Dogs northern entrance, she enhanced the south drive and the Castleground area. The farmhouse of Castleground was rebuilt in 1874, in brick with stone window facings, gothic gables and sculpted wooden bargeboards, followed by a row of six cottages in the same style to the west of Zeals House behind Manor Farm House, which was considerably extended. To give a sense of arrival a new lodge at the entrance of the long, horse chestnut-lined drive was built in rock-faced stone with tall stone chimney stacks and a stone cartouche bearing the date 1879 with Julia's initials. Lofty gate piers and black wrought iron gates enhanced the appearance of this scenic route to Zeals House winding past fields of south downs sheep behind estate railings. The final improvement to the approach was a picturesque dry-stone arch, modelled on one at Stourhead, which had been in a decaying state before Julia restored it to its former beauty.

The Christian faith had played such a life-enhancing role in Julia's life that she wanted to give a substantial donation to the Church of England. An opportunity arose when she was asked if she would like to donate a new organ for Salisbury Cathedral. When she was twenty-six years old, she had a season ticket to the 1851 Great Exhibition in Hyde Park, regularly visiting the spectacular pavilions.[284] There she would have seen and heard the magnificent organ built by Father (Henry) Willis. This organ is

Zeals House south drive, dry-stone arch.

now in Winchester Cathedral.[285] It was to Father Willis she turned to build a new organ for Salisbury Cathedral in 1876.[286] This extraordinary gift is still in situ today, giving beautiful sound in the lofty early thirteenth-century masterpiece.

Apart from religion and keeping the village social cohesion together with attendance at the established church, Julia's passion was to improve education. Her new schoolroom was put to good use, but in addition she wanted to endow a school in Salisbury to improve education. To this end Julia donated £5,000.[287] The funds were released on her death to set up a private grammar school in Salisbury.[288] It was renamed the Chafyn Grove School in her honour and remains as a highly respected co-ed preparatory school.[289]

Aware of the changing political landscape and of the softening of landlords' powers over the community, Julia saw her role as keeping everything steady and in good shape to hand over. Her father had brought her up thinking that his daughter would inherit, before Chafyn was unexpectedly born, so she knew how to manage the estate. She was strong and capable.

Having succeeded in achieving what she could to help her religious and educational passions, Julia had another goal. She would become involved in politics.

CHAPTER THIRTY-THREE

Politics

During Benjamin Disraeli's government in 1883, Lord Randolph Churchill and John Gorst set up The Primrose League, named after Disraeli's favourite flower, to draw the working class into politics and to uphold and support God, Queen, and the Conservative cause. In Wiltshire, Sir Henry Ainsley-Hoare of nearby Stourhead became a Tory and stood unsuccessfully for the seat of East Somerset. He was increasingly involved in the Primrose League and was a speaker at events.[290] The league initiative was very popular and had more members than the trade unions because women were allowed to join.

Julia saw this as an opportunity to give political guidance to the village and to have a meeting place for women. In consequence, she built a village hall in 1888. Zeals did not previously have a hall and it was something that she had long thought of adding to the local facilities. It was built abutting the almshouses on Chafyn-Grove land. As was the pattern with her behaviour, the village were delighted to have a village hall, but Julia kept it mostly for her own use, for the Primrose League and the occasional concert. It was only allowed to be used for events of which she approved.[291] Non-conformist meetings were banned. No doubt she would have involved Sir Henry Hoare to advise and attend as a guest speaker, but in the first meeting in the new hall, Julia as the ruling counsellor was the presiding officer over the local branch, and the speaker. The subject of her speech was Joseph Chamberlain: 'When Julia read from his book at her inaugural address, she had to cover it in thick paper so that she would not have to touch it. Her speech was first rate, speaking for more than an hour. Her allusion to Mr Chamberlain was by no means complimentary.'[292]

Her role in the league gave Julia a purpose and a public voice. The Primrose League had its own anthem and remained in existence until 2004.

The agricultural depression continued into the 1880s, when refrigerated container ships were able to import cheap meat, further upsetting the home-grown market. There was further movement away from the village into towns but Julia carried on with her life knowing the crisis would pass and that the estate was well funded. The gloomy outlook for tenants was lifted momentarily for the Queen's Golden Jubilee celebrations in 1887. It began with a peal of bells at 6 a.m., a church service and the planting of an oak tree. Later in the day Julia entertained one hundred in her yard and the White family had two hundred for dinner at Manor Farm. Bonfires were lit in the evening.[293] From the charity she had set up with Chafyn she continued to make donations, latterly to the benefit of the Grove Buildings opposite the church in Mere, and refurbishments including a new roof and interior work to Mere Church, both executed in 1892 after her death.

Changes as to how women were perceived were slowly developing. Julia's own environment and the wider world were changing around her, though she had been in tune with social demands when she started her schoolroom. The lines of demarcation for the social hierarchy were becoming blurred. The industrialists, the new middle class, were chipping away at the edges, buying or building their own country houses to take advantage of their new leisure.

In mid-Victorian England, the landed gentry, the upper-middle class, were not generally ambitious. Their lives were determined by continuity and stability, with the aristocracy above them and the middle-class professionals below them. The family motto was 'Ny Dessux Ny Desseux', neither above nor beneath. Each layer of social order was strictly adhered to, accepting and indeed admiring of those above, dismissive of the layer beneath, but respectful of tenants and employees. When Julia and Chafyn were on their dahabieh on the Nile, they were not invited on to any of the aristocrats' boats. Lord Scarborough, Lord Spencer and others ignored them. Likewise, when Chafyn and Julia were having dinner alone in their hotel in Granada they amused themselves with speculating about the identity of two men and a young boy, obviously British, at another table. They nicknamed them 'Brown, Jones and Policeman'.[294] Intrigued, Julia discovered they were Welsh, named James and Robinson, one with a son, attorneys from Lovells, and that there was a legal firm of that name in Wells. Although it was innocent amusement, they were highlighting the divisive attitude of the social boundaries, which would soon be broken down.

Each generation has its cultural and political obstacles to overcome, but in late Victorian England Julia's world was changing at a pace. She was too ingrained or too old to understand people's aspirations and was against voting rights being extended again in 1888, as tenants would be less likely to conform to their religious and political restrictions. Church attendance had been in decline for some time as a more democratic way of life and political reform was emanating from the towns. In the sleepy west country, cultural nudges lagged behind.

It would be long after the Victorian period before women had the vote in 1918, but adjustments to the role of women and girls had started slowly from the 1870s, by people like Julia setting up their own school groups for girls, endowing education and involving women in political discussion in the Primrose League. For Julia, her obsession with church attendance and using political meetings to persuade those who could vote to vote Tory, was a way of keeping control of the Zeals estate. Non-conformist religions were rising, especially the Methodist and Congregational chapels, and tenants were no longer in fear of being given notice to quit if they voted the 'wrong' way.

At Ferne, Tom Grove had stepped out of his comfortable existence of the landed gentry to pursue his ambition of joining the aristocracy through being a member of parliament. Indeed, there were many former members of parliament in both the Grove and the Chafyn-Grove families, but he wanted to be a baronet, and his life's plan revolved around this vanity. He had achieved that and had lost his seat. Grove still had to continue selling off periphery parcels of land to keep his debts in check, and when there was nothing left to sell outside of Ferne, he started selling items from the house including two Romney portraits of his grandmother and Aunt Chafin, having copies made. When his wife died, he set on marrying a wealthy widow. The first attempt failed but he then married the widowed Frances Best. She paid many of the bills. Although he had a good land agent in Jackson, the latter's role was to manage the estate, not to advise.

In 1885, Tom Grove, missing the Houses of Parliament, took on the expense of another campaign for a seat. As a Liberal he fought the seat of Wilton, the stronghold of the Earls of Pembroke, against Sidney Herbert Jnr, the Tory candidate. This soured the longstanding relationship between the families, but Herbert was pleased when Grove voted against his own party on the Home Rule Bill. The issue caused the Liberals to split and Grove joined the breakaway Liberal Unionist Party. Having won against Herbert with a majority of 822, he was confident of an increased majority of over 1000 when he reapplied for the Wilton seat in 1892. His opponent was Lord Folkestone, a supporter of Lord Salisbury and Tom Grove had to fight a fierce campaign. A letter from Isaiah Maggs Jupe, a prominent non-conformist at Mere, provoked many abstentions from polling, giving rise to a riddle: 'Why is the South Wilts election the most notable from a Biblical point of view? Answer: Because after perusing a <u>Mere</u> letter from Isaiah it altered the <u>Fokes-tone</u> and numbers forsook the <u>Grove</u>.'[295]

Having lost the Wilton seat to Lord Folkestone by 407 votes, Grove successfully applied to become a Wiltshire County Councillor, unable totally to break away from politics but suffering a sharp decline in political power. When the bank refused any more funds, Tom Grove still kept his lifestyle going, with his wife's help, until his death in 1897. He died intestate leaving his widow in a precarious position. The prosperous Ferne estate, purchased in 1563 by Robert Grove, had taken one generation to unwind.

Tom Grove's son Walter inherited the baronetcy and a bankrupt estate. When he planned to marry Agnes Fox-Pitt, the daughter of the landowner of the vast Rushmore Estate, General Augustus Pitt-Rivers, Tom Grove objected, aiming for a larger dowry. The two fathers met to discuss their differences and love found a way.

Following the death of Tom Grove, the remaining contents were sold at auction followed by the house. Walter's allowance together with his shooting and hunting invitations had long since dried up and Ferne was so encumbered it had to be sold. Walter and his wife Agnes moved to Sedgehill House, which was still in the family's possession.[296] The Ferne estate was purchased in 1902 and resold to the 13th Duke of Hamilton in 1914. The house was used by his wife Nina as a domestic animal sanctuary for city pets during the Second World War. In a dilapidated state, Ferne House was demolished in 1965.

At Zeals, Julia had kept the estate in good order and as always had taken her duties seriously. Being active with the Primrose League, church and schooling, she had left behind the anxiety and self-doubt of her former years. Through strength and determination, she created a fulfilling life for herself.

In 1890, feeling unwell she went to her doctor and probably the family's London doctor in Manchester Road in London, and was diagnosed with cancer. She remained at Zeals for a while with her live-in companion, Miss Caroline Bazeley, but then went to Bath as she had better treatment there.

Julia would not live to see Zeals House again.

CHAPTER THIRTY-FOUR

Legacy

Julia Elizabeth Chafyn-Grove died in Bath in 1891, aged sixty-six, having been mistress of Zeals House for 26 years. At her death it was reported: 'Her kindness to the poor was proverbial: and her loss will be mourned by them as that of a most kind and considerate friend.'[297]

Julia's memorial
at Zeals church.

At the reading of her will, there was a message to her tenant farmers: 'We have always bound together by kind feelings and if I have ever hurt anyone of them, by word or deed, I here ask their forgiveness. It has been done inadvertently, if at all.'[298]

Richard White, the tenant farmer at Manor Farm, was hurt. His name in Julia's will had been crossed out. She had reprimanded him about his irregular church attendance. When he explained that his wife was low church so he had to alternate Sunday observance, she failed to understand that loyalty to his wife took precedence over loyalty to his landlady.[299]

The executors were George Troyte-Bullock the heir, Chafyn's friend Arthur Myers late of the Coldstream Guards, and the Rev. Calcraft Wyld, a Michell relative. In her will, Julia was as generous in death as she was in life. All of her executors were left legacies and she looked after local people and the church clergy.

This formidable woman was both kind and generous, but on her own terms. She was also 'a rather frightening lady, but if she took a liking to someone, she was wonderful'.[300] When interviewing prospective tenants, they had to be Church of England, Tory and in favour of the South West Wilts Hunt.[301] At her funeral her lawyer announcing that Miss Grove, as she was known in the village, had requested him to announce that she hoped to be forgiven, was unusual.

Julia was generous with a warm heart but a cold personality; she lacked awareness of how her stiffness was perceived. She took life and herself seriously, avoiding over-friendliness with tenants to retain their respect, whereas Chafyn would laugh and joke with them and they loved as well as respected him. She seemed incapable of small talk. Her apparent control belied the insecurities she had, being inclined to morose self-reflection when alone for too long, and unhappily aware of her own mistakes in her life choices. But in later life, Julia overcame her tragedies and created her own lasting place on the estate. She left many charitable donations and became part of the legacy of Zeals village – and Zeals House.

Julia's commitment to duty was paramount, and in step with the demands of the Victorian era. It was duty that stopped her from taking a long journey to Australia to join Chafyn when it was offered. But if she had gone, she would have arrived too late to see him. Remaining unmarried was partly out of choice, but also duty, not wanting to lose the Chafyn-Grove name and risk the management of the estate being swallowed up by a husband. It would have been his legal right.

Her real problem was loneliness and being under-stimulated. In an energising environment as she enjoyed in Granada, in Egypt and in her meetings with Alfred Morrison, she was at her best. Morrison, four years older than Julia, could have been a good match for her if the friendly relationship had developed. There was obviously an attraction, Alfred appreciating Julia's knowledge of art and artefacts and her enjoyment of his significant collections while she enjoyed the stimulating conversations. Towards the end of her diary, she refers to him as Alfred rather than Mr Morrison. They were both of gentry families – the Morrisons considerably wealthier, the Chafyn-Groves much longer established. But Chafyn's death and her all-consuming grief would have put an end to any escalation in the friendship as she concentrated on duty and keeping the estate in order for her cousin, George Troyte-Bullock whom she relied on more and more. On Alfred's side, the drawback was Julia's age as Alfred also had a duty to perform – he had to produce an heir. His single status was probably due to his shyness of women, which Julia often mentioned, but he met, through the Pembroke family, the daughter of the Wilton parish vicar, Mabel. He married her in 1866 when he had reached the age of 44. She was 18 years old, and soon an heir, Hugh, was born, followed by other siblings.

Having jolly people around was uplifting for Julia – like the Murphys – the trio her brother steered clear of and was embarrassed by. She loved Chafyn who was a good-humoured companion but of a different generation, with his own life and interests to pursue, and not always there for her.

Julia was a woman of her generation with its regulated restrictions, finding her freedom galloping across the downs in the Wiltshire countryside even in torrential rain. But she was open to eccentric behaviour, like taking sheep for a walk with Chafyn on the Nile, treating them like domestic pets. She thought nothing of jumping on a donkey to ride off on the hills to the temples on the Nile or to stand on a chair in the middle of the schoolroom to make a speech on harvest home day in front of a horrified audience. Pushing the boundaries of the social order, Julia sometimes befriended people she liked regardless of their class, whereas Chafyn rigidly stuck to those he was at school or university with, and army officers.

Of Chafyn's friends, Arthur Bowen Richard Myers, born in Tenby, Pembrokeshire in 1838, stayed in touch with Julia and was a comfort to her. He became an army surgeon in the Coldstream Guards before retiring having married Blanche Molesworth in 1878. But before he married, he wanted to go back to the Nile region where he so much enjoyed his time with Chafyn and Julia. He planned to travel by camel – with bottles of claret for the journey – into the Sudan on a hunting expedition for lions and elephants with the Hubrians. The trip was undertaken in the winter of 1874-5, with three young colleagues from the Coldstream and two others, The Earl of Ranfurly and Charles Arkwright. The hunting was successful but Ranfurly died of dysentery near the end of the journey, with Myers later saying the trip was irresponsible. He wrote a book about the sporting tour and died in 1921.

Hoffman, as he was always referred to by Chafyn, who sadly had to return home without his friend and travelling companion, would have taken the first available mail steamer from Bombay to London, clutching Chafyn's diary of their adventurous trip to give to Julia at Zeals on his return. Henry Westwood Hoffman was born in Kent in 1835. He married three years after returning from the fateful trip and lived in Putney working as a medical examiner. He and his wife Georgia Danton had five children, two boys following their father to Trinity College Cambridge, one becoming a doctor and the other an architect. He died in 1922.

Julia was the last member of the family to bear the Chafyn-Grove name. The family had struggled for generations to raise healthy children to keep the estate going, losing so many in infancy. They ran out of heirs to bear the name. The dilemma was a contrast to their Ferne cousins. At Ferne House, where each generation had multiple healthy children, the Groves came to the end of the line too: they had not run out of heirs but of money.

Just before Julia died, a property in Mere on the south side of Castle Street was being demolished in 1890. It was a 15th-century building in poor repair and being used as a barn. Further excavation revealed a 'handsome stone fireplace on which were sculpted two shields, one containing an emblem of the Trinity, similar to that on the balcony in Mere Church, the other plain, but probably the arms of the founder had been erased. In each corner and in the centre was a quatrefoil.'[302] There was also a smaller fireplace, 'less ornate and devoid of shields but of similar construction'. There seemed no doubt that the ancient building had been for ecclesiastical use 'probably for the Dean as Rector of Mere'.[303] As the land was on the Zeals Estate, Julia was asked, just before the end of her life, what she would like to do with both fireplaces. She asked for them to be sent to Church House, Salisbury, back to the house where Thomas Chaffyn as Mayor in 1547 and member of parliament for Salisbury reconstructed the dwelling house and ran the family's sheep mercer's business so many centuries before.[304]

Julia's gift had taken the Chafyn-Grove story full circle.

PART V

TROYTE-BULLOCK

CHAPTER THIRTY-FIVE

Troyte-Chafyn-Grove

George and Alice Troyte-Bullock supported Julia assiduously in her later life, but when she died, they were in no hurry to move into Zeals House, preferring to live at the family home of North Coker in Somerset.

George Troyte-Bullock, with his distinguished red hair and red beard, inherited the North Coker estate when his father, George Bullock, died in 1885. He and Alice, his second wife, had moved into the manor leaving their rented house in Sedgehill where some of their children were born.[305] George became a Fellow of the Society of Antiquaries, as well as Justice of the Peace for the County of Wiltshire. But these worthy positions were undermined when in the same year as he became Sheriff of Dorset in 1888, elected county councils were set up, leeching away the landed power base. The 1890s became a decade of anxiety for country landowners. The power that Julia enjoyed in the mid-Victorian period was ebbing away by the time she died in 1891 to be replaced by a less authoritative and more democratic tone.

The annoyances of the mid-Victorian years for the middle classes centred on the unreliability of the Post Office and the railway schedules, which would constantly change without notice. Towards the end of the century communications were more efficient, with the canal system and rail freight moving industrial products around the country and to ports as the country steered away from being an agricultural economy towards an industrial one. Improved communication made movement of people as well as goods much easier. In 1884, the latest Reform Bill was passed, giving 60 per cent of the male population the vote, so there were considerably more serious topics of conversation for the gentry other than mislaying a few letters and parcels.

North Coker House, Somerset.

The Bullock family lived in the village of East Coker near Yeovil in Somerset. Historically, the family were engaged in the manufacture of sailcloth. There were many towns engaged in making nautical equipment in the West Country, Dorset having an extensive coastline and the ports of Weymouth and Poole. George Bullock Senior of East Coker died in 1786 leaving his estate to his son John, who married Sarah, the sister of the late George Warry of Shapwick, Somerset.[306] They had three children: Hannah, Mary and George Junior.[307] As the only son, he would inherit North Coker Manor from his father. He followed the family tradition of public service, becoming Deputy Lieutenant for the County.[308] In 1826 he had married Maria Caroline Chafyn-Grove of Zeals, sister of Major William Chafyn-Grove of Zeals.[309]

George changed his name to keep the name of Troyte from a previous Royal Assent from the will of a relative, the Revd Edward Berkely Troyte of Huntsham Court, Devon. Later, in compliance with cousin Chafyn's will, he became Troyte-Chafyn-Grove, but as soon as the obligation was discharged, all his children reverted to the use of Troyte-Bullock.

By the time George Troyte-Bullock inherited the Zeals estate he was seventy-one years of age. The following year the Liberal government had returned an overwhelming majority in the general election in 1892 enabling the introduction of sweeping changes to the way land was taxed, with the electorate demanding a more democratic society. The Reform Bill of 1884, together with boundary changes, had already begun to diminish the power of the rural landlord. The franchise had been extended to the village men of Zeals who had been given a vote and a voice, no longer living in fear of their landlord or the fear of God. The age of abstinence and thrift was giving way to a new style of living, with more freedoms and a softening of religious strictures.[310]

Gladstone's government was chipping away at landlords' privileges with Bills giving tenant farmers the right to shoot hares and rabbits, and for landlords to compensate vacating tenants for improvements they had made to property.[311] Taxation on land values and ground rent were considered, but death duties were favoured by the Chancellor of the Exchequer, Sir William Harcourt, in 1894. Initially set at 8 per cent this was considered manageable, despite complaints. The agenda of levelling down was unstoppable.

The newly named Troyte-Chafyn-Grove family pondered the future of Zeals House. It was very important to keep the estate and the house for historic and family reasons, but other than using the house for field sports they were left an old-fashioned, shabby house by Julia, who had done little maintenance since she took over in 1865. The heavy drapes and tables covered in fringed cloths, the tapestries and excessive clutter were out of fashion and discarded. Julia had not warmed to the patterned wallpapers and fabrics by the mid-Victorian taste-maker William Morris and the Arts and Crafts movement, favouring traditional Victorian schemes, multi-coloured flowered wallpapers with borders and picture rails. Morris and Co. led the change from solid mahogany to lighter, simple, honest furniture in vernacular woods. By the Edwardian era smaller, lighter tables, desks and chairs with spindly tapered legs were in fashion, some furniture being embellished with delicate satinwood marquetry. The muted palette of dark greens and reds gave way to natural climbing and trailing foliage on wallpapers with fruit and flower motifs. The English house favoured organic forms which evolved from the 1890s to the end of the Edwardian period with lighter greens, silver greys and mauves in the swirling patterns of the Art Nouveau period. Victorian halls were filled with potted palms in cachepots and conservatories stuffed with ferns and palms became a feature of fashionable country houses. The conservatory at Zeals House was on the west side of the house facing the round pond with its island and rose arbours.

Zeals House, panelled bedroom, *c*.1915.

Zeals House, the boudoir, *c*.1915.

George decided that the best option was to let Zeals House, thus preserving the shooting and connection to the South West Wilts Hunt. A prospective tenant, Captain Percy Browne, made an offer to rent Zeals House initially for a period of five years from October

223

1893. George hesitated but was reassured by Squarey that it was a very good offer. Capt. Browne became a popular figure in the Zeals village before leaving to fight in the Boer War at the end of the century. He returned to a hero's welcome at the end of the war in 1902 and there was a great celebration for his safe return. Manor Farm was covered in flags and bunting to welcome him back to the village where he was much loved.[312]

Balancing his options in the undercurrent of political change, George Troyte-Chafyn-Grove remained a model estate owner. He returned an ancient stained-glass window he found at Zeals House to Mere Church where it was added to the south windows of the sanctuary in 1893.[313] At some time in the past it had been removed, possibly by Julia Chafyn-Grove, to make way for her west wall Chafyn memorial window.[314] In 1900 he gave Silton Church a new bell cage and a treble bell, still in the belfry.

Four years later celebrations took place in the villages of Zeals and Silton for the diamond jubilee of Queen Victoria. To celebrate the event, George built some thatched cottages in Silton to be called the Victoria Cottages. He also built a new house on the site of the former Hookhill Farm. When completed in 1899, the stone house with fifteen acres of garden was called Silton Lodge.

George and Alice's son and heir Edward George (Eddie) married in January 1898. He and his new wife Grace Amy Margaret Batten took possession of Silton Lodge. Their first child, a daughter, Elizabeth Grace (known as Betty) was born in the same year, in December.[315]

Built in the Victorian style, Silton Lodge became a favourite home for the family, which grew to include a son and heir – George Victor, born in 1900 – followed by another daughter, Winifred Mary. Eddie, as he was known in the family, took over responsibility for the parish affairs of Silton, where he was 'a most conscientious magistrate and he and his wife completely immersed themselves in village affairs'.[316]

As well as her husband's work in the community, Grace Troyte-Bullock was also involved in the running of the school and the parish, distributing charitable donations, including Julia's donation of coal and clothing. There were meetings to discuss how the village would celebrate the Coronation of King Edward VII. Grace offered to give the children tea and a souvenir of the event.[317] A dinner would be given for the adults, and after tea the children would have games and Grace would give out the commemorative Coronation Day medals.

The hamlet of Silton was experiencing a dwindling population in line with other rural communities, but it did have a village school, and Eddie's name was added to the book of school managers. By

1905, a new vicar, Revd Barnes-Lawrence, arrived and Eddie became chairman of the managers responsible for 'the school building, hedging and fencing of the recreation ground and the water supply from the well'.[318] School attendance was strictly regulated for childhood illnesses, the school once closed for five weeks because of an outbreak of whooping cough.[319] Children were barred from school if they had symptoms of typhoid or typhus fevers, scarlet fever, diphtheria, measles, mumps, chicken pox, phthisis (consumption), ringworm, impetigo, smallpox or verminous conditions.[320] With no inoculations and limited medical understanding, many of these diseases would end in child mortality. In such cases, clothing was disinfected. It was considered that illness was due to poor sanitation. Silton did not suffer badly from some of the more deadly childhood diseases.

Provided they spent six months of a year in school, children were allowed to be in part-time employment at ages twelve to fourteen, and eleven to thirteen for agricultural work, providing much needed extra hands at harvest time. As well as arable, the village also had dairy and sheep, the animals being less labour-intensive than arable.

At this time various items were removed from Zeals House and taken to Silton Lodge. They included a spring stuffed sofa on walnut legs and three pillows from the pink bedroom, four framed prints

Troyte-Chafyn-Grove family. *c.*1905 (Maria Caroline née Chafyn-Grove seated left. George with hat, Alice with umbrella).

from the library, a volume of Hoare's *History of Modern Wiltshire* from the schoolroom, books, papers, some china, and chairs from the servants' quarters. Interestingly, a set of Chippendale chairs was dispatched to Silton Lodge, not from the dining room but from the servants' hall, proving they were completely out of fashion. Taken from the large drawing room were a pair of white and gold chairs on casters with stuffed seats and backs upholstered in light green cord silk, and some chairs on cabriole legs stuffed and covered en-suite.[321] Two large oil paintings were also removed to Silton, one of Major William Chafyn-Grove, and the other of his daughter, Julia Elizabeth. Further items went to North Coker House from the library and King Charles rooms.[322] With George running the Zeals part of the estate and Eddie the Silton part, the family grew again when Grace gave birth to a daughter, their fourth child, Cecily Violet, in 1907.

When Zeals House became empty again, in 1905 George removed more items to North Coker. These included a three-quarter-length portrait in a black and gold frame of Anne Coker, wife of Harry Chafyn Grove who inherited Waddon Manor, along with a flowerpiece oil painting from the servants' hall.[323] At the same time two antique armorial helmets over the door in the entrance hall were removed to the Chafyn-Grove Chapel in Mere Church.

Another tenant was found in 1911. Edmund Sebag-Montefiore rented the house having signed a lengthy formal inventory from Messiters of every item in the house.[324] But during the tenancy there were many contentious letters from Sebag-Montefiore's solicitor to Rawlence and Squarey, who were accused of acting 'too zealously in Mr Troyte-Chafyn-Grove's interests'.[325] He was asked to roll the drives, which he considered the responsibility of his landlord.

Edmund set about renting an extra kitchen garden area and wanted to erect primitive fencing to keep the sheep out. But it was made clear to the tenant that the fencing could only be of an approved 'strained wire' design. The wily Squarey, at the end of his life, (he died in 1911) would have explained that only a permissible type of fencing was acceptable as it had to be easily collapsible during the hunting season. As Edmund's young son Geoffrey had also taken up hunting with relish, Squarey gambled that the father would pay the extra cost for the 1,936 yards of fencing which had to be purchased from a manufacturer in Birmingham with accompanying netting. The sheep could be kept off the vegetables but this was not guaranteed during the hunting season. The produce from the kitchen garden for Zeals House was important – but not as important as hunting. As Squarey predicted, Sebag-Montefiore agreed.

Despite the minor grievances, the Sebag-Montefiore family enjoyed living at Zeals House. Edmund's son Geoffrey would have a long association with the house. Into the future he would share his love of hunting with George and Alice's granddaughter Betty, the eldest daughter of their son Eddie Troyte-Bullock.

George Troyte-Chafyn-Grove died in 1913 at the age of eighty-four. He did not live long enough to see his eldest daughter Mabel Cecily marry (for the first time), becoming Mrs John Hammond at the age of fifty-three.

After the First World War Zeals House was let again.[326] There were death duties to be paid, by then at the rate of 15 per cent and items had to be sold off to cover the cost. It appears that North Coker House, occupied by George Bullock's third son Cecil John Troyte-Bullock, was let or sold in 1920, when the entire contents were disposed of at auction.[327] The house was converted into flats at a later date.

Having inherited the estate, and with the First World War imminent, Major Edward Troyte-Bullock decided to keep his family in the more manageable Silton Lodge. 'Troops were marching through Zeals village on their way to training camps, the coast and France with the village people turning out to cheer them.'[328]

As the Commander of the 1st Battalion of the Dorset Yeomanry, and becoming Lieutenant Colonel in 1914, Edward was called up for duty.[329] He set sail for Egypt.

CHAPTER THIRTY-SIX

Edward

'The spectacle of the Yeoman of England and their fox-hunting leaders, striding in extended order across the Salt Lake and the open plain, unshaken by the gruelling they were getting from shrapnel, which caused many casualties, is a memory that will never fade.'[330]

Dorset Yeomanry Officers. Edward, front row, fifth from left, no. 15, with Dorset Yeomanry Officers before leaving for Gallipoli.

By April 1915, the Gallipoli campaign was in stalemate. A plan was devised to knock the Ottoman Empire out by capturing Constantinople (now Istanbul). There were Allied troops on the Aegean coast with the Australian and New Zealand forces (ANZAC) hemmed in at the north of the Gallipoli peninsula and British and French forces to the south at Helles. At both locations there had been heavy casualties on both sides. A new campaign by Lord Kitchener to invigorate the Mediterranean Expeditionary Force was devised with a landing on Suvla Bay by the New Army and Divisions of the Yeoman (Territorial) Army based in Egypt. Success would mean that allied ships could pass through the Dardanelles reach the Turkish capital.

The new assault was scheduled for 6th August in the crescent-shaped sandy Suvla Bay. Two destroyers, the *Grampus* and the *Bulldog*, discharged up to 500 men at a time into shallow-bottomed boats built with landing drawbridges. There were three separate landing stations and by moving at night before moonrise, they hoped to be unseen by Turkish snipers. Intelligence showed only 1500 Turkish troops at Suvla, the British forces totalled 20,000. The rest of the Turks were waiting for an invasion but were 30 hours march away at the tip of the peninsula. The objective of the mission was to secure the hills which surrounded the bay, including Chocolate and Scimitar hills, and from the top of the ridges hold a tactical advantage over any advancing

Turkish troops. To complete this task, it was essential to gain ground on the hills before the Turks were alerted and started their march to Suvla. The whole battle was supposed to last for 36 hours.

It was mismanaged from the start. The troops landed in darkness with the officers finding it difficult to locate their soldiers. Unaware of their surroundings and with unclear maps to guide them, some waded to the shore as the lighters grounded. Although the first encounter was successful but with heavy casualties, by the morning the scene was chaotic. The planning took no heed of the unfriendly terrain, the strong leadership of the Turkish Army by Mustafa Kemal, or the logistical problems of supply. Digging in was difficult in the rocky terrain, covered with gorse and scrub oaks with uneven ground over a dried-up salt lake and ravines. The men pressed forward with only a pint of water to last in the heat of the day. Getting supplies of water, rations and equipment to the troops proved hazardous.

On 7th August there was little progress. Two hills had been taken but at the cost of 1700 casualties. The elderly Commander Lieutenant General Sir Frederick Stopford did not go ashore and failed to give clear orders, qualifying instructions with the words 'if possible', leaving the chain of command in chaos.

8th August would have been the last day when the mission to take the top of the ridges with little opposition was possible before the Turkish troops arrived from the tip of the Peninsula that evening, but Stopford's orders were not forthcoming. Concerned at the lack of progress, Sir Ian Hamilton, commander of the Mediterranean Expeditionary Force, wanted an advance to the ridges immediately, but Stopford's plan was to wait until the following day. Orders were finally given in the early evening of the 8th with the 32nd Brigade marching to Tekke Tepe ridge in darkness over rough terrain. When they arrived, the Ottomans had reached the top of the ridge before them and charged the exhausted troops with bayonets, resulting in severe losses.

It was against this backdrop that Lieutenant Colonel Edward Troyte-Bullock landed in Suvla Bay with the 1st Battalion of Dorset Yeomanry as part of the 2nd Mounted Division (but without their horses) on 15th August. The plan was for the 2nd Mounted, and the 29th Division brought up from nearby Helles, to secure Scimitar Hill in the largest battle of the campaign. The troops were now under Major General Beauvoir De Lisle, Stopford having been dismissed by Kitchener.

The troops grouped in orderly lines 'advancing with echoes of the Charge of the Light Brigade minus the horses.[...] Even though casualties soon mounted, the lie of the ground in this area offered some protection from the deadly Turkish fire, enabling the advance to gain some ground. The crest of Scimitar Hill was once again captured, but also, once again, when the troops gained the top, Turkish enfilade fire was so accurate that the position could not be held.'[331]

Following the attack on Scimitar Hill on 21st August 1915, Edward sent a letter to Major Goodden a week later:

The Dorset Yeomanry paraded with the 2nd Mounted Division, about 3pm and marched across about 2 miles of open salt marsh in attack formation, until reaching cover at the bottom of Chocolate Hill, where they halted and rested. About 4pm the 2nd South Midland Mounted were given orders to advance and capture Scimitar Hill about 2 miles distant, with the Brigade on its right to join in the final attack on the Turkish trenches. At 4.30pm we moved off, 1st line Berks Yeo, followed by the Dorset Yeo then 3rd the Bucks Hussars with the Brigade machine gun sections bringing up the rear over undulating ground. Through scrub, some burnt, some burning from the effect of shell fire from our navy warships in the Bay. We crossed the advanced trenches on Chocolate Hill held by the South Wales Borders and Enniskillen Fusiliers, who had already made an attack, got into the Hill, but had been driven off by Turkish shell fire. The Turks kept up heavy fire, long range indirect artillery shells and bullets rained on us. Casualties were light and we got to the plateau edge at the top of the Hill. Here we halted in a dry ditch and under cover of banks, partially thrown up by the Infantry in their earlier attack and organised for the final rush. About 30 SW Borderers under a Captain joined us. Our Brigadier then joined us and said he would go across to some of the brigade, who had moved too far to the left. They would yell and shout when they made their final charge and this would be the signal for us to make our assault including the SW Borderers in a single line. The Brigade on our right never got within a mile of Scimitar Hill to support us. The men were falling all around and I knew the attack had failed so I withdraw our men still alive and as many wounded as possible to the edge of the plateau, where we dug in and found a defensive position to repel any counter attack.

Once established, being the only Dorset Yeomanry officer alive and unwounded, I with my orderly and batman went off in search of other pockets of Troops, first meeting a group of SW Borderers and then in a ravine a dressing station, where we found a wounded SW Borderer Major, who had telephone communication with his HQ back in the British Advance Trenches. We discussed the situation and agreed we could not hold the position in daylight without reinforcements and if none arrived, we would retire at daybreak. I returned to my own men and about 3.30am some infantry arrived, took over the line and I was ordered to retire. I marched those I had assembled, some 50 in all, after our attack failed, back to the British forward trenches carrying our wounded. On arrival I found Lt Col Grenfell of the Bucks Yeo, who after our Brigadier had been killed, took command. He provided a guide and the Dorset Yeomen retired to the back of Chocolate Hill, where we had rested during the advance.[332]

Major Goodden took over temporary command of the Regiment and Edward the Brigade, consisting of the remaining Dorsets Bucks and Berks.[333] As a result of the very heavy losses by the 2nd Mounted Division by early September it became two Brigades, Lieutenant Colonel Troyte-Bullock commanding the 2nd of these. The Dorset Yeomanry, all volunteers and many fighting for the first time, suffered heavy losses. Of eight officers, Edward was the only one to survive from the Dorset Yeomanry (Queen's Own), and the casualties of the failed August Offensive were 21,500.

On 7th October 1915, Edward was sent home suffering from dysentery. On his journey back to Zeals House where Grace had taken over the school management and parish responsibilities while Edward was away. He was haunted by the loss of his officers and men – the volunteer Dorset farmers.

On the Salt Lake in the aftermath, a Yeomanry medical officer wrote:

What a scene of desolation – dead men, mules, rifles, ammunition, helmets and emergency rations lay everywhere. As we marched slowly along, we came across some of our dead and hastily buried them while it was possible. Most of these had not fired off any ammunition, as they had been killed by shell fire long before they were within rifle range of the enemy. It was sad work, burying these men, mostly yeomen farmers in the prime of life and of splendid physique – the senseless slaughter of war seemed appalling when viewed calmly after the excitement of battle was over.[334]

Gallipoli resulted in the loss of 115,000 killed or wounded. Of this number, half were British and Irish, the other half Allied troops from the dominions of Australia, New Zealand, (ANZAC), India, and Newfoundland – and French. The Turkish Army suffered many wounded and 65,000 dead.

The regimental history records of Troyte-Bullock at Scimitar Hill: 'Never was a desperate attack more gallantly led, never was the call of a commander more bravely answered by the men of the Dorset Yeomanry when Colonel Troyte-Bullock, acting under superior orders assaulted and captured the enemy's first line trenches.'[335]

On 3rd June 1916, Edward received a letter from Downing Street:

The King has been graciously pleased to give directions for the following appointments to be Companions of the Most Distinguished Order of St Michael and St George, for services rendered in connection with Military Operations in the Field. (Entry No. 77) Lt. Col. EDWARD GEORGE Troyte-Bullock, Dorset Yeo.[336]

Having recovered from illness, Eddie was once again posted for active service in 1917 to Northern France. He regularly wrote letters home, with many requests for papers, old magazines, and the local gazette to be sent to him. In June he wrote 'Don't forget I have no library or books like you have at Zeals.' Although he had received a bundle of *Illustrated* papers he became frustrated at the slowness of the mail. Unable to write about his military activities, his letters were dominated by requests for information about life at home.

'The Quaker Oats have not arrived yet. It is marvellous how long parcels from home take to get here! My silk underclothing (which I badly want) has not reached me. When were they sent off? Parcels from Salisbury come in 4 days. You might wake them up at the Mere P.O. about it.'

Eddie's love of the countryside is evident in his letters as he describes species of birds and plants he finds while walking in the neighbourhood. He was also concerned about his wife Grace working too hard in the hospital and his children's education at various schools in Dorset and Devon. To his eldest daughter Betty, who was at Sherborne School in Dorset, he wrote: 'It is important to work hard and be well educated. You should learn to speak French as it's a useful language spoken in many parts of the world.'

In mid-summer Eddie's thoughts were leaning towards the harvest at Zeals and Silton. He wrote to Betty:

How are the crops looking? What on the hay prospects? Is there much grass on the Silton fields? Are the fields being rolled properly? Have the Batten's brought their cows? Which fields are they putting up for hay? Have they altered the fencing at all? What has been done with the Silton furniture and pictures? Are they ever looked at? What a catechism I have to go through to find out anything!

In July, Eddie's concerns returned to his clothes.

My dear Betty, I should so much have liked to have had the cuffs of my 2 silk shirts turned up – quite an easy job with a sewing machine before they were sent, I really think with 2 grown-up daughters – one of them might have done them properly and not stitched over the frayed edges. Am now going about with ragged cuffs. You will find you will need to do a lot of work mending and stitching besides all sorts of other things if you propose marrying a poor man. Your loving Dad.

But Betty was not destined to marry a poor man.

Once home at the end of the First World War, Edward learned that his neighbour at Clouds House in East Knoyle, Percy Wyndham, had been killed, a year after succeeding his father.[337] Even closer to Zeals, at Stourhead, Henry Hugh Arthur Hoare and his wife Alda lost their only son and heir Henry (Harry) Hoare. There had been a big party at Stourhead for Harry's coming of age in 1909 but when the war broke out, he immediately signed up to the Dorset Yeomanry.[338] With their son fighting for King and Country,

Sir Henry and Lady Hoare helped to look after wounded soldiers who were sent home recuperating at a Red Cross Hospital in Mere, set up in The Grove Buildings opposite St. Michael's Church. Built in 1892 as an infant and technical school after Julia's death, and with her endowment, the buildings had been converted.[339] An operating theatre and a place for tuberculosis patients was built nearby, but later demolished. Grace Troyte-Bullock helped the sick and wounded in-patients as a Quartermaster for the Voluntary Aid Detachment in the hospital.[340] Alda's 'Dear Tommies' were driven to Stourhead, shown the house and pictures, given tea, where there might be music and a chance to fish on the lake.[341]

Harry Hoare was sent to Gallipoli with the Dorset Yeomanry 'but succumbed to pneumonia and paratyphoid, and was repatriated to Stourhead. When fit, he returned to Palestine in November 1917 where he was shot through the lungs in the Battle of Mughar Ridge. He died of heart failure a few days later in hospital in Alexandria.'[342]

A little later Sir Henry wrote: 'Our only and best of sons. He never grieved us by thought, word or deed.'[343] Harry Hoare's death was a blow from which his parents never recovered. Sir Henry and Alda stayed on at Stourhead for another thirty years but with no direct heir, the decision was made to hand the estate over to the National Trust.

Edward was still haunted by the losses of the Dorset Yeomanry. Out of the ranks of 301 soldiers, 191 were saved or wounded, 110 had lost their lives. He knew them all well, having led them in weekend training and summer camps over the years.

Bill Woodhouse wrote: 'I have heard it said that, after the first day's engagement after landing in Gallipoli my grandfather, mounted, read out the casualty list with tears pouring down his face.'

In 1918, Edward received a Territorial Declaration.

Left to right: Mrs Thompson, George Troyte-Bullock (later George Troyte-Chafyn-Grove), Dowager Mrs John Grove of Ferne, Miss Grove, Thomas Fraser Grove and Mrs (Alice) Troyte-Bullock.

CHAPTER THIRTY-SEVEN

Troyte-Bullock Family

When Edward and Grace eventually made the move into Zeals House in 1920, automobiles were better suited to longer journeys and Edward's children would invite friends for weekends. They would either arrive by car or be collected from Gillingham Railway Station. With motoring becoming widespread, the countryside became more accessible. Once weekend guests arrived at Zeals, they could enjoy endless scenic walks, fishing on the lake for perch and trout, picnics on the island of the round pond amongst the rose arbours, as well as croquet in the summer months. Indoor recreations would include taking pot luck in the billiard room, music around the grand piano in the hall and card games. Life was swell.

The attractions of Zeals for the younger Troyte-Bullock generation were the shoot, boating on the lake, the addition of a grass tennis court, and hunting with the South West Wilts Hunt. Walks through the woods would be carpeted with bluebells in the spring, followed in the summer with a white cloud of wild garlic.

Zeals House, ivy-clad with car, *c*.1905.

Zeals House, round island pond with rose arbour.

The woodland paths would take the young ones past the icehouse to the gazebo, a two-storey outbuilding with a sweeping panorama of the Blackmore Vale in Dorset.[344] Here they could take afternoon tea. Now called the folly, the gazebo had been rebuilt in brick in a canted shape in the 19th century and likely to have been the work of George Devey. It bears a resemblance to another canted garden folly, The Bay House, built later by him at Coombe Warren in Kingston-upon-Thames for Bertram Currie in 1870-1872. In the winter, skating on the lake was a popular pastime until the ice was broken up and taken into the icehouse.

As the 'bright young things', the younger generation of the 1920s were having fun, but Edward was beleaguered by financial worries and, set in his ways, bewildered at the swiftly changing threats to the family's way of life. Finding it difficult to adjust to new inventions, he never learnt to drive, although he had a Lancaster car in the coach house. Mistrusting technology, he thought that the horse as a means of transport would never be superseded.[345]

With the prospect of rising costs and falling rents, the life of the country gentleman was in free fall. The farmers and labourers supported and emboldened Prime Minister David Lloyd-George, whose ambition was to grab the power from country landlords. Edward saw his children and their friends and young relatives of the next generation enjoying life without the burden of memories of

Zeals garden folly, restored.

the First World War, but unknown to them, there was an economy drive in the household. When Edward's chauffeur lost his cap, he was concerned that his employer would be annoyed as it was only a week old and he would have to spend money on replacing it.[346] But Cecily, with her love of horses and hunting wanted her own beagles and her father could not bring himself to refuse her, his youngest daughter.

Edward's life was forged in the countryside, in the West Country Somerset, Dorset and Wiltshire counties he had been born into. As a local Deputy Lieutenant and Justice of the Peace, he never sought London life or belonged to a London Club, preferring to be a member of the Dorset County Club in Dorchester and the Dorset and Wiltshire Naval and Military Club. Consequently, without the vibrant conversations of London Club life, sharing concerns and solutions with other landowning members, he was isolated in his rural abode. Edward would not have wanted to alarm his wife Grace, although she would have been aware when he queried bills or asked her to reduce the number of servants in the house. Grace was an ideal wife, carrying out parish duties for the community, as was expected of her. Her grandson, Bill, recalls that most of the servants found her formidable, although she was always very gentle with him. She was concerned for her husband's health. He constantly had a pipe in his mouth, and in the evening in his study he would smoke cigars.

It was in 1926 that Edward learned of his eldest daughter Betty's attachment to his former tenant Edmund Sebag-Montefiore's son, Geoffrey. The two shared a love of hunting and love for each other. When Geoffrey's mother died and sister Clara (Clarissa) married, the family reluctantly left Zeals. Then the War came and Geoffrey joined the 9th Lancers where he was disabled, losing the use of an arm. His Regiment were 'kindness itself to me'.[347]

Geoffrey, five years older than Betty, lived in Portman Square in London and worked for his father Edmund and other partners at Joseph Sebag & Co., a successful stock and share brokerage in the City at 7 Angel Court, E.C.2, started by his grandfather. The family was prosperous and distinguished. When Geoffrey proposed marriage to Betty on 1st January her father Eddie was delighted for her but there were difficulties to be overcome, notably from his father Edmund and from Edward's stern sister Mabel, who was Chafyn's goddaughter and referred to by Julia as 'a dear'. Geoffrey wrote regularly to Betty at Zeals, sometimes twice a day.

My darlingest Betts. Here I am back again and Oh! how I miss you up here. I'll hate it tomorrow morning when there is no you to go and see before I go to the City. Why the devil couldn't your foul Aunt Mabel be broader minded? I can't become a Christian. I heartily wish I could but I can't any more than you become a Jewess. I simply can't abide intolerance and really she was just about as beastly to me as it was possible to be. I know you are very fond of her and I promise that I'll stick just as much from

Geoffrey Sebag-Montefiore's certificate.

your Aunt as it's possible for any human being to stick. I do hope that your Aunt realises that I at least behave like a gentleman.[348]

'I have had a long conversation with your Mama on the telephone. She was on great form and pray God she stays in it with you. I really am terribly fond of her as she's been a real good friend to me. I think your parents and Eddie [Edmund] are dining tomorrow night, and are going to the play.'

Geoffrey was anxious to hear the results of the meeting of the two families who were known to each other for many years. Following the family meeting, Geoffrey wrote:

My darlingest Betts, You will have got a wire from me telling you about Father. In the office this morning he adopted the attitude of 'pained but acquiescent'. He was 'quite nice' but that's all. He said I had better dine with him tonight. Well! We dined together tonight. He asked me what I wanted to drink and I told him a whisky and soda. He said, 'Wouldn't you like a bottle of

Aunt Mabel's wedding. From left to right – Back row: Edward Troyte-Bullock, Cecil Troyte-Bullock, Rosa Troyte-Bullock née Caulfield, Hugh Troyte–Bullock, the bride Mabel Hammond née Troyte-Bullock, John Hammond. Middle row: Alice Troyte-Bullock, Grace Troyte-Bullock neé Batten, Joan Troyte-Bullock née Acland, Centre in shawl: the dowager Alice Troyte-Bullock, far right with flowers, Margaret Troyte-Bullock, bridesmaid, daughter of Hugh and Rosa. Front row: Eddie and Grace's children: Betty, Mary, Cecily and George.

champagne?' I said 'all right'. He ordered a bottle and he raised his glass and said 'here's to the health of your young woman". Old devil isn't he? He talked about Zeals and the old days all dinner. Incidentally, he remarked that my step – as he always calls Alice – would dislike giving up half her pearls!! Then he got to real business. I will go to Dodd's tomorrow for a ring for you.

The following morning,

When he was ultra-haughty Father told me that if any son of mine was baptised, he'll cut him out of his Will. That did depress me terribly. Well! I got on to the baptismal stunt with him tonight. I told him why I wanted any children we had to be brought up by you in your religion was because it was your job to look after that side of their education and I was utterly against interfering with it. If in the unlikely event of your consenting to let them be brought up in my religion, they would merely develop into atheists. Father said with regard to girls that he didn't care a damn what they were, but with regard to boys he didn't want them baptised at birth and would never permit it. If I insisted, they would be cut out of his father's Will. He said that when they reached the age of discretion, they were to be allowed to choose their own religion – either yours or mine. Personally, I think that's fair. That they would adopt your religion I've no shadow of doubt. That they will not be ashamed of mine is my earnest hope.

Geoffrey planned to go to Zeals at the weekend to explain the baptism situation to Eddie, 'probably on Sunday, but if necessary, we would have to give up hunting on Saturday'.

'My own darlingest Betts, one thing is certain. Father is delighted I am marrying you and is very pleased to see me happy at last. If you play your cards right he'll give us anything we want within reason. He adored Zeals and is very fond of you all. He often regrets the old days. Eddie [Edmund] wants you to see 55 Lower Belgrave Street soon as someone else is after it.'

During the engagement, Geoffrey regularly invited members of the Troyte-Bullock family to London to go to the theatre and a restaurant. Mostly it was Betty and her mother Grace, but Geoffrey also invited Aunt Mabel and her husband John Hammond. Imagining Grace had 'one or two rows over the telephone with Aunt Mabel', Geoffrey learned that the Aunt had declared, 'I don't care two hoots about the play.' To Betty, he wrote: 'I know you are fond of them so if your Aunt wants to see you anytime, I'll always get out and let her if she doesn't want me there. I'll do that for you. As to how your Aunt Mabel and Uncle will treat me only time will tell.' The wedding took place on 8th March 1927, but not in a church. Later the couple had one child, a boy, Peter.

Following the marriage of his eldest daughter, Edward resumed going over the account books in his study. Reading newspapers, he learnt about estates being sold or relinquished. Stowe in Buckinghamshire, the former Duke of Buckingham's country estate before his bankruptcy in 1848, was sold to a philanthropist in 1921, and subsequently proposed as a gift to the nation but it was rejected without an endowment. It was sold to the Governors of what would become Stowe School. Eventually, the magnificent Stowe Gardens would be handed over to the National Trust.

Closer to home, Viscount Portman had rebuilt his family seat, Bryanston in Blandford, Dorset, in 1899, spending £200,000 building a new house doubling the size of the original, securing the architectural services of Richard Norman Shaw to execute the project.[349] 'The Portman family suffered six successive deaths in 29 years, bringing them to their knees financially through inheritance tax. In 1925 there was a 14-day sale of the contents and the house was shut up empty for several years.[350] Later it became, and remains, Bryanston School.

With the repercussions of the Wall Street crash of 1929, Edward's problems escalated. After the First World War, the Roaring Twenties in America was built on optimism. There was a boom in the industrial sector of automobiles, iron, steel and of retail, so as the stock market soared city people borrowed money to invest in it. The subsequent success, excess and opulence in cities across America was addictive, so the more the stock market rose the more frenzied the borrowing. When the prices dropped, frantic selling resulted in the crash. Simultaneously, outside the cities in America's rural agricultural communities there was a decline in earnings because of overproduction. The Great Depression spread across the Atlantic.

By 1930, Eddie was overwhelmed. Aside from trying to balance the books, Edward was worried about his wayward son and heir, George Victor, who was not behaving responsibly. Edward had worked hard to keep the estate together and had lost confidence in his son's commitment. Reluctantly, and angry with his son, he came to the conclusion that the only solution was to sell Zeals House. He put the house on the open market.

CHAPTER THIRTY-EIGHT

Vernon Mann

The Great Depression of the 1930s brought about by the American financial crash reverberated around the world, resulting in increased taxation and poor farming conditions in England. Tenants were

Drawing of Zeals House, *c*.1930.

relinquishing their properties as they were unable to pay their rents. With the agricultural economy collapsing, more and more people were seeking employment in the towns and cities. Former farm labourers, with the benefit of a much-improved education system, would be encouraged to become clerks. The country estates that survived had other sources of income, either land elsewhere in cities where rents were increasing, or some other industrial-related investment or ownership. An aristocrat, with a title and a landmark estate, could attract a wealthy American heiress to prop up his heritage, but for the landed gentry, entirely supported by the agricultural community, the only way was to sell off assets.

The proposed sale of Zeals House attracted a buyer. His name was S. Vernon Mann, surely the American Samuel Vernon Mann III from Queens, born in New York in 1900.[351] He breezed into Zeals bursting with ideas. On his list were a room for a Frigidaire, more en-suite bathrooms and substantial alterations to the garden layout. The architectural practice of Rolfe and Peto of Bath was instructed to make drawings for alterations to the house mainly reusing existing rooms.[352]

William Rolfe and Gilbert Eyre Peto of Bath had a thriving practice in cottages, houses and alterations in the 1930s. Both partners were related to the successful Victorian architectural practice of Ernest George and Harold Peto; Rolfe through Samuel Morton Peto's wife and Gilbert as a nephew of Harold. They had worked nearby at the Peto family house in Wiltshire, Iford Manor.[353]

The large drawings convey the rambling L-shaped floor plan of Zeals House and the proposed alterations.[354] Existing and proposed floor plans were drawn up in 1931 from July to September. External dimensions are the same as the house designed by George Devey as no alterations to the facades had been carried out since he finished his rebuilding work on the main house in 1863 and the schoolroom extension in 1869. The only external alteration sought by Rolfe and Peto was to the central drawing room window. It was proposed that this window be made into a French door, in line with the modern trend, which was to lead to a new, ambitious terrace arrangement. These drawings are the earliest evidence available of Devey's floor plan of the house.

Internally, most of Vernon Mann's alterations involved an expansion of the vast servants' area, going against the trend for fewer live-in staff. He wanted eight new servants' bedrooms to be added to the second floor over the parlour wing. A few modern practical features were proposed, like a telephone room in the entrance hall and a sewing room with a built-in linen cupboard. Also proposed was a change of use of two large rooms on the first-floor mezzanine. Devey had placed the library and billiard room on this level to take advantage of the extensive views of the park and fields beyond. For Vernon Mann they were to be converted into extra bedrooms.

A new back staircase was proposed entered by a door from the front entrance courtyard. The service area with the Victorian rooms for various multi-functional tasks was surprisingly unchanged architecturally, but a large room marked 'heating' was added within the existing area. Wherever space allowed, fitted cupboards were to be installed in the corridors and fitted wardrobes added to the bedrooms. The master bedroom was allocated for Mrs Mann and the adjoining dressing room for the master was to the north, the oriel window overlooking the front of the house. On the second floor, the butler had his own en-suite bathroom. Another large bedroom was allocated for a 'manservant', the American equivalent of a valet.

Having been recreated as a Victorian house, the alterations to Zeals appear modest. A more up-to-date design might have been expected, bearing in mind that by 1931 Art Deco and Modernist houses were being built on both sides of the Atlantic. The amount of space for servants and the use of the servants' area with small rooms for brushing and drying, cold store, sink, and boots, appears formal.

Externally, there was a proposed move away from the eighteenth-century landscaped parkland towards colour and structure. On the sloping land to the East, a rose garden was to be created, enclosed by balustrading, stone steps with ornamental urns. Mr Mann would benefit from a good view of this from the oriel window in his dressing room. These balustrades were to continue all around the house. The last set of drawings in September 1931 includes a wildly ambitious scheme to move the front entrance encompassing Devey's battlemented porch to a new north access with a cloistered approach. Included was a large area for flowers. The plan of the service area included a flower room with its own sink for arranging flowers for inside the house. Devey liked to use classical motifs in brick with stone features in garden buildings, surrounded by stone balustrades as appears in his designs for the flower garden and orangery at Coombe Warren in Kingston upon Thames in 1870-1872.[355]

The proposed alterations to the garden were old-fashioned, as English gardens had moved away from the cluttered multi-coloured planting and sectioning of the mid-Victorian years. In the house, the plans retained a formal way of living. But Samuel Vernon Mann III no doubt wanted the quaintness of the mellowed stone manor house, with the coats of arms emblazoned in stone on the south wall, as a romantic idyll. He wanted a slice of old England.

There were many successful Americans in England to snap up whatever antiquities, paintings and sculptures the London auctions had to offer. The aristocracy fared better from the increased unearned income than the gentry, as they had more to sell off when necessary. Many sold their London mansions, and some, like Devonshire House, were demolished. The English gentlemen's Grand Tour acquisitions bought cheaply from impoverished European aristocrats were now being sold on to Americans to furnish their New York mansions and their Newport retreats.[356] Wealthy Americans with new money soaked up the Poussins, Van Dycks, Breugels, Rembrandts, Rubens, Holbeins, and Raphaels, as well as whole libraries of books.

Vernon Mann's plan for the house included the layout of Devey's design that retained the Great Hall in the medieval part of the house. The servants' area was rambling. It included separate rooms for fuel, heating, laundry, boots, a cold store, sink, kitchen with cooker, pantry, brushing and drying, a cloakroom, a coat room and two lavatories. In the servants' hall wheeled trollies were used to pass food from one end of the table to another.[357]

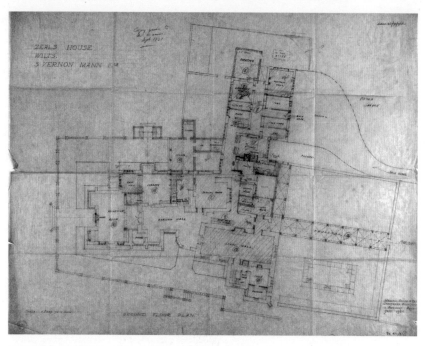

Zeals House plan – ground floor, 1931.

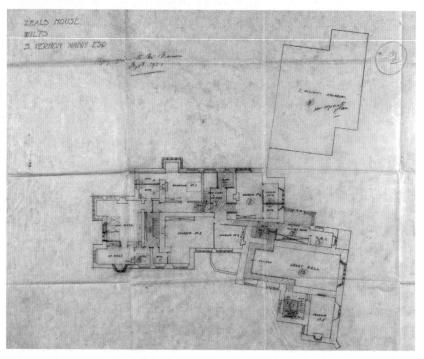

Zeals House plan – first floor, 1931.

The sale did not go through. As Vernon Mann had put so much thought into exuberant plans for the proposed purchase, it is unlikely he would not have proceeded with the purchase. More probable is that the property was withdrawn from sale and other sources were found for much needed funds. In 1930, the Chafyn-Grove Romney portraits and possibly house contents and books from the library were auctioned at Christies in London.[358] Throughout the 1930s, cottages and farms on the Zeals estate were being sold off, one by one, mostly to the tenant occupiers, depleting the estate's acreage.

The importance of holding on to Zeals House was, once again, the priority as Edward struggled to keep his footing. He was on a slippery slope.

CHAPTER THIRTY-NINE

Memoir

Edward and Grace's youngest daughter Cecily was thirteen years old when the family moved from Silton Lodge to Zeals House. Being the youngest of the four children, she was indulged. She spent most of her time in the stables at Zeals House in her late childhood, 'when she wasn't eating cold mutton and pickles in the servants' hall'.[359] At the age of sixteen, 'she hunted with her pack of beagles when mounted on a stubby cob with everyone else on foot as they should have been.'[360]

When Cecily married an army officer, Richard (known as Dick) Woodhouse, they were stationed in Egypt, so took their young child Bill to Zeals House to be under the care of her parents. The heat was having an adverse effect on their first child, born in 1933.

Bill Woodhouse, the grandchild of Lieutenant Colonel Edward Troyte-Bullock, remained at Zeals House into the late 1930s looked after by his grandmother, Grace. His memoir reveals daily life at Zeals House as seen from the perspective of a young child

Cecily with beagles at Zeals House stables.

and provides a fascinating account of the running of the house and the servants' activities.

> The day would start with a nursery breakfast. Then I would accompany grandmother along a stone-flagged passage to the kitchen where there were windows high above two huge sinks. These seemed to be in constant use with a small army of scullery maids toiling amidst steam and clatter and chatter. Undercooks were all around preparing vegetables and stirring large pans.[361] [...] After detailed planning of the day's menus with Grace, cook would write everything down on a large blackboard which hung in the kitchen for everyone to see. [...] The garden provided the house with all its vegetables and fruit in season (except tropical fruit) and similarly house pigs and chickens were kept and a few house cows. There were no deep freezers or even a refrigerator but there were lots of cool larders and dairy rooms and for winter everything would be preserved by bottling, salting and waterglass.[362]

Although groceries were delivered, sometimes Grace would drive into Gillingham in her Austin to shop for some provisions, taking young Bill with her. They would leave the stable yard, drive through the park, under the stone bridge to the tall iron gates by the south Lodge (no longer part of the Zeals Estate), or if in the northerly direction to Mere they would take the north drive past Black Dogs to go to Walton's Emporium.

On other occasions Bill would be driven to Zeals village when Grace had to look at some problem with one of the almshouses or attend to church business. On returning to the stable yard the Austin was garaged in one of the three coach houses. The other two were occupied by Edward's Lanchester, rarely used, and a remaining carriage. As previously mentioned, in his mid-seventies, 'Edward could never quite accept that horseless carriages were here to last.'[363] Grace, meanwhile, adapted to the telephone, the wireless and electric light. Extraordinarily, Zeals House was still lit by gas until the mid-1930s. Outside, the estate yard was responsible for maintaining the lake and the house, stables, farm buildings and bridges, the provision of gates and fencing. Besides the sawmill there were joiners, carpenters, painters, plumbers, plasterers, glaziers and tilers, all of whom were kept busy. The head gardener led a team of seven gardeners and apprentices from his potting shed. They looked after the walled kitchen garden, the greenhouses, the peach houses, the lawns, the flower beds, and the rose arbours that were a feature of the island in the round pond.[364]

But some incidents were confusing for a young child. 'Long Live the King' preparations were being made for the forthcoming Coronation, with flags and bunting being erected and Bill's grandfather receiving mugs, medals and silver spoons to be distributed. The excitement ended in 'gloom and muttering' without explanation.

Like all country families, the Troyte-Bullocks liked sports and for Bill, the lake was a 'wondrous world'. 'Starting with the exquisite little boathouse with its tiled roof nestling into the bank keeping the boat clean and dry ready to be stepped into from the quay side. The clear green water reflected light such as you will only find in those rare natural grottos. A rather fine rowing skiff and a green punt were nurtured in the magical building. Granny taught me to fish for perch and trout in the lake. She was a great fisherwoman and encouraged all her grandchildren, she also had the run of the Stourhead lakes courtesy of old Sir Henry Hoare who was a great friend.'[365]

Bill's grandparents had stopped hunting in the late 1930s, 'although the South West Wiltshire Hunt still met at Zeals and a kill near the house had me bloodied at the age of four. Granny enthusiastically followed the otter hounds and I remember splashing through the Stour at an early age. It is clear that the local hunts provided the backbone of the Cavalry and one can see why Cavalry officers were given so much encouragement to hunt.'

Bill rarely saw his grandfather who spent a great deal of his time in his study, trying to balance the books. Sometimes, Bill's grandmother would have something to discuss with Eddie and she would take her grandson down the passage to knock on his study door.

'Granny had a Jack Russell called Patch, and Poppa a slightly rougher haired older one called Spot, and they couldn't stand the sight of each other, so Patch would be shut out and, if Granny thought there might be a row, so was I. If she thought it was going to be an amicable discussion I was allowed in, to Poppa's discomfort as he then felt he had to watch what he said and hated me fiddling with things.'[366]

Despite the financial restrictions, Zeal House had many guests and family visitors. On one occasion when the whole family were gathered, it was time for the annual cull of the young rooks in the lime trees along the drive. 'This was done with .22 rifles and I was most impressed with Uncle Geoffrey's prowess with his rifle used with one arm. The other arm having been shattered by a German sniper when he was a young Lancer fresh out of Sandhurst.'[367]

'At the end of the phoney war things were looking serious. Aunt Mary came back from Malta, which was about to earn its George

Cross for heroism under siege.'[368] Her husband Jack D'Aeth was killed serving in the Mediterranean fleet.

In the Spring of 1940 my sister Sally, and I were dumped at Zeals while my parents hunted for a house to buy for the duration.[369] Meanwhile, the house, the gardens and the estate fell unusually quiet as all able-bodied men and women were called up. Leslie the pantry boy, aged sixteen, was suddenly footman, butler and everything else including plumber, on a fast-learning curve. Ethel did her best to be all things at once, including housekeeper and nanny to me at one stage. As with all large houses in the land that didn't have schools evacuated to them, Zeals House was requisitioned for military use and the Grenadier Guards were billeted to what was now a very empty house. The officers behaved and were treated as house guests and the men used the servants' quarters and the house became alive again. General Percival and his staff were also billeted with us.[370]

The Woodhouses bought a house and at this time Bill went away to school, but he returned to Zeals House for holidays. 'When the Grenadier Guards left, the house again became very empty and I had my own little bedroom looking down to the lake. The most evocative sounds of Zeals to me are the thump of the ram pumping water into the huge tank in the tower, and the quiet of the evening or the dawn, with the sound of ducks on the lake.'[371]

CHAPTER FORTY

Requisitioned

The ailing Edward Troyte-Bullock was pleased to have the house returned after the 6th Battalion of the Grenadier Guards left, but his peace was short lived. In 1941 there was a plan to house the Air

Ministry at Zeals House. Rawlence and Squarey wrote to Captain Cleeve, Staff Captain Quartering, at Bulford Camp, Salisbury on 29th December 1941 on behalf of Edward. 'Colonel Troyte-Bullock is outraged at the thought of his being evicted from Zeals House for the Air Ministry and says he will use every endeavour to stop such eviction. Can you re-consider this matter and let Colonel and Mrs Troyte-Bullock remain where they are? Remember, he is nearly 80 years of age and his wife not far short.'[372]

The appeal was unsuccessful and another requisition was causing Edward further anguish. It was not long before the Air Ministry had begun to inspect the area of Zeals and Stourton with a view to requisitioning land for an aerodrome, which would swallow up 266 acres from Zeals, 88 of which were part of Manor Farm, and 264 from Stourhead.[373] Convenient locations were sought in Wiltshire for operational units for support and training as they were initially considered to be too far from the Continent for offensive operations, although they could reach the Channel.[374] Edward was against the idea. On 23rd May 1942 he wrote: 'It would deprive the occupants of the land, of quiet enjoyment, two farms would be detrimentally affected and the shooting would naturally be destroyed.'[375] As a former military man, Edward would be expected to do all he could to

Zeals House architectural drawing, 1905.

help the Second World War effort, but once again, field sports were the priority.

At Stourton, Sir Henry Hoare was similarly against the aerodrome.[376] The 7th Devonshire Regiment had moved into Stourhead, twenty officers billeted in the house, the men in the stables and Memorial Hall. Reluctantly, he gave permission for the temporary airfield, to be called RAF Zeals, as eventually did Edward Troyte-Bullock. He was not to cave in lightly and attempted a different tactic. On 29th November 1942, Rawlence and Squarey wrote: 'We regret to have to complain that at the above aerodrome site, we understand from the owner of the Estate, Colonel Troyte-Bullock that coursing meetings take place on this site Sunday afternoons, and of course, hares followed by dogs of all descriptions, not only run across the site of the aerodrome, but other lands in the occupation of the owner and his tenants. Will you be good enough to stop this please?' Edward was hopeful that if disruption of his shoot would not stop the aerodrome, then the danger of hare coursing running over the proposed airfield land would make the Air Ministry think twice. The Staff Captain, Salisbury Plain Area, Bulford, Wilts, knew that farmers were against hare coursing so he asked in a letter on 30th November: 'Will you please say if you have received any specific complaints from surrounding farmers or land owners as to damage done by the hares? If you have, would you be good enough to give particulars.'

Rawlence and Squarey conceded on 2nd December 1942: 'We have received no specific complaints from surrounding farmers, but, of course, they do strongly object to dogs of all descriptions coursing hares from the aerodrome site on to land which they occupy, and as we told you in our letter, Colonel Troyte-Bullock, the owner of the Estate, is very much upset about it.'[377]

Later in the month, young Bill Woodhouse was on school holiday and staying at Zeals House on 29th December 1942. 'Grandfather, now eighty, was fading fast. He died of bronchial pneumonia in his sleep whilst I was staying. Granny as usual bore all these trials and tribulations with amazing fortitude.'[378]

Following Edward's death, his widow Grace presented Silton Church with a Bishop's Chair in his memory, made of fifteenth-century bench ends from a church in Cornwall.[379]

The aerodrome and the occupation of Zeals House for the duration of the war went ahead with the requisition agreement signed by Grace Troyte-Bullock on 25th March 1943. Excluded were the tapestry room and the peacock room for some of Grace's piled up furniture, which was locked in these two rooms. Other exclusions included 'the dairy, cooling house and cowsheds, all buildings west of yard, and garden cottage'.[380]

Grace planned to move into The Chantry in Mere for the duration but because the house was rented, she had to wait a few weeks until the tenants left. In the meantime, she stayed locally with friends and put the furniture she needed for the Chantry in storage at Waltons in Mere. It was inconvenient, and she worried about the pictures, trying to get them valued for insurance purposes. These included the Romney portrait of Elizabeth Chafyn-Grove (Aunt Chafin), two small oval pictures, a portrait of Mrs Grove, the wife of Hugh Grove by Honthorst, a lady playing the mandolin on a wood panel, horse portraits, and an old map.[381] Grace also worried about insurance for her dairy stock and was told the government were not responsible for bomb damage or blast. When she took her possessions out of storage some items were damaged, including Julia's prized drawing room tapestry, which had rotted panels. Meanwhile, her son, George Victor had moved into Manor Farm House with his wife and baby son Charles, and took the valuable stamp collection to the bank for safe keeping.

Grace became the District Representative of the Women's Land Army. While at Zeals House the Air Ministry were soon erecting electrical poles, and underground cables in various farms and the park. Also requisitioned by the Air Ministry was the clock tower wing, stables with five bedrooms above them, two dog lodges and squash racquet court, the conservatory near the house, and greenhouses.

Once settled in the Chantry, Grace kept an eye on Zeals House. There was a plan to dig a trench from the house to the lake across the park as more water was required at RAF Zeals and on one occasion she found the RAF officers had drained the round pond and dumped the resulting mud in the lake so they could use the pond as a bathing pool.[382] Knowing the water system was complicated and supplied water to the two large fields on the east of the house, she soon put a stop to these activities.

In July 1940 a German Heinkel 111 crashed at Huntingford, killing the crew. Then in October 1940 a Hurricane was shot down, crashing at Wellhead, the pilot surviving with severe burns. In March 1941 a German bomber crashed near Kingston Deverill and in July that year a British bomber crashed at Lower Mere Park Farm.

'The RAF Zeals airfield opened on 21st May 1942 where Spitfires and Hurricanes were based. It was later used by the US Airforce, as well as Canadian and New Zealand squadrons.' In Zeals village, the local people welcomed the US Air Force who were based at Stourhead, the American officers being kind to the local children by giving them chocolate and oranges. The airfield served as a base for a number of different authorities including the RAF's night fighters, the U.S.A.A.F. and latterly the Fleet Air Arm. Not very successful from a service point of view, the all-grass runways with few standings had a drainage problem, which meant the airfield suffered from excessively muddy conditions and at certain times it was virtually unusable, 'as the Americans discovered in the autumn of 1943'.[383]

Spitfires were used to escort Allied bombers on their return missions from occupied northern France and the western approaches, on one occasion shooting down an Fw190 north of Dieppe. Several squadrons arrived and left from Colerne in Wiltshire and Ibsley in the New Forest in Hampshire.[384] When missions were often abandoned because of waterlogging, focus turned to a training regime with forced marches.[385] Weather permitting, flying sorties resumed over the French coast.

In June 1944 King George VI visited Zeals House and inspected the troops in the park, prior to Grace signing a new requisition order in July for south lodge on Gillingham Road, the south drive, rock arch, the peach house and the heated greenhouse.

On 10th July 1944 a Mosquito overshot Zeals airfield and crashed at Pen Selwood, the two crewmen surviving. It was a foggy day and the incident was followed by a tragedy. A USAAF Norseman was refused permission to land because of poor visibility. Coming in to land over Stourhead, the plane hit the conical roof of Alfred's Tower, which was sliced off, the resulting crash killing all the American crew on board.[386]

'Soon after Christmas 1944 a unit was set up at Zeals to teach Dakota pilots how to pick up a glider from the ground without landing the tow aircraft. It was an American idea where for some years mail had been collected from outlying townships in such a way. The decision to teach the art had (I believe) a connection with a large number of gliders that were left where they landed after being used in the D-Day invasion.'[387]

The villages of Stourton and Zeals were not raided and night sirens rarely occurred, but the take-offs and landings during the night raids would have been audible to all the local people. The site was surrounded by tall beech woods, which, although being camouflage, would cause problems for the pilots.

Crews were taken to RAF Zeals for glider training and on 19th February 1945 several on board a Dakota TS436 were returning to their base in RAF Leicester East, having completed their course. With visibility down to 100 feet, the pilot took off setting his course in and out of cloud but failed to reach a safe height before the plane hit a clump of beech trees sixty feet high on top of a knoll. All twenty servicemen on board were killed except the pilot, the scene of the crash later marked with a memorial that survives to this day.

The last tenant at RAF Zeals was the Royal Navy, who arrived in April 1945 from a base in Somerset that was being closed. As was the custom, The Royal Navy Air Station Zeals was renamed HMS Hummingbird, a training station within the Fleet Air Arm.[388] On New Year's Day 1946, Hummingbird was decommissioned, the site returning to agricultural use. Some buildings remained for farm storage and the control tower was converted into a private house.[389] In 1945-6 the glider training school was taken over by the Admiralty and closed down early in 1946. After the war, the names of the twelve local men who had died for their country were added to the war memorial in The Square in Mere.[390]

Bill Woodhouse wrote: 'One heard stories of pheasants being pursued by jeeps full of tommy-gun-firing airmen and of hand grenades being rolled down rabbit holes. No doubt these things did happen but if you conscript a lot of young men from every sort of background and then ship them thousands of miles from home to fight someone else's war it reflects well on them that they behaved as well as they did.'[391]

CHAPTER FORTY-ONE

George

Edward and Grace's only son, George Victor, inherited a much-reduced estate. He had been landed with heavy death duties to pay, which had increased to a maximum of sixty per cent by 1939.[392] Following his father's death, he was advised by the family's agents, Rawlence and Squarey, now run by Norman Rawlence, to sell a portion of the Silton Estate to pay the taxes. Two farms amounting to 679 acres were sold at auction and a smaller farm of eighty-three acres to a resident tenant farmer. The breaking up of the hamlet ended the one-thousand-year history of the Silton estate.

George had been a wild child. Bill Woodhouse wrote: 'The children were forbidden to swim in the lake because my grandfather felt they might be ensnared in the weed. George, in front of his sisters, climbed to the peak of the boathouse roof and dived off plunging deep into the green waters. He stayed down as long as his breath would allow and by the time he came up his sisters were convinced their father had been right and their only brother had drowned.' On the occasions when Bill accompanied his grandmother in her car to go shopping, he was 'regaled with stories of how my Uncle George had ditched his sports car at this bend or had crashed at this bridge. The impression given was that her only son had been pretty wild, which was confirmed by some of my mother's stories.'

George was born in 1900 at the beginning of a new century, and although he liked hunting and shooting when in the countryside, by the mid-1920s the place to be was America. He took a steamer to a buzzing New York and it appears he went from there to Canada to visit his uncle, Hugh Ambrose Troyte-Bullock, who had emigrated to Wolfville, Kings County, Nova Scotia and married Rosa Caulfield.[393] From there George went to New York and met an actress called Dorothea Quigley. Taking no notice of his father's wrath he brought her back to England becoming engaged to be married in March 1927. Edward did everything he could to dissuade George from what he thought would be a disastrous union. He regarded the American actress as highly unsuitable for his only son. Ignoring paternal advice, George married Dorothea in St. Mark's Church, North Audley Street in Mayfair in May 1927, the Troyte-Bullock family members hostile to the new arrival. A year later, the pair were in Court, Dorothea petitioning for an uncontested divorce. George returned to Zeals alone.

While his father was doing all he could to keep the house going for his son to inherit, the heir lived a carefree life. George spent most of his time socialising in London but by the outbreak of the Second World War he was back at Zeals House, having married Nina Yolande Rathbone, considered by the family to be preferable

Major George Victor Troyte-Bullock.

to the first wife but not a vast improvement. The pair had moved into Manor Farm adjacent to Zeals House for the duration of the requisition. Fortunately, Edward had let Manor Farm in 1937 but not Manor Farm House, as the new tenant farmer, Richard Stratton, lived nearby at Kingston Deverill so had no need of accommodation. With his mother nearby at The Chantry in Mere, George was also on hand to watch over the behaviour of the RAF officers. During this time, the couple's only child was born in 1942, Charles Hugh Troyte-Bullock.

In 1940, George was in the Rifle Brigade preparing to ship to Norway to repel the Germans on that front but the Germans moved too fast and the battle of Narvick had been fought and lost before the Rifle Brigade arrived.[394] He later became a Captain in the Rifle Brigade and at the end of the war became a major.

When the RAF officers moved out of Zeals House in 1945, the decision was made to continue living at Manor Farm and let Zeals House. A lease was agreed with Stroud Boys' Preparatory School, but before the school moved in, George Victor wanted Zeals village to celebrate the end of the war with a party at Zeals House. He wrote to his tenants to suggest a deduction of £1 from the next quarter's rent to 'help you celebrate victory and to thank all those who helped to achieve it, and especially in memory of all those who gave their lives'.[395]Further celebrations took place for Queen Elizabeth II's Coronation in 1953, when George and Nina hosted a large dinner for the village at Zeals House.

After Stroud school left, Zeals House was leased again to a girls' finishing school and there were signs that George Victor was settling into being a good landlord. Eventually, George and Nina moved back into Zeals House in 1956 with their young son, Charles. Saving Zeals House was once again the priority and because it was in a dilapidated state, it was deemed unlettable. In the same year Silton Lodge was advertised in *Country Life* and sold.[396]

Nina preferred to be in London rather than at Zeals. She was extravagant and loved partying, shopping, and living the high life. George would accompany her to London regularly and they carried on living as if money would never run out. It may appear their attitude was irresponsible, but self-indulgence and extravagant behaviour gave them an outlet from the constant threat of the demise of their way of life.

Having decided to reinstate the family at Zeals House, in order to raise funds George and Nina decided to sell Manor Farm

House, which in previous generations was known as one of the best and most successful farms in Wiltshire.[397] It is likely the home farm acres were gradually reduced until it became necessary to sell the Manor Farm House as well. The Queen Anne house was purchased in 1959 by Leigh Holman on a twenty-one-year lease and later the freehold was purchased. He was the first husband of the *Gone with the Wind* actress Vivien Leigh, who regularly visited the house.

A year later, George died of a heart attack at the age of sixty, leaving the widowed Nina at Zeals House with eighteen-year-old Charles. Death duties and a diminished estate made keeping the house unsustainable, but they attempted to keep afloat by selling items from the house and any remaining parcels of land and cottages. The final decision to sell the house was made jointly between Nina and her son Charles. It was a sad day and Charles went to see his Aunt Sally (Cecily's daughter and Bill Woodhouse's sister) at her place of work in London in the mid-1960s to tell her of the decision. They had tried to stay afloat but were drowning in debt.

Even if George and Nina had been frugal there seems little doubt the estate would still at some stage have had to be sold. For the Troyte-Bullock family members who remembered the family living at Zeals House there were so few sentimental objects left. Silver with the family logo, pictures and jewellery were all probably slipped into auction houses to buy a bit more time, including, it is assumed, Charles II's gift of a salt centrepiece.

Zeals House was for sale for a lengthy period, until a buyer was found in 1968. In the same year Grace Troyte-Bullock died at the age of ninety-three. She remained at the Chantry in Mere, effectively the dower house, for the rest of her life, enjoying the long, low Tudor house, dominated by the tall towers and clock bells of St Michael's Church to the north.

Nina and Charles moved to Waddon House, in Portesham, Dorset, which the Chafyn family had owned continuously since 1700, and on and off since 1400. Charles Troyte-Bullock changed his name to Chaffyn-Grove, adding an extra letter to differentiate him from the original family.

Having cleared their possessions, Charles Chaffyn-Grove closed the door on a way of life that was out of time and an estate steeped in family history and debt, leaving a hollow, lifeless Zeals House.

Charles remained at Waddon Manor for life. He married twice, his second wife bringing a son and a daughter from a previous marriage, but he had no natural children of his own. This mild-mannered man allegedly turned the attic floor at Waddon House into an elaborate train set.

He died in 2014 – the last member of the family who had lived at Zeals House.

PART VI

DEPARTURE

CHAPTER FORTY-TWO

For Sale

During the 1960s there was little demand for country houses which had been designed to house multiple servants, with Victorian architecture in particular viewed unfavourably.

In 1965, the Grove family mansion for five hundred years, Ferne House in Donhead St. Andrew near Shaftesbury, was demolished. It had been used in the Second World War as a refuge for evacuated

Zeals House from the far east.

domestic pets from cities and was in a dilapidated state. Without a buyer, Zeals House may well have suffered the same fate. The future of Zeals House was in the balance when it finally found one. It was purchased in 1968 by Alex Garnett Phippen from Devon who brought new money, ideas and enthusiasm to repair and refurbish the house. He hoisted a flag onto the flagpole on the top of the tower; he had arrived and was in residence. The scale of the task ahead was indicated by the fact that there were still Second World War Nissen huts in the kitchen courtyard which had not been cleared.[398]

Cultural change turned houses like Zeals, with its Victorian rambling architecture, into white elephants. Unfashionable in the mid-twentieth century, many country houses and buildings were demolished. Even George Gilbert Scott's St. Pancras Station, a magnificent Victorian edifice, was in danger of being razed. Kenneth Clark, writing in 1962, observed of Victorian Gothic houses, '[...] only recently have we begun to notice these monsters, these unsightly wrecks stranded on the mud flat of Victorian taste.'[399]

As Zeals has been for sale several times in recent years, the sales brochures give clues as to the changing style of interior furnishings over more recent decades. Most noteworthy is that Devey's internal fittings appear to have remained intact. As some of Devey's landmark larger country houses have been demolished, or altered for commercial use, Zeals House provides a fascinating invitation into his world, as a preserved authentic example of his work with no stylistic architectural diversions from his earlier country houses. There is no evidence of Julia's involvement in any of the interior features of Devey's ceilings, chimney pieces or panelling. Even the arched open doorways were the architect's standard format in the high-Victorian era. Whereas some owners would have taken out some of Devey's fixtures and the heavy oak panelling, there appears to be no inclination towards modernising by any of the later occupants, and there is no evidence of the Troyte-Bullocks adding anything to the house other than the conservatory, although they removed many free-standing items. Bearing in mind that Zeals House survived the impact of two World Wars and two schools, it is remarkable that the house still has so many original Devey features. Both internally and externally, the house is relatively unchanged since he constructed the substantial additions in 1863. In the servants' hall there still exists an ancient food trolley on wheels used to pass food from one end of the table to the other. The Great Hall was retained by Garnett Phippen but by 1994 an estate agent's plan reveals that it had acquired a false ceiling. The rambling servants' quarters with all the various rooms for the preparation and preservation of food and for grooming were still retained in their original state in the medieval part of the house.

Alex Garnet Phippen purchased Zeals House with eleven hundred acres of land, carefully restoring the house over the years. He liked to hold jousting tournaments on the east lawns with one particularly large public event in 1972. During the refurbishment, Garnet Phippen made some discoveries in the house. One was the priest hole, only accessible by treading over open floor joists, and another was a secret cellar in the basement. He opened the door which was locked with a large key and trod cautiously down a few steps to find an empty cellar room perfectly dry and preserved.[400]

He planned to live in the house for life, but his business, a chain of laundry shops, was hit hard by 1970s selective employment tax. By 1976 Zeals House was for sale again, as advertised in *Country Life* by Pearsons/Hamptons, with thirty acres.[401] The house may have been saved but at the cost of a break-up of the estate.[402] An article in *The Daily Telegraph* about the proposed sale by Pearsons/Hamptons said it was 'in the market for only the second time in five hundred years'.[403] The sale of the house was followed in 1977 by a disposal of the contents, which included all furnishings in the house, as well as bags of peat in the outhouses and a lone jousting lance.[404]

Since then, the house has changed hands many times. The property was for sale again in 1979 with John German Ralph Pay, advertised in *Country Life* as 'an impressive and historic house in a fine parkland setting with a lake and great sporting potential' with fifty-nine acres,[405] Three years later, Zeals was offered by Strutt and Parker with sixty acres and a separate lot of eighty-one acres of pasture.[406] By the end of 1982 Michael Hanson, reviewing the property market for country houses in *Country Life*, commented that there was a gradual growth in sales, and that Zeals House 'was sold comparatively quickly in what was still, in the summer, a difficult market'.[407] It was sold by Strutt and Parker that year and again in a subsequent year. Zeals House, once the powerful heart of a thriving village, at the time of writing stands empty.

CHAPTER FORTY-THREE

Devey's Contribution

The dates for George Devey's architecture at Zeals House have been misinterpreted. The only published biography of Devey to date is by Jill Allibone (1991) in which she barely mentions Zeals. She dates his buildings by invoices, and credits the work at Zeals at 1866-1872 to William Chafyn-Grove (Chafyn) and his sister Julia Chafyn-Grove, following the success of the almshouses in 1865.[408] The date of the almshouses is correct. Chafyn commissioned them in 1864 and they were built in 1865 but only after the rebuilding of Zeals House was completed. The date of the first invoice in 1866 would have been caused by a delay until probate was granted after Chafyn died.

T. H. Baker wrote that the house was rebuilt entirely by Julia, but in a slip-note at the back of his book, by way of apology he wrote in 1898: 'Mr George Troyte-Chafyn-Grove has called my attention to the fact that the enlargement of the house was carried out, not by

Zeals House, north-east elevation, clad in foliage.

the late Miss J. E. Chafyn-Grove, as stated in vol. xxix., p. 337 of the Wiltshire National History and Archaeological Magazine, but by her brother, William Chafyn-Grove in 1862-3. The date of the oldest part of the house is 1380.'[409]

George Troyte-Chafyn-Grove was at Zeals House regularly during the building work and his dates line up with the family's diaries. Julia then brought Devey back for further extensions after Chafyn's death; the new wing reveals the date 1869 embedded in stone in the rear wall of the courtyard. It is unlikely that Julia would have waited until 1872 to settle the invoice for Devey's work, so it is possible that Devey built a cottage which her diary reveals was considered and rebuilt the old crumbling gazebo into a two-storey folly in brick with a canted front, a style which he had used before for the garden folly at Coombe Warren, but to date, nothing has surfaced to prove it. There is also a cottage in Zeals village called Swiss Cottage, with diagonal lofty brick chimneys in the Devey style, commissioned by Julia in 1870 for the Zeals' curate, but there is no evidence of the name of the architect.

The manor house of Zeals is an important part of Wiltshire's architectural history and one of the County's Grade I listed houses. In Walter Godfrey's *The Work of George Devey*, his only reference to Zeals House is also brief: 'In Wiltshire are Zeals House, Mere, an excellent building of stone...'[410]

Zeals House was a successful example of a compact, integrated Victorian country house. George Devey synergised the medieval, seventeenth-century, eighteenth-century and Victorian elements in his substantial rebuilding and extending of the house, so that it blends into one picturesque mass. Over time, the old and the new have mellowed together.

It is a tribute to Devey that his work created a successful building, and with Zeals House's Grade I listing it should remain so, as a monument to a great Victorian architect and a fine example of the domestic Tudor-Gothic architecture of our built environment. His historical knowledge and application of the Tudor Gothic was at its height in this period of his architectural maturity. He expertly blends light and shade, as well as horizontal and vertical elements. His experiments with textures and visual effects which began at Betteshanger in 1856 resulted in a pot pourri of materials and architectural styles to choose from. Applied decoration at Zeals House is more carefully chosen with the benefit of Devey's experience and remains serenely picturesque.

The photographs of Zeals House under construction and when completed are a rare combination to have survived. They were placed in an album, not in Devey's loose box of papers.[411] He must have been pleased with the result but more likely he wanted to retain the images so that he could reprise some features for a future house. The architect's influence from Zeals can be seen in his later houses. The square-inside-a-square panelling style later resurfaced in the dining room at Goldings, Hertfordshire (1871-1877) and on a chimney breast at 25 Lennox Gardens, London, (1886).[412] The positioning of the tower, clock tower and pointed gables of Macharioch House (1873-1877) share the styling of Zeals House from the previous decade.

In the 1870s, as agricultural landed estates like Zeals were suffering a decline, Devey embarked on his busiest decade, with emerging plutocrat clients. He was commissioned to build two new large houses, Goldings in Hertfordshire for Robert Smith and his largest country house, Hall Place (1871-1874) in Leigh, Kent, for Samuel Morley MP, a hosiery manufacturer. The budget was 'unrestrained'.[413] The interior decorative elements were of the highest quality. The towers were more numerous and loftier than Goldings, the chimney stacks higher. Hall Place incorporates the characteristics of the Tudor Gothic style, the irregular plan, gables and turrets at varying heights.[414] Walter Godfrey in dense Edwardian tone remarks: 'It is a tribute to the architect's power and an indication of the greatness of his genius that he was perfectly equal to all the demands which these larger enterprises made upon his resources, and that their perfection and charm are not less in every particular than in the smallest cottage which he built.[415]

Mark Girouard suggests that 'Devey's very large country houses are his weakness and are depressingly shapeless.'[416] But they were built at a time when an enormous house was a status symbol which could disguise a lack of pedigree. As country houses, they are now out of fashion. Betteshanger House is now Northbourne Park Preparatory School, Hall Place is a venue for exhibitions and weddings, and Goldings is Hertfordshire County Council's Surveyors' offices. Coombe Warren in Kingston-upon-Thames was demolished in 1926 for suburban redevelopment. The smaller of Devey's houses like Zeals and Wilcote House in Oxfordshire are viewed as a more manageable size for modern family living, even though the massive former servants' quarters, sometimes half the house, need considerable adaptation.

As Devey continued his country house practice, the younger architects Richard Norman Shaw and Eden Nesfield scoured the Weald area of Kent and East Sussex for vernacular ideas to create an Old English style they deemed suitable for the countryside.[417] Both young architects were considerably influenced by Devey's work there.[418] Inspired by the tile-hung and half-timbered medieval buildings, they were also studying Devey's interpretation of them. The variety and imagination of Devey's chimneys, which he drew obsessively, were a main feature of his Weald buildings.[419] Devey was an important influence on Shaw, especially for his country houses.[420]

One of the architects chosen for the redevelopment in the 1880s of the 'Chelsea fields' of Lennox Gardens and Cadogan Square, Devey worked alongside G. E. Street, R. N. Shaw, J. J. Stevenson, Ernest George and Harold Peto. He was in favour of individually styled houses and the Flemish gables with stone dressings first used at Betteshanger were reprised in the tall narrow houses of these garden squares.

> Turning to the English Country House. In this direction the debt which the twentieth century owes to the nineteenth and to such great architects as Richard Norman Shaw, Eden Nesfield, George Devey and Philip Webb cannot be exaggerated. They relit the torch which is being carried on by a new generation of men, among whom Mr Lutyens fills a large place. Their work was essentially that of pioneers. They not only re-established principles of traditional domestic design which had been drowned in the fervours of the Gothic Revival but they set out to rediscover the right uses of materials. As men of their time, they had to adjust to the new outlook to an infinite variety of pressing problems in the planning and equipment of houses.[421]

Because Devey was involved in several styles of architecture and tended to work in isolation, it has been difficult to pigeon-hole him. The wide span of his work encompassed the Weald cottages, lodges, stables, alms house, schoolrooms, Tudor Gothic country houses and the Queen Anne movement. Gavin Stamp refers to Devey as 'an enigmatic and shadowy character in the history of Victorian domestic architecture'.[422] But there are signs that he is coming out of the shadows.

Victorian country houses are once more appreciated for their high ceilings, beautifully proportioned rooms and solid construction.

Architects of the Victorian period are being reappraised. In 2018, writing in *Apollo*, Charles Holland reassesses Devey's work, especially at Betteshanger and suggests, 'Devey's work holds much to interest us today.'[423] In 2020, on the centenary of George Devey's birth in 1820, Timothy Brittain-Catlin observed in *The Victorian*, 'This influential figure is again arousing interest among architects.'[424]

Rarely in the best of health, Devey was unhappy in his private life. He was engaged to Flora Hoskins, the daughter of the vicar at Chiddingstone when he was working in the Weald in 1857, but it was broken off and she later married Newton Streatfield who also became a vicar. Devey was heartbroken. When Streatfield died in 1866, he again asked the widowed Flora to marry him and was once more rejected. Jill Allibone suggests that the rejection was likely caused by Devey's unorthodox religious beliefs.[425] Heartbroken again, he poured his energy into his workload, which was considerable, requiring regular visits to his projects scattered across the country.

During the later years of his life, from 1881, Devey lived in the Lavender Hill district of Battersea, South London, in Ashley Lodge. It was demolished to make way for urban redevelopment *c.*1900. The house was built *c.*1800 speculatively and was rented to various tenants over the years.

Ashley Lodge, Battersea.

Planning to retire, he purchased an early Georgian house with panelled rooms overlooking the sea in Hastings to be near his brother. It had a paved terrace and summer houses at either end, but he did not live long enough to take possession. In 1886, he contracted bronchitis. Nursed by his cousin Clara Egg in his brother's house, he was unable to recover from the illness and in November he died of pneumonia.[426]

Writing of the architect's output, Mark Girouard observed, 'By the time of his death [George Devey] had designed more country house work than Shaw, Nesfield and [Philip] Webb put together.'[427]

CHAPTER FORTY-FOUR

Local Legends

When the clock strikes 12, the black dogs on the north lodges at Zeals House come down to drink the water. This tale is an old Mere legend probably invented for children.

The Great Hall was the scene of an execution of a 'Cromwellian spy by Royalist supporters who can apparently be heard on dark stormy nights, according to a property market review by Huon Mallalieu on haunted houses for sale in *Country Life*.[428] It is interesting to note that it is the only time Zeals House has been the subject of an article in *Country Life* other than in the property section in estate agents' advertisements.

Another story involves a young woman dressed in a grey cloak. She descends the staircase and leaves by the front door, then walks through the park to the woods beyond the lake. The story has been passed down the generations. The young lady is thought to be the ghost of a daughter of the house on her way to elope with a man she had met in Zeals village, who was never heard of again.[429] The alleged disappearance has evolved into a ghost story. All daughters of the house would be accounted for, but servant girls, if unhappy

Black Dog gate pier.

in service, often left without warning and without staying in touch with anyone in the household below stairs. In February 1876 a skeleton of a young woman was found in the wood on the far side of the lake by the dry-stone arch. It was removed and interred in Zeals churchyard.[430]

A letter written from a member of the Troyte-Bulllock family while living at Zeals House tells of a pistol and a satin shoe underneath the floorboards discovered while electricity was being installed in the servants' quarters in 1936, so there could have been a murder, the skeleton by the lake having a bullet hole in the head; it could have been a servant girl, and it could have been an elopement that went wrong.

Any empty Victorian house can appear sinister, it is easy to conjure up ghostly images. As in Jane Austen's *Northanger Abbey*, such conjurations are likely to be fanciful and emerge from over-stimulated imaginations.

Epilogue

In February 2021 a local West Country magazine, *The Blackmore Vale*, highlighted the plight of the empty Zeals House, with an article entitled 'Prestigious Past and Desperate Decay'.[431] This was followed in June 2021 with an article in *Private Eye*'s 'Nooks and Corners', which stated that Zeals House is 'a rare example of a domestic property with a surviving medieval range'.[432] Both articles highlight Historic England's addition of Zeals House to their register of Buildings at Risk. SAVE Britain's Heritage also highlighted the house's plight with a press release.

Like many manor houses inhabited by the same gentrified family over multiple generations, Zeals is a rise and fall story. The Chafyn-Grove family story parallels the histories of many similar estates, from their best years to their demise. The rise through trade to gentry, increasing land holdings as an investment to provide an income to keep the house running. But unlike the aristocratic families, the gentry were less cushioned against events beyond their control.

Tracing the history of Zeals House through the Tudor, Stuart and Georgian periods reveals an upward graph of status, income and land holdings. The culmination of many generations of caretaking took Zeals House to the boom Victorian years, peaking in the

Zeals House. North drive to Black Dogs.

mid-1860s where much of this story was written, as more records are available from that period.

Diaries are enlightening to gain an overview of the social atmosphere and characters of a period. The male diaries of the Chafyn-Grove family are less introspective than Julia's. Major William Chafyn-Grove's reflected on events in a male world. His son Chafyn's diaries were, it would seem, written to be entertaining and enlightening, with self-discipline and no alterations, regularly recorded on a daily basis. Julia's diaries were written in arrears, sometimes two weeks after events as she muddled dates, in one instance two succeeding Sundays were both called Palm Sunday, but they were more reflective and enlightening about her character. All the diaries are obsessed with the fear of illness and close monitoring of the weather. Staying indoors if it was too cold or too wet would prevent a life-threatening disease. There was the constant danger of the emotional loss of child and adult mortality as well as the practical consideration of running out of heirs.

From the 1870s there was a slow melting away in the fortunes of the landed gentry. Agricultural decline, rising industrialisation, and several Reform Acts in a series of political manoeuvres decreased the value of their land holdings. Levelling down had electoral momentum and there was no going back.

From Edwardian times to the mid-twentieth century, families who had suffered from losing heirs through war and financially through crippling death taxes, officially labelled estate duty, were abandoning their former estates or in the case of some of the great aristocratic houses, handed them to the National Trust. Although running out of money was predominately caused by death duties, on occasions it was human failure from poor financial management, gambling or over-indulgence as a few black sheep roamed amongst the flock on the country estates. Like Ferne House, many gentry houses were demolished.

When Zeals House was sold out of the Chafyn-Grove/Troyte-Bullock family, their status as landlords, acquired over five centuries, disappeared. The automatic respect and obedience of the estate tenants and within the village could no longer be taken for granted, as the family's hold over the lives of farm workers, maintenance men, gardeners and domestic servants evaporated. Now the Chafyn-Grove name is mostly forgotten, except for the highly respected Chafyn-Grove Preparatory School in Salisbury which still bears the name, along with remaining endowments in Zeals village and Mere from Julia's generosity. Without the estate, respect for the family dwindled away. As the Chafyn-Grove/Troyte-Bullocks relinquished the house, any remaining deference for the landlord's family members vanished. Their status was withdrawn; they became powerless.

It was Zeals House that held the power.

Abbreviations

DHS	Dorset History Centre
FSLS	Frome Society for Local Study
MEREM	Mere Museum
MHS	Mere Historical Society
NLA	National Library of Australia
RIBA	Royal Institute of British Architects
SHC	Somerset Heritage Centre
UOS	University of Sheffield
VCH	Victoria County History
WANHM	Wiltshire Archaeological and Natural History Magazine
WBR	Wiltshire Buildings Record
WSHC	Wiltshire and Swindon History Centre

Zeals Estate Map in 1994

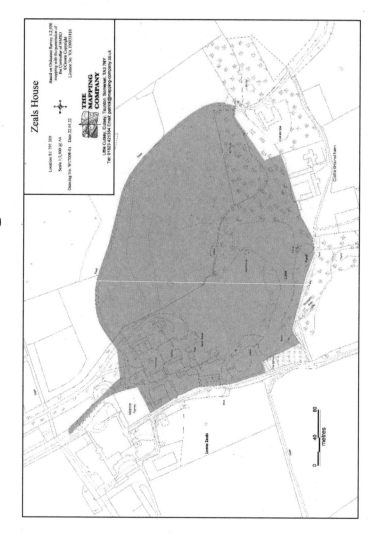

Zeals House

Location ST 797 319

Scale 1:2,500 @ A4

Drawing No. W17008-01   Date 22.04.22

Based on Ordnance Survey 1:2,500 mapping with the permission of the Controller of HMSO ©Crown Copyright
Licence No. VA 100053116

THE MAPPING COMPANY

Little Cutsey, Cutsey, Taunton, Somerset, TA3 7NY
Tel: 01823 421354 Email: patrol@mapping-company.co.uk

0   40   80
metres

Zeals Estate map *c.* 1994.

Family Trees

Chafyn / Chafyn-Grove Family Tree

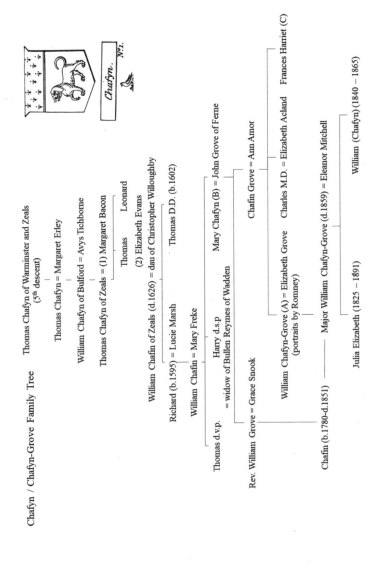

Thomas Chafyn of Warminster and Zeals
(5th descent)

Thomas Chafyn = Margaret Erley

William Chafyn of Bulford = Avys Tichborne

Thomas Chafyn of Zeals = (1) Margaret Bacon

Thomas   Leonard

(2) Elizabeth Evans

William Chafin of Zeals (d.1626) = dau of Christopher Willoughby

Richard (b.1595) = Lucie Marsh   Thomas D.D. (b.1602)

William Chafin = Mary Freke

Thomas d.v.p.

Harry d.s.p
= widow of Bullen Reymes of Wadden

Mary Chafyn (B) = John Grove of Ferne

Chafin Grove = Ann Amor

Rev. William Grove = Grace Snook

William Chafyn-Grove (A) = Elizabeth Grove
(portraits by Romney)

Charles M.D. = Elizabeth Acland   Frances Harriet (C)

Chafin (b.1780-d.1851) ———— Major William Chafyn-Grove (d.1859) = Eleanor Mitchell

Julia Elizabeth (1825 – 1891)   William (Chafyn) (1840 – 1865)

Troyte-Bullock Family Tree

Major William Chafyn-Grove (d.1859) = Eleanor Mitchell

William (Chafyn) (1840 – 1865)

Julia Elizabeth (1825 – 1891)

Maria Caroline = George Bullock

George Troyte-Bullock = Alice Welby-Gregory
(changed name on succession to Troyte-Chafyn-Grove)

Lt. Col. Edward Troyte-Bullock (1862-1942) = Grace Batton

George Troyte-Bullock (1900-1956) = Nina Yolande
(sold Zeals in 1968)

Charles

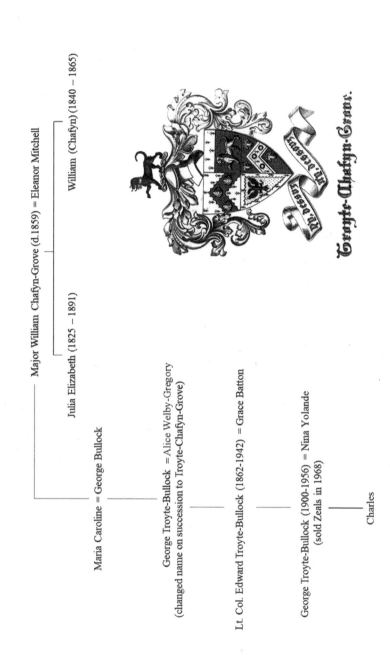

Troyte-Chafyn-Grove.

Endnotes

1. Nikolaus Pevsner and Bridget Cherry, *The Buildings of England, Wiltshire* (London: Penguin Books, 1975), p. 603.
2. Julian Orbach, Nikolaus Pevsner and Bridget Cherry, *The Buildings of England, Wiltshire* (New Haven and London, Yale University Press, 2021), p. 827-8.
3. Chippenham, Wiltshire and Swindon History Centre, WSHC.865/577. *The Journal of Julia Chafyn-Grove*, Vol. II, Spain and Wiltshire 1864-1865.
4. Ruth Newman and Jane Howells, *Salisbury Past* (Andover: Phillimore, 2001), p. 22.
5. *Wiltshire Archaeological and Natural History Magazine (WANHM)* vol xliv, no. clxxv, December, 1941, p. 479. C. R. Everett, 'Notes on the Diocesan Church House, Salisbury'.
6. *A History of the County of Wiltshire (VCH)* ed. By R. B. Pugh, vol. 5 (London: Oxford University Press, 1957), p. 36.
7. *City of Salisbury*, ed. By Hugh Shortt (London: Phoenix House Ltd., 1957), p. 50.
8. Nicholas Cooper, *Houses of the Gentry 1480-1680* (New Haven and London: Yale University Press, 1999), p. 6.
9. Historic England, Zeals House, Zeals. < https://britishlistedbuildings.co.uk 1318497-zeals-house-zeals>.
10. *Mere: A Wiltshire Country Town*, ed. by Norah Rutter and others (Shaftesbury: The Blackmore Press, 1975), p. 22.
11. William Harvey and George William Marshall, *The Visitation of Wiltshire, 1565* (Memphis: General Books, 2012), p. 6.
12. George Macaulay Trevelyan, *English Social History*, 1944. (London: Book Club Associates, 1973), p. 88.

13. *WANHM*, vol. 29 (Devizes: C. H. Woodward, 1897), pp. 322-324. T. H. Baker, 'Notes on the Documentary History of Zeals'.

14. Trevelyan, *English Social History*, p. 61.

15. Rev. J. E. Jackson, 'Charles Lord Stourton' *WANHM*, vol. 8 (Devizes: Henry Bull, 1864), pp. 304-306.

16. Rev. J. E. Jackson, 'Charles Lord Stourton' pp. 304-306.

17. *VCH Wiltshire*, ed. by R. Benson and H. Hatcher, 18 vols (London: Oxford University Press, 1962) pp. 200-206.

18. Timothy Mowl, *Elizabethan and Jacobean Style* (London: Phaidon Press, 1993), p. 93.

19. Richard Colt Hoare, *The History of Modern Wiltshire*, 8 vols (London: John Nichols & Son, 1822), vol 1, p. 12.

20. Richard Colt Hoare, *The History of Modern Wiltshire*, p. 12.

21. *Mere: A Wiltshire Country Town*, pp. 11-13.

22. John and Pamela McCann, *The Dovecotes and Pigeon Lofts of Wiltshire* (Salisbury: The Hobnob Press, 2011), pp. 135-139.

23. *The Visitation of Wiltshire, 1623*, ed. by George W. Marshall (London: George Bell & Sons, 1882), pp. 51, 57.

24. Richard Colt Hoare, *The History of Modern Wiltshire*, p. 33.

25. Note: Referred to as Thomas D.D. (Doctor of Divinity) to differentiate from the numerous Thomas Chafyns.

26. John Walker, *The Sufferings of the Clergy during the Great Rebellion* (London: F. Nicholson, 1714), p. 66.

27. A. G. Matthews, *A revision of John Walker's Suffering of the Clergy during the Grand Rebellion, 1642-60* (Oxford: Clarendon Press, 1988), p. 371.

28. Edward Hutton, *Highways and Byways in Wiltshire* (London: Macmillan, 1917), p. 230.

29. *WANHM*, vol. ii, 1855, p.30.

30. Charles Spencer, *To Catch a King* (William Collins, 2017), p. 219.

31. Richard Ollard, *The Escape of Charles II after the Battle of Worcester* (London: Constable and Co., 1986), p.116.

32. Richard Ollard, *The Escape of Charles II after the Battle of Worcester*, p. 116.

33. T. H. Baker, *Notes on the Documentary History of Mere*, WSHC.Mer.940, 1898, p.55.

34. Charles Spencer, *To Catch a King*, p. 219.

35. Richard Colt Hoare, *The History of Modern Wiltshire*, pp. 33-37.

36. T.H. Baker, 'Notes on the Documentary History of Mere', WSHC/Mer.940,1898, p.54.

37. Dorset History Centre (*DHS*), Rev. G. W. Saunders and Rev. R. G. Batelot, 'Letter from E. G. Troyte-Bullock', *Somerset & Dorset Notes & Queries*, vol 19, (Sherborne: J.C. and A. T. Sawtell, 1929), pp. 20-21.

38. Trevelyan, *English Social History*, p. 277.

39. Saunders and Bartelot, 'Letter from E. G. Troyte-Bullock', pp. 20-21.

40. Richard Colt Hoare, *The History of Modern Wiltshire*, p. 33.

41. *A Tale of Two Manors, Zeals a Wiltshire Village*, ed. by Gwyneth Jackson and others, (Somerset: Dickins, Printers, 1997), p. 97.

42. John and Pamela McCann, *The Dovecotes and Pigeon Lofts of Wiltshire*, p. 138.

43. Mary Chafin, *Original Country Recipes* (London: Macmillan, 1979), p. 7.

44. Trevelyan, *English Social History*, p. 280.

45. Richard Colt Hoare, *The History of Modern Wiltshire*, p. 15.

46. Helen Kaufman, *Conscientious Cavalier* (London: Jonathan Cape, 1962), p. 145.

47. Ibid. p. 145.

48. Kaufman, *Conscientious Cavalier*, p. 9.

49. WSHC. 865/40. Leases, land in Mere and Broughton, 1648.

50. WSHC. 865/28. Forty deeds relating to houses in specified streets in Mere, 1537-1794.

51. WSHC. 865/103. Four deeds relating to a house in West Waddon near Manor House, 1595-1663.

52. *Historic England, Zeals House, Zeals.* <https://britishlistedbuildings.co.uk/1318497-zeals-house-zeals>.

53. John Newman and Nikolaus Pevsner, *The Buildings of England, Dorset* (London: Penguin, 1975), p. 149.

54. William Chafen, *Anecdotes and History of Cranborne Chase, 1818.* (Wimborne: The Dovecote Press, 1991), p. 11.

55. The original part of the house bears similarities to the early part of Mells Park, Somerset (before substantial Victorian additions) by Ireson built in 1725, burnt down and subsequently demolished in 1917. The date, being built at the same time as the orangery is a further indication.

56. *A Tale of Two Manors*, p. 119.

57. Peter Fitzgerald, *Nathaniel Ireson of Wincanton, Architect, Master Builder and Potter* (Wimborne Minster: The Dovecote Press, 2016), p. 29.

58. WSHC.865/292.
59. *WANHM*, vol ii, 1855, pp. 29-30. T. H. Baker, 'Temporary Museum at the Council Chamber, Salisbury, List of Articles Exhibited, September 13th 1854 (on loan from William Chafyn-Grove of Zeals, Wiltshire).
60. *Burke's Landed Gentry*, ed. by Bernard Burke, ed., 2 vols (Oxford: Harrison and Sons, 1863), p. 608.
61. Richard Colt Hoare, *The History of Modern Wiltshire*, p. 37.
62. Trevelyan, *English Social History*, p. 314.
63. *The Burlington Magazine*, vol. 47, July 1930, p. 328. A. C. R. Carter, 'Forthcoming sales at Christies'. This article appears in 1930 when a later occupant of Zeals House offered to Christies a pair of portrait paintings which had been passed down to generations of Chafyn-Groves as part of the house. This portrait was purchased by Frederick L. Jack and was subsequently given to the Museum of Fine Arts, Boston. It was accessioned in 1935 (the companion portrait of Elizabeth Chafyn-Grove was unsold and remained at Zeals House).
64. *Burke's Landed Gentry*, Bernard Burke, ed., 8th edition. 2 vols (London: Harrison and Sons, 1894), p. 840.
65. *The English Chronicle*, as quoted in *The History of Parliament: The House of Commons, 1754-1790*, ed. J. Brooke, 1864.
66. WSHC. 865/294. Architectural drawings with detailed measurements by Joseph Saunders.
67. Engraving of Zeals House 1822, p. **. [check page no., pic11]
68. WSHC. 1641/110. *Will of William Ghafyn-Grove*, 1793.
69. *The Grove Diaries*, ed. by Desmond Hawkins, (Wimborne: The Dovecote Press, 1995), p. 39.
70. Steven Parissien, *Regency Style* (London: Phaidon Press, 1992), p, 12.
71. Parissien, *Regency Style*, p. 19.
72. Pauline Agius, *Ackermann's Regency Furniture and Interiors* (Marlborough, Wiltshire: The Crowood Press, 1984), pp.11-13. *The Repository of Arts Journal* was published 1809-1820.
73. *The Grove Diaries*, p. 175.
74. Ibid. p. 108.
75. Ibid. pp. 43-46. Thomas Grove Snr. had married Charlotte Pilfold, whose sister Elizabeth married Timothy Shelley. Percy Bysshe Shelley was their son.
76. *The Grove Diaries*, p. 73.
77. Ibid. p.86.
78. *The Grove Diaries*, p. 52.

79. Ibid. p. 102.
80. *The Grove Diaries*, p.105.
81. Ibid. p.108
82. Ibid. p.109.
83. *The Grove Diaries*, pp. 121, 173.
84. Two of Charlotte's sisters had died, Marianne in 1806 when her dress caught fire, aged 14, and Louisa, the youngest, in 1810, probably of scarlet fever, also aged 14.
85. *The Grove Diaries*, p. 175.
86. Equivalent to £94,000 today.
87. Equivalent to £235,000 today.
88. Wiltshire-opc.org.uk. 2014.
89. *The King's England, Wiltshire, Cradle of Our Civilisation*, ed. Arthur Mee (London: Hodder and Stoughton, 1943), 253.
90. Referred to as Major William Chafyn-Grove to differentiate from his uncle William and son William.
91. Singlestick was a kind of martial art using a wooden stick. It was used in training soldiers to use backswords.
92. Anon. *The Salisbury and Winchester Journal*, August 1814.
93. Trevelyan, *English Social History*, p. 470.
94. William Chafen, kinsman, the Chafen family having branched off from Zeals House.
95. WSHC. 865/570/1. *Journal of William Chafyn-Grove, Paris, 1819.*
96. WSHC. 865/570/1. 1819.
97. The Groves of Ferne, often referred to the Chafyn-Groves as a junior branch of the Ferne family, or the Groves of Zeals. To keep the identity of the Chafyn family alive, they often used the name Chafin as a Christian name.
98. Adrian Tinniswood, *His Invention so Fertile, The Life of Sir Christopher Wren* (London: Jonathan Cape, 2001, p.3.
99. WSHC. 865/574, *Diary of William Chafyn-Grove*, 1825.
100. WSHC. 865/574, October 1825.
101. Note: Thomas Grove Jnr. married 2nd wife, Elizabeth Hill of Gloucester in 1824.
102. WSHC. 865/574, 1825.
103. Note: From loose notes attached to WSHC. 865/574.
104. *The Grove Diaries*, p. 166.
105. Ibid. p. 112.
106. Ibid. p. 171.
107. WSHC.865/570/4. *The Diary of William Chafyn-Grove, 1831-1832.*

108. WSHC.865/570/4. *The Diary of William Chafyn-Grove,* 1831-1832.

109. *The Bristol Cable,* October, 2017. Steve Mills, 'The Bristol Reform Riots'.

110. Mills, 'The Bristol Reform Riots'.

111. North Coker House, Near Yeovil, Somerset, the home of her daughter Maria Caroline and her husband, George Bullock.

112. WSHC.865/570/4, *The Diary of William Chafyn-Grove,* 1831-1832.

113. Grove refers to Dr. John Grove of Close Gate, Salisbury

114. WHSC. 865/570/4.

115. *The Grove Diaries,* p. 172.

116. When William Beckford had left Fonthill for Bath he built a new house, Lansdown Tower.

117. WSHC 865/570/4, *Diary of (Major) William Chafyn-Grove,* Salisbury, 1831. p. 8.

118. Mayor Charles Pinney was acquitted. WSHC.865/570/4.

119. WSHC.865/570/4.

120. WSHC.865/570/4.

121. White was the tenant farmer at Manor Farm.

122. WSHC. 865/570/4, *Diary of William Chafyn-Grove,* Bath, 1832.

123. Sir Richard Colt Hoare, *The History of Modern Wiltshire,* 8 vols (London: John Nichols and Son, 1822), p. 35. This engraving is reproduced on page 8, illustration 4.

124. WSHC. 865/570/4.

125. *The Grove Diaries,* p. 188.

126. Trevelyan, *English Social History,* p. 493.

127. David Longbourne, *The Book of Mere, Portrait of a Wiltshire Town,* (Halsgrove, Wellington, Somerset: 2004, p. 51. Zeals became a separate parish in 1894.

128. *Wiltshire Archaeological and Natural History Magazine,* vol. xxviii, p. 210.

129. Nikolaus Pevsner and Bridget Cherry, *The Buildings of England, Wiltshire* (Penguin Books, London, 1975), p. 348.

130. *Silton, Records of a Dorset Village,* ed. by Silton Women's Institute (Castle Cary Press, Somerset, 1983), p. 128.

131. *A Tale of two Manors, Zeals,* p. 25.

132. Revd William Frederick Chafyn-Grove left a daughter Mary Anne, who married George St. Lo in her father's Melbury Abbas Church.

133. Emma Gatehouse, *Julia Chafyn-Grove and the Role of Elite Women in the Nineteenth Century,* History Dissertation HY6001, Bath, 164393.
134. WSHC. 865/596.
135. Helen Kaufman, *Conscientious Cavalier* (London: Jonathan Cape, 1962) p. 9.
136. Ibid. p. 9.
137. Ibid. p. 249.
138. WSHC.1641/118. *Will of (Major) William Chafyn-Grove,* 1852/Codicil 1857.
139. *Vimeira Magazine,* ed. William Chafyn-Grove, (Sydney: Wellbank and Reading, 1865), p.121. Sydney, Australia. National Art Library (NLA).
140. Peter Todd, Private collection.
141. Charles-Henry Grove was the ninth of the ten children of Thomas Grove Snr and Charlotte née Pilford.
142. WSHC. 865.522/521.
143. John Venn and J. A. Venn, *Alumni Cantabrigienses* (Cambridge: Cambridge University Press, 2011), p. 165.
144. Kenneth Clark, *The Gothic Revival* (London: John Murray, 1962), p. 45.
145. *Fonthill Revisited, A Cultural History,* ed. by Caroline Dakers, (London: UCL Press 2018), p. 149.
146. The Marquess of Westminster was created Duke of Westminster in 1874 by Queen Victoria.
147. *Country Life,* 8/4 1971, p. 812. Mark Girouard, *'The Rural Architecture for the Rich, George Devey in Kent II'.*
148. Josephine Walpole, *Art and Artists of the Norwich School* (Woodbridge, Suffolk: Antiques Collectors' Club, 1997), p. 85.
149. Jill Allibone, *George Devey, Architect, 1820-1886* (Cambridge: The Lutterworth Press, 1991), p. 18.
150. *Journal of the Royal Institute of British Architects,* 1906, 3rd series, vol xxi, no. 19. Walter Hindes Godfrey, *'George Devey, A Biographical Essay'.*
151. *Architectural Association Journal,* 24/266, April 1909, p. 96. James Williams, *'George Devey and His Work'.*
152. John Newman, *The Buildings of England, West Kent and the Weald* (London: Penguin Books Ltd. 1976), p. 115.
153. Jill Allibone, *George Devey, Architect,* p. 42.
154. *Journal of the Royal Institute of British Architects,* 3rd series, no. 22, 5 December, 1914, p. 66. W. S. Perchon, *'University of Sheffield Collection of George Devey's Drawings'.*

155. Christopher Hussey, *English Country Houses, Late Georgian, 1800-1840* (London: Country Life Limited, 1955), p. 193.

156. *Journal of the Royal Institute of British Architects*, W. S. Perchon, p. 66.

157. Walter Godfrey, *The Work of George Devey* (London: B. T. Batsford, 1907), p. 3.

158. Jill Allibone, *George Devey, Architect*, 1820-1886, p. 42.

159. WSHC.865/577. *The Journal of Julia Chafyn-Grove*, 1864-1865, p. 107.

160. WSHC.865/577. *The Journal of Julia Chafyn-Grove*, 1864-1865, p. 90.

161. *Architectural Association Journal*, 24/266, April 1909, p. 95, James Williams, '*George Devey and His Work*'.

162. *Journal of the Royal Institute of British Architects*, 8/19, 1906, p. 508, Walter Hindes Godfrey, '*George Devey, A Biographical Essay*'.

163. *Journal of the Royal Institute of British Architects*, Walter Hindes Godfrey, '*George Devey, A Biographical Essay*, p. 516.

164. *Country Life*, 8/4 1971, p. 812. Mark Girouard, '*The Rural Architecture for the Rich, George Devey* in Kent II'.

165. Equivalent of approximately £6.7 million today.

166. WSHC.865/577. *Journal of Julia Chafyn-Grove*, 1864, pp. 7-8.

167. Built for Prince Albert's 1862 Exhibition, replaced by the Albert Hall.

168. University of Sheffield. (UOS), Photograph album of houses by George Devey, 1850-1890.

169. WSHC.865/570/8. *Diary of William Chafyn-Grove, Vol. II, Egypt. 1864.* Note: All quotations in this chapter from this diary unless otherwise referenced. (vol. i, the first part of the voyage, is missing).

170. John White was the tenant farmer of the Manor Farm at Zeals.

171. Revd Charles Townsend, Vicar of Mere Church.

172. James Bruce, 8th Earl of Elgin, at the time of his death in November 1863, Viceroy of India.

173. Murray's Handbook for Egypt Guide, published by John Murray in 1847.

174. R. E. Foster, *Sidney Herbert, Too Short a Life* (Gloucester: The Hobnob Press, 2019), pp. 56-57.

175. R. E. Foster, *Sidney Herbert, Too Short a* Life (Gloucester: The Hobnob Press, 2019), pp. 432-433. Note: Lady

Herbert would eventually convert to become a Roman Catholic in 1865.

176. Befriended by Julia.

177. Ann England. Julia's maid from Zeals House.

178. Shipping Agent

179. P & O paddle steamer *Syria* was built in Northam, Southampton in 1863 specifically for the Southampton-Alexandria route.

180. NLA. *Vimeira Magazine,* ed. William Chafyn-Grove (Sydney: Reading and Wellbank, 1864-1865), p. 14.

181. WSHC.865/577. *The Journal of Julia Chafyn-Grove,* vol ii, Spain, 1864. All quotations in this chapter are from this Journal unless otherwise referenced. (vol. i is missing).

182. NLA. *Vimeira Magazine,* ed. by William Chafyn-Grove (Sydney: Reading and Wellbank, 1865), p. 15.

183. WSHC.865/577. *The Journal of Julia Chafyn-Grove*, Vol. II, Spain and Wiltshire. 1864. All quotations in this chapter are from this Journal unless otherwise referenced.

184. The six daughters of Charles-Henry and Eliza Grove: Emily Charlotte, b. 1832, Agnes, b. 1841, Alice, b. 1843, Elizabeth, Julia and Philippa (called Phyllis).

185. WSHC. 865/577. pp. 7-8.

186. Ibid.

187. *The Diary of Charlotte Downes, 1857,* ed. John William Lane and Valerie Lane Kay, 2 vols (Ardleigh, Colchester: Claret Jug Publications, 2014), p. 387. Charlotte Grove married The Revd Richard Downes.

188. A portrait of Gussy Hoare aged 14 hangs at Stourhead, painted by Frederick Leighton.

189. WSHC.865/577. *The Journal of Julia Chafyn-Grove,* vol. ii, 1864. All quotations in this chapter are from this Journal unless otherwise referenced.

190. Stephen Anderton with Alan Power, *Stourhead* (National Trust Books, London, 2019), p. 72.

191. Alfred's Tower on the Stourhead Estate on the Wiltshire/Somerset border. King Alfred's Tower was built to commemorate the end of the Seven Years' War and the accession of George III by Henry Hoare II in 1772 and is 161ft. (49m) high. The architect was Henry Flitcroft.

192. WSHC. 865/577. p. 21.

193. Caroline Dakers, *Clouds, The Biography of a Country House* (Yale University Press, New Haven and London, 1993), p. 72.

194. A portion of this 'queer lot' is now in the British Museum.
195. WSHC. 865/577. p. 25.
196. Babington House, Somerset, now a hotel.
197. WSHC. 865/577. p. 30.
198. WSHC.865/570/9. *The Diary of William Chafyn-Grove,* Australia, Ceylon and Bombay. All quotes in this chapter are from this diary unless otherwise referenced.
199. WSHC.85.577. The Journal of Julia Chafyn'Grove, Vol. II, Spain and Wiltshire. All references quoted in this chapter are from this Journal unless otherwise stated.
200. Tom Grove went to Sherborne School.
201. WSHC. 865/570/9. *Diary of William Chafyn-Grove,* Vol II, Australia, Ceylon and Bombay, 1864-1865. All quotations in this chapter are from this diary unless otherwise referenced.
202. NLA. *Vimeira Magazine,* ed. by William Chafyn-Grove (Sydney, Australia: Reading and Wellbank, 1865), p 167.
203. NLA. *Vimeira Magazine,* contributor, James Attwood, ed. by William Chafyn-Grove, (Sydney, Australia: Reading and Wellbank, 1865), p. 103.
204. Chafyn is informed by a later letter from Chisholm that Mrs Chisholm had lost her baby. Her constant sickness on board was likely to have been morning sickness rather than sea sickness.
205. The *Duncan Dunbar,* eight months later in August 1865 was shipwrecked off the coast of Brazil and sank, all passengers surviving under difficult circumstances.
206. Perthdps.com. con-wa38.
207. Sir John Young, Governor of New South Wales. Later Governor of Canada.
208. C.S.S. *Shenandoah* was part of the US Confederate Navy and fired the last shot in the American Civil War. In 1864-1865, in an effort to disrupt the Union's economy she raided commercial ships around the world, mostly whaling ships. She docked in Williamstown, Melbourne on 25th January 1865 to fill her storerooms and complement where Capt. Waddell signed up stowaways as crew. The Shipping Articles show 40 crew enlisted when out of territorial waters, but before departure 19 of the crew deserted, some giving statements of their service to the United States. In Liverpool, in November 1865, she surrendered.
209. John Herring Snr, prolific painter of farmyard scenes.

210. St Pauls Church designed by Victorian ecclesiastical architect Richard Cromwell Carpenter in 1848.

211. St Michael's Church. Arts and Crafts architect George F Bodley and Victorian architect William Burges both worked at St. Michael's Brighton in 1860-1 and 1893-1895 respectively.

212. *Census 1861*. Thomas King, Coachman at Zeals House.

213. WSHC. 865/577. *The Journal of Julia Chafyn-Grove*, Vol II, Spain and Wiltshire 1864-1865. All references in this chapter are from this Journal unless otherwise referenced.

214. Druce's furniture bazaar, Baker Street, London.

215. WSHC. T.H. Baker, MER 940.1898. p. 67.

216. The du Boulay family of Donhead Hall, Donhead St. Mary, Shaftesbury, Dorset

217. The Hussey family of Salisbury. James Hussey married Tom Grove's sister, Henrietta.

218. WSHC.865/570/9. *Diary of William Chafyn-Grove*, Australia, Ceylon and Bombay 1964-1965. All quotations in this chapter are from this diary unless otherwise referenced.

219. Sir Frederick Pottinger (1831-1865), police inspector in N.S.W., known for his fight against bushrangers.

220. Named after William Govett, an early surveyor of the upper Blue Mountains, 1831.

221. WSHC. 865/577. *Journal of Julia Chafyn-Grove*. Vol. II. Spain and Wiltshire. 1984-1865. All quotations in this chapter are from this journal unless otherwise referenced.

222. Rector of Stourton

223. WSHC. 865/570/9. *Diary of William Chafyn-Grove*. Vol. II. Australia, Ceylon and Bombay. 1864-1965. All quotations in this chapter are from this diary unless otherwise referenced.

224. A year later in 1866, the A.S.N.C *Cawarra* (built in Glasgow in 1864), sank in a fierce gale off Newcastle, N.S.W. with the loss of 60 souls. One passenger survived.

225. P & O *Northam* built in 1858.

226. This photograph, probably sent to Julia at her request, was taken after he had been in the bush for four months, where he would have had long hair and a long beard as seen in the image of Chafyn in this chapter.

227. WSHC.865.577. Journal of Julia Chafyn-Grove, Vol. II, Spain and Wiltshire, 1864-1865. All quotations are from this journal unless otherwise stated.

228. The dowager, Mrs John Grove, Tom Grove's mother.

229. WSHC. 865/570/9. *Diary of William Chafyn-Grove,* Vol. II, Australia, Ceylon and Bombay. 1864-1865. All quotations in this chapter are from this diary unless otherwise referenced.

230. WSHC. 865/570/9. *Diary of William Chafyn-Grove,* Vol. II, Australia, Ceylon and Bombay, 1864-1865. All quotations in this chapter are from this diary unless otherwise referenced.

231. WSHC. 865/577. *Journal of Julia Chafyn-Grove,* Vol. II, Spain and Wiltshire, 1864-1865. All quotations in this chapter are from this Journal unless otherwise referenced.

232. Julian Orbach, Nikolaus Pevsner and Bridget Cherry, *The Buildings of England, Wiltshire* (New Haven and London: Yale University Press, 2021), p. 287.

233. S S *Baroda*, a passenger/cargo ship of the British India Steam Navigation Co. Ltd. Arrived in Bombay 4th November, 1865.

234. WSHC. 865/570/9. *Diary of William Chafyn-Grove,* Vol. II, Australia, Ceylon and Bombay. 1864-1865. All quotations in this chapter are from this diary unless otherwise referenced.

235. WSHC. 865/570/9. *Diary of William Chafyn-Grove,* India, 1865. p. 198.

236. David Powell Snr. of Hampstead. Family friends of the Chafyn-Groves. David Powell Jnr. was with Chafyn in Sydney and Melbourne.

237. Lord Edward St. Maur, second son of Edward Seymour, 12th Duke of Somerset (b. 1841, d. Yellapoor, India, December 1865).

238. Capt. Henry Brand, (b. 1841, left Coldstream Guards in October 1865). Became Liberal MP for Stroud, later 2nd Viscount Hampden and 24th Baron Dacre on death of father 1892. In 1895 became Governor General of N.S.W., Australia, d. 1906.

239. Anne de Courcy, *The Fishing Fleet* (Weidenfeld & Nicolson, London, 2012), p. 195.

240. Lieutenant W. C. Grove (lost) Imperial War Museums Tablet, iwm.org.uk

241. *Memoirs of a Victorian Farmer,* ed. Michael McGarvie (Frome Society for Local History, 1990), p. 9.

242. Over-scaled pieces of furniture and porcelain featured in the Great Exhibition in 1851 and seeing such pieces displayed, well-heeled visitors copied them, but they had been deliberately over-scaled as exhibition pieces only.

243. Historic England, Zeals House, Zeals, https://britishlistedbuildings.co.uk. 1318497-zeals-house-zeals>.

244. *Property Review, Salisbury*, c. 1972, p, 119, Mere History Society (MHS). 324/B. Anon. '*Zeals House, a Tudor house with a Cromwellian Ghost*', (interview with Alex Garnet Phippen).

245. Equivalent to approximately £132,000 today.

246. Neville Wilkinson, *The Guards' Chapel* (London: The Chiswick Press, 1938), p. 192.

247. Lieutenant W. C. Grove (lost) Imperial War Museums Tablet, iwm.org.uk.

248. This window is now at Waddon Manor, Portesham, Dorset.

249. *Journal of the Royal Institute of British Architects*, 3rd series vol xiii, no. 19, 1906, Walter Hindes Godfrey, '*George Devey, A Biographical Essay*', p. 524.

250. *Architectural Association Journal*, 24/266, April 1909, p. 95. James Williams, '*George Devey and His Work*'.

251. Jill Allibone, *George Devey, Architect*, p. 51.

252. Mark Girouard, *The Victorian Country House* (New Haven and London: Yale University Press, 1979), p. 19.

253. *Memoirs of a Victorian Farmer* ed. Michael McGarvie (Frome Society of Local Studies, 1990), p. 105.

254. *Royal Institute of British Architects*, 8/19, 1906, p. 50. Walter Hindes Godfrey, '*George Devey, A Biographical Essay*'.

255. *Architectural Association Journal*, 24/266, April 1909, p. 100. James Williams, '*George Devey and His Work*'.

256. *A Tale of Two Manors*, p. 98.

257. *Census Returns*, R.G. 9/1324, Zeals House, Mere, Wiltshire, 1861.

258. *Census Returns*, Zeals House, 1881.

259. The cottage referred to could have been Swiss Cottage in Zeals village, which reprises many of Devey's cottage features, including the diagonal chimneys as seen on the almshouses.

260. *The Tale of Two Manors*, p. 98.

261. *Country Life*, 8/4 1971.Mark Girouard, '*The Rural Architecture for the Rich, George Devey in Kent II*', p. 812.

262. Nicholas Cooper, *Houses of the Gentry*, 1480-1680 (New Haven and London: Yale University Press, 1999), pp. 61-64.

263. *Property Review*, Salisbury, c. 1972. MHS. 324/B. Anon. '*Zeals House, A Tudor House with a Cromwellian Ghost*', (Interview with Alex Garnet Phippen), p.119.

264. John and Pamela McCann, *The Dovecotes and Pigeon Lofts of Wiltshire* (Salisbury: The Hobnob Press, 2011), p. 136.

265. *A Tale of Two Manors*, p. 107.

266. *Property Review,* Salisbury, c. 1972, MHS.324/B. Anon. *'Zeals House, A Tudor House with a Cromwellian Ghost',* (Interview with Alex Garnet Phippen), p. 119.
267. WSHC.865/577, *Diary of Julia Chafyn-Grove,* 1864, pp. 1-4.
268. WSHC.865/564. 1905.
269. Later used extensively on Devey's Queen Anne London townhouses in the 1880s.
270. This report is in the same location as the secluded priest hole, confirming Charles II's stay.
271. *Commonplace Book and Journal,* compiled 1885-1895, T. H. Baker. Somerset History Centre, (SHC), (A/SBS/1).
272. Referred to later as the Tapestry Room.
273. *Commonplace Book and Journal,* T. H. Baker. SHC. compiled 1885-1895. (A/ABS/1).
274. Arthur Mee, *The King's England – Wiltshire* (London: Hodder and Stoughton, 1939, reprinted 1943), p. 393.
275. *WANHM,* vol.II, 1855, pp.26-30.
276. Trevelyan, *English Social History,* p. 552.
277. *Memoirs of a Victorian Farmer,* ed. by Michael McGarvie, (Frome Society for Local Study, 1990), p. 104.
278. James Holden, *Wiltshire Gate Lodges* (Gloucester: The Hobnob Press, 2018), p. 103.
279. WSHC. 865/602. *Julia Chafyn-Grove,* Certificate of visit to the Holy Land, 1873.
280. WSHC .865/596. *Julia Chafyn-Grove,* Theological Extracts, 1847.
281. *The Grove Diaries,* p. 234.
282. *A Tale of Two Manors,* p. 100.
283. *Memoirs of a Victorian Farmer,* p. 101.
284. WSHC. 865/598. *Julia Chafyn-Grove,* Season Ticket for the Great Exhibition, 1851.
285. Salisbury Cathedral, North Transcept Noticeboard.
286. Salisbury Cathedral, Julia's donation acknowledged on the North Transept Notice Board.
287. Approximately £650,000 in today's money.
288. WSHC. PR/Zeals St. Martin/2948/7. *Will of Julia Chafyn-Grove.*
289. *The Journal,* Salisbury, 10/6 1976, Anon. *'Chafyn-Grove Remembers the Lady from Zeals',* p. 9.
290. Stephen Anderton with Alan Power, *Stourhead* (London: National Trust Books, 2019), p. 121.
291. *A Tale of Two Manors,* p. 98.

292. *Memoirs of a Victorian Farmer*, p. 105.

293. *A Tale of Two Manors*, p. 192.

294. WSHC. 865/577. *Journal of Julia Chafyn-Grove*, Spain, 1964, p. 30.

295. *Commonplace Book and Journal*, 1892, T. H. Baker. SHC. A/ABS/1.G.828. p. 334.

296. Tom Grove initially withdrew consent to Walter and Agnes's marriage as the dowry was too modest, but love and negotiation won the day.

297. *Silton, Records of a Dorset Village*, p. 17.

298. *Memoirs a Victorian Farmer*, p.105.

299. Ibid. p. 104.

300. *A Tale of Two Manors, Zeals*, p. 100.

301. Ibid. p. 122.

302. WSHC. T. H. Baker, MER.940.1898. Short Notes. p. 3.

303. Ibid.

304. The medieval Church House, Salisbury, was rebuilt into a workhouse and latterly is an event venue.

305. George's first wife, Emily Portman, had died after only a few months of the 1856 marriage.

306. *Burke's Landed Gentry*, 1914.

307. George Bullock, (1798-1885). Hannah m. in 1827, the Revd. Rowland Huyshe, Mary m. in 1828, the Revd. Henry Michell.

308. *Burke's Landed Gentry*, 1914.

309. Maria Caroline Chafyn-Grove *(1797-1866)*.

310. Asa Briggs, *A Social History of England* (London: Weidenfeld and Nicolson, 1983), p. 231.

311. David Cannadine, *The Decline and Fall of the English Aristocracy* (New Haven and London: Yale University Press, 1990), p. 68.

312. *A Tale of Two Manors, Zeals*, p. 110. Manor Farm was known as The Parsonage from 1781-1831 on Land Tax Returns.

313. C.E. Pointing, F.S.A. MER.940.1898. p. 7.

314. *Silton*, p. 37.

315. Julia's godchild Eddie's siblings were his elder sister Mabel Cecily (Chafyn's goddaughter) and the younger Isabel Annie, Evelyn Mary (poignantly born on 12th November 1865, the day before Chafyn died), Hugh Ambrose, Cecil John, and Alice Christine.

316. *Silton*, p. 18.

317. *Silton.* p. 109.
318. Ibid. p. 95.
319. Ibid. p. 97.
320. Ibid. p. 97.
321. WSHC. 865/564.
322. WSHC. 865/564.
323. WSHC. 865/564. 1905.
324. WSHC. 1265/117.
325. WSHC. 1265/117.1911-1912.
326. *A Tale of Two Manors, Zeals*, p.97.
327. WSHC. 865/566.
328. Silton. p. 177.
329. Silton. p. 101.
330. Captain Wedgwood Benn (later killed), 1/1 County of London Yeomanry, from *The Naval Memoirs of Admiral of the Fleet Sir Roger* Keyes (London: Thornton Butterworth, 1934), p. 421
331. Stephen Chambers, *Suvla August Offensive* (Barnsley, South Yorkshire: Pen and Sword Military, 2011), p. 173.
332. Wessex Yeomanry, 2015, on the 100th anniversary of the attack on Scimitar Hill.
333. On 22nd August Major Goodden was wounded in the head, and evacuated, but died a month later.
334. Teichman, O., *The Diary of a Yeoman M.O.* (London: Fisher Unwin Ltd., 1921).
335. Note accompanying sale of medal.
336. Extract from *London Gazette Supplement*, 3.6.1916. pp. 55-59.
337. Caroline Dakers, *Clouds, The Biography of a Country House* (New Haven and London: Yale University Press, 1993), p. 193.
338. Stephen Anderton with Alan Power, *Stourhead* (London: National Trust Books, 2019), p. 142.
339. David Longbourne, *The Book of Mere, Portrait of a Wiltshire Town*, (Wellington, Somerset: Halsgrove, 2004, p. 76.
340. *Mere, A Wiltshire Country Town* ed. by Norah Rutter and Others, (Shaftesbury, Dorset: The Blackmore Press, 1975), p. 64.
341. Stephen Anderton and Alan Power, *Stourhead* (London: National Trust Books, 2019), pp. 143-144.
342. Ibid. p. 144.
343. Adrian Tinniswood, *The Long Weekend, Life in the English Country House between the Wars* (London: Jonathan Cape, 2016), p. 3.

344. Garden folly, recently restored. No longer part of the Zeals Estate.
345. Recollections of Bill Woodhouse.
346. Recollections of Bill Woodhouse.
347. Geoffrey Sebag-Montefiore, letters 1926.
348. Geoffrey was educated at Eton College and Sandhurst.
349. Andrew Saint, Richard Norman Shaw (New Haven and London: Yale University Press, 2010), p. 355.
350. Stephen Anderton and Alan Power Stourhead (London: National Trust Books, 2019), p. 147.
351. Samuel Vernon Mann III, New York, USA. geni.com
352. *Who's Who in Architecture,* Frederick Chatterton, ed., (London: The Architectural Press, 1923), p.195, p. 211.
353. RIBA Drawings, V & A, Rolfe and Peto, Bath.
354. RIBA Drawings V&A., Rolfe and Peto for Zeals House, 1931. PA411/6/1-16.
355. Walter Hinds Godfrey, *The Work of George Devey* (London: B. T. Batsford, 1907), p. 12.
356. David Cannadine, *The Decline and Fall of the British Aristocracy* (New Haven and London: Yale University Press, 1992), p. 112.
357. David Longbourne, *The Book of Mere,* (Wellington, Somerset: Halsgrove, 2004), p. 52.
358. A.C. R. Carter, ed., 'Forthcoming Sales at Christies', *The Burlington Magazine,* 47, July 1930, p. 238. The portraits of William Chafyn-Grove and his wife Elizabeth Chafyn-Grove of 1789-1780.
359. *A Tale of Two Manors*/Bill Woodhouse, p. 107.
360. Ibid. p. 107.
361. *A Tale of Two Manors*/Bill Woodhouse, p. 101.
362. Ibid. p. 104.
363. Ibid. p. 108.
364. Ibid. p. 104.
365. Ibid. p. 107.
366. Ibid. p. 106.
367. Ibid. Geoffrey Sebag-Montefiore had married Elizabeth Grace Troyte-Bullock (known as Betty), eldest daughter of Edward and Grace.
368. Ibid. Mary Winifred Troyte-Bullock, middle daughter of Edward and Grace married Jack D'Aeth.
369. Ibid. p. 107. Sally, Bill's sister, born on holiday in Devonshire on one of her parents' visits to Zeals on leave.

370. Ibid. pp. 8-9.
371. Ibid. p. 109.
372. WSHC. 1265/129. Grace Troyte-Bullock was 66 years of age in 1941.
373. *A Tale of Two Manors*, p. 181.
374. David Berryman, *Wiltshire Airfields in the Second World War* (Newbury, Berkshire: Countryside Books), p. 13.
375. WSHC.1265/129.
376. Stephen Anderton and Alan Power, *Stourhead* (London: National Trust Books, 2019), p. 146.
377. WSHC. 1265/129.
378. Ibid. p. 109.
379. *Silton*, p. 39.
380. Letter from Mere & Tisbury Rural District Council to Rawlence and Squarey, 26th February 1943. WSHC. 1265/129.
381. WSHC. 1265/135.
382. WSHC. 1265/132.
383. Bernard Pike, from *The Michael Tighe Memorial Archive*, MHS.453.63.
384. Wiltshire Airfields in the Second World War, p. 233.
385. Ibid.
386. Stephen Alderton and Alan Power, *Stourhead* (London: National Trust Books, 2019), p. 146.
387. Bernard Pike, from *The Michael Tighe Memorial Archive*, MHS. 453.63.
388. *Wiltshire Airfields in the Second World War*, p. 240.
389. Ibid. p. 242.
390. David Longbourne, *The Book of Mere, Portrait of a Wiltshire Town* (Wellington, Somerset: Halsgrove, 2008), pp. 141-142.
391. Memoir of Bill Woodhouse, *A Tale of Two Manors, Zeals*, p. 110.
392. David Cannadine, *The Decline and Fall of the British Aristocracy* (New Haven and London: 1990), p. 97.
393. Hugh Ambrose Troyte-Bullock was the second son of George and Alice Troyte-Chafyn-Grove.
394. Memoir of Bill Woodhouse. *A Tale of Two Manors*, p. 108.
395. *A Tale of Two Manors*, p. 193.
396. DHS. D-635/1. RON/2/2/Silton/4.
397. Ibid. p. 119.
398. *Property Review, Salisbury* (c.1972), p. 119. MHS.234B. Anon, 'Zeals House, A Tudor House with a Cromwellian Ghost'.

399. Kenneth Clark, The *Gothic Revival, An Essay in the History of Taste* (London: John Murray, 1962), p. 9.

400. *Property Review, Salisbury,* (c. 1972), p. 119. MHS.234B. Anon. *'Zeals House, a Tudor House with a Cromwellian Ghost'.*

401. *Country Life,* 23 September 1976, p. 5. (supplement), 'Zeals House for Sale advertisement by Peasons/Hampton and Sons'.

402. *Country Life,* 30 December 1982. Michael Hanson, *'The Market Report, Year of the Disappearing Doldrums'.*

403. *The Daily Telegraph,* 1 December 1976, p. 23. Arthur Bowers, *'Houses and Estates'.*

404. Pearsons Brochure, 15 June 1977. MHS. *Sale of Contents of Zeals House.*

405. *Country Life,* 21 June 1979, p. 57. (supplement) MHS.237/9. 'Zeals House for Sale Advertisement by John German Ralph Pay'.

406. *Country Life,* 13 May 1982, p. 33. (supplement), 'Zeals House for Sale advertisement by Strutt and Parker'.

407. *Country Life,* 30 December 1982. Michael Hanson, 'The Market Report, Year of the Disappearing Doldrums'.

408. Jill Allibone, *George Devey, Architect,* (Cambridge: The Luterworth Press, 1991), p. 157.

409. WSHC. T. H. Baker, MER.1898. (supplement, p.3).

410. Walter Hindes Godfrey, *The Work of George Devey,* (London: B. T. Batsford, 1907), p. 30.

411. UOS.MS.281.

412. Walter Hindes Godfrey, *The Work of George Devey,* p. 15/ RIBA.PB.818/3/(6).

413. Jill Franklin, *The Gentleman's Country House and its Plan, 1835-1914* (London: Routledge and Kegan Paul, 1981), p. 262.

414. Robert Kerr, *The Gentleman's House* (London: John Murray, 1864), p. 387.

415. *Journal of the Royal Institute of British Architects,* 8/19, 1906, p. 516. Walter Hindes Godfrey, *'George Devey, A Biographical Essay'.*

416. Mark Girouard, *The Victorian Country House* (New Haven and London: Yale University Press, 1979), pp.84-95.

417. Mark Girouard, *Sweetness and Light, The 'Queen Anne' Movement, 1860-1900* (Oxford: The Clarendon Press, 1977), p. 25.

418. Gavin Stamp and André Goulancourt, *The English House 1860-1914 (*London: Faber and Faber Limited, 1976), p. 50.
419. Andrew Saint, *Richard Norman Shaw* (New Haven and London: Yale University Press, 2010), p. 100.
420. Henry Russell-Hitchcock, *Architecture, Nineteenth and Twentieth Centuries* (London: Penguin Books, 1958), p. 453.
421. Lawrence Weaver, *Country Life Library – Architectural Monographs – Edwin Lutyens* (London: Hudson & Hearns Ltd. Printers, 1913), p. vii.
422. Gavin Stamp and André Goulancourt, *The English House 1860-1914, The Flowering of English Domestic Architecture* (London: Faber and Faber Limited, 1986), p. 50.
423. *Apollo,* 6 August 2018, Charles Holland, 'The Eclectic Country Houses of George Devey', and *Apollo,* July August, 2018, pp. 30-31, 'George Devey was a Magpie with a Painters' Sensibility'.
424. *The Victorian,* the magazine of the Victorian Society, No. 63. 3/2020. Timothy Brittain-Catlin, 'George Devey: The Architect as Artist and Archaeologist', pp. 4-7.
425. Jill Allibone, *George Devey, Architect,* p. 51.
426. Jill Allibone, *George Devey, Architect* (Cambridge: The Lutterworth Press, 1991), p. 134.
427. Mark Girouard, *The Victorian Country House* (New Haven and London: Yale University Press, 1979), p.83.
428. *Country Life,* 8 December 1994, p. 56. Huon Mallalieu, 'The Property Market, Haunted Houses for Sale', ed. Melanie Cable-Alexander.
429. David Longbourne, *The Book of Mere* (Halgrave, Wellington, Somerset: 2004), p. 52.
430. Ibid.
431. *The Blackmore Vale Magazine,* 21 February, 2021, pp. 16-18. Steve Keenan, *'Prestigious Past and Desperate Decay'.*
432. *Private Eye,* Nooks and Corners, 11-24 June 2021, No. 1549, p. 23.

Bibliography

Allibone, Jill, *George Devey, Architect, 1820-1886* (Cambridge: Lutterworth Press, 1991)

Anderton, Stephen and A. Power, *Stourhead* (London: National Trust Books, 2019)

Arius, Pauline, *Ackermann's Regency Furniture and Interiors* (Marlborough, Wiltshire: The Crowood Press, 1884)

Aslet, Clive, *The Last Country Houses* (London: Book Club Associates, 1982)

Beamish, Derek, *et al.*, *Mansions and Merchants of Poole and Dorset* (Poole: Poole Historical Trust, 1976)

Benson, R. and H. Hatcher, ed., *A History of the County of Wiltshire (VCH)* vol. vi (London: Oxford University Press, 1962)

Berryman, David, *Wiltshire Airfields in the Second World War* (Newbury, Berkshire: Countryside Books, 2009)

Briggs, Asa, *A Social History of England* (London: Weidenfeld and Nicolson, 1983)

Brodie, Antonia, *et al.*, eds, *Dictionary of British Architects 1834-1914* (London and New York: Continuum, 2001)

Burke, Bernard, ed., *Burke's Landed Gentry* (London: Harrison and Son, 1863)

Burke, Bernard, ed., *Burke's Landed Gentry* (London: Harrison and Son, 1894)

Cannadine, David, *The Decline and Fall of the British Aristocracy* (New Haven and London: Yale University Press, 1990)

Cannadine, David, *Victorious Century: The United Kingdom 1800-1906* (London: Allen Lane, 2017)

Coldstream, Nicola, *Medieval Architecture* (Oxford: Oxford University Press, 2002)

Chafin, Mary, *Original Country Recipes* (London: Macmillan, 1979)

Chatterton, Frederick, ed., *Who's Who in Architecture* (London: The Architectural Press, 1923)

Clark, Kenneth, *The Gothic Revival* (London: John Murray, 1962)

Collins, Bruce, *Wellington and the Siege of San Sebastian 1813* (Barnsley: Pen and Sword Books, 2017)

Colvin, Howard, *The Biographical Dictionary of British Architects, 1600-1840* (New Haven and London: Yale University Press, 2008)

Cooper, Nicholas, *Houses of the Gentry, 1480-1680* (New Haven and London: Yale University Press, 1999)

Cornforth, John, *The Inspiration of the Past* (London: Viking, 1985)

Crook, J. Mordaunt, *The Rise of the Nouveaux Riches* (London: John Murray, 1999)

Dakers, Caroline, *Clouds, The Biography of a Country House* (New Haven and London: Yale University Press, 1991)

Dakers, Caroline, ed., *Fonthill Recovered* (London: UCL Press, 2018)

Dodd, Dudley, Stourhead: *Henry Hoare's Paradise Revisited* (London: Head of Zeus Ltd., 2021)

Fitzgerald, Peter, *Nathaniel Ireson* (Wimborne: The Dovecote Press, 2016)

Foster, R. E., *Sidney Herbert: Too Short a Life* (Gloucester: The Hobnob Press, 2019)

Franklin, Jill, *The Gentleman's Country House and its Plan*, 1835-1914 (London: Routledge and Kegan Paul, 1981)

Fraser, Antonia, *Charles II: His Life and Times* (London: Weidenfeld and Nicolson, 1993)

Gemmett, Robert J., *William Beckford's Fonthill* (UK and USA: Fonthill Media, 2016)

Gere, Charlotte, *Nineteenth-Century Decoration, the Art of the Interior* (London: Weidenfeld and Nicolson, 1989)

Girouard, Mark, *Elizabethan Architecture* (New Haven and London: Yale University Press, 2009)

Girouard, Mark, *Sweetness and Light, The 'Queen Anne' Movement, 1860-1900* (Oxford: Oxford University Press, 1977)

Girouard, Mark, *The Victorian Country House* (New Haven and London: Yale University Press, 1979)

Girouard, Mark, *Life in the English Country House* (London and New Haven: Yale University Press, 1978)

Godfrey, Walter Hindes, *The Work of George Devey, Architect* (London: B. T. Batsford, 1907)

Gomme, Andor and Alison Maguire, *Design and Plan in the Country House* (New Haven and London: Yale University Press, 2008)

Hall, Neil G. M., *Salisbury in the Great War* (Barnsley, South Yorkshire: Pen and Sword Books, 2016)

Hawkins, Desmond, ed., *William Chafen, Anecdotes and History of Cranborne Chase, 1818* (Wimborne: The Dovecote Press, 1991)

Hawkins, Desmond, ed., *The Grove Diaries, 1809-1825* (Wimborne: The Dovecote Press, 1995)

Hawkins, Desmond, *Shelley's First Love* (London: Kyle Cathie Limited, 1972)

Hawkins, Desmond, *Cranborne Chase* (Wimborne: The Dovecote Press, 1998)

Hibbert, Christopher, *The English, A Social History 1066-1945* (London: Guild Publishing, 1987)

Hill, Michael, John Newman and Nikolaus Pevsner, *The Buildings of England: Dorset* (New Haven and London: Yale University Press, 2018)

Hitchcock, Henry-Russell, *Architecture: Nineteenth and Twentieth Centuries* (London: Penguin Books Ltd. Pelican History of Art, 1858)

Hoare, Richard Colt, *The History of Modern Wiltshire*, Vol. I, (London: John Nichols and Son, 1822)

James Holden, *Wiltshire Gate Lodges* (Gloucester: The Hobnob Press, 2018)

Hussey, Christopher, *English Country Houses, Late Georgian, 1800-1840* (London: Country Life, 1955)

Hutton, Edward, *Highways and Byways in Wiltshire* (London: Macmillan, 1919)

Jackson, Gwyneth F., *The Tale of Two Manors: Zeals, a Wiltshire Village* (Somerset: Dickins Printers, 1997)

Kaufman, Helen A., *Conscientious Cavalier, Colonel Bullen Reymes, 1613-1672* (London: Jonathan Cape, 1962)

Kerr, Robert, *The Gentleman's House* (London: John Murray, 1864)

Kluz, Ed, Tim Knox, *et al.*, *The Lost House Revisited* (London: Merrell, 2017)

Lasdun, Susan, *Victorians at Home* (London: Weidenfeld and Nicolson, 1981)

Longbourne, David, *The Book of Mere* (Wellington, Somerset: Halsgrove, 2008)

Marshall, George W., ed., *The Visitation of Wiltshire*, 1623 (London: George Bell and Sons, 1882)

Matthews, A. G., *A Revision of John Walker's Suffering of the Clergy during the Grand Rebellion*, 1642-60 (Oxford: Clarendon Press, 1988)

McCann, John and Pamela, *The Dovecotes and Pigeon Lofts of Wiltshire* (Salisbury: The Hobnob Press, 2011)

McGarvie, Michael, ed., *Memoirs of a Victorian Farmer, Richard White of Mells, Norridge and Zeals* (Frome: Frome Society for Local Study, 1990)

Maroon, Fred. J., *The English Country House, A Celebration* (London: Pavilion Books, 1988)

Mee, Arthur, *The King's England – Wiltshire* (London: Hodder and Stoughton, 1943)

Moore, Andrew, *The Norwich School of Artists* (London: HMSO, Norfolk Museums Service, 1995)

Mowl, Timothy, *Elizabethan and Jacobean Style* (London: Phaidon Press, 1993)

Mowl, Timothy, *William Beckford, Composing for Mozart* (London: John Murray, 1998)

Musson, Jeremy, *The English Manor House* (Aurum Press, 1999)

Muthesius, Stefan, *The High Victorian Movement in Architecture, 1850-1870* (London and Boston: Routledge & Kegan Paul, 1972)

Myers, Arthur B. R., *Life with the Hamran Arabs* (London: Smith, Elder & Co., 1876)

Newman, John and Nikolaus Pevsner, *The Buildings of England: Dorset* (London: Penguin, 1975)

Newman, Ruth and Jane Howells, *Salisbury Past* (Andover: Phillimore, 2001)

Ollard, Richard, *The Escape of Charles II after the Battle of Worcester* (London: Constable, 1986)

Oswald, Arthur, *Country Houses of Dorset* (Tiverton: Dorset Books, 1994)

Parissien, Steven, *Regency Style* (London: Phaidon Press, 1992)

Peill, James, *The English Country House* (London: Thames and Hudson, 2017)

Pevsner, Nikolaus and Bridget Cherry, *The Buildings of England: Wiltshire* (London: Penguin Books, 1975)

Placzek, Adolf K., ed., *Macmillan Encyclopedia of Architects*, vol. i (New York: Free Press, Macmillan Publishing Co. Inc., 1982)

Pugh, R. B., ed., *A History of the County of Wiltshire*, vol. v [VCH] (London: Oxford University Press, 1957)

Rogers, Malcolm, *Montacute House* (London: The National Trust, 2000)

Russell, Una and Audrey Grindrod, *The Manor Houses of Dorset* (Wimborne Minster: The Dovecote Press, 2007)

Rutter, Norah V., *et al.*, *Mere, A Wiltshire Country Town* (Shaftesbury: The Blackmore Press, 1975)

Saint, Andrew, *Richard Norman Shaw* (New Haven and London: Yale University Press, 1976)

Saumarez Smith, *Eighteenth-Century Decoration, Design and the Domestic Interior in England* (Weidenfeld and Nicolson, 1993)

Shepherd, Valerie, ed., *The Poems of William Barnes* (Nottingham: Trent Editions, 1998)

Sidney, Mary, *Historical Guide to Penshurst Place* (Tunbridge Wells: Goulden & Curry, 1903)

Silton Women's Institute, *Silton, Records of a Dorset Village* (Castle Cary Press, 1983)

Spencer, Charles, *To Catch a King: Charles II's Great Escape* (London: William Collins, 2017)

Stamp, Gavin, *The English House 1980-1914: The Flowering of English Domestic Architecture* (London: Faber and Faber, 1986)

Stapylton, H. E. C., *The Eton School Lists, 1791-1877* (London: Simpkin, Marshall & Co., 1884)

Steel, John and Michael Wright, *The English House* (Woodbridge, Suffolk: Antique Collectors' Club, 2007)

Summerson, John, *The Classical Language of Architecture* (London: Thames and Hudson, 1980)

Summerson, John, *Architecture in Britain, 1530-1830* (New Haven and London: Yale University Press, 1993)

Thornton, Peter, *Authentic Décor, The Domestic Interior 1620-1920* (London: Weidenfeld and Nicolson, 1984)

Tinniswood, Adrian, *His Invention So Fertile, A Life of Christopher Wren* (London: Jonathan Cape, 2001)

Tinniswood, Adrian, *The Long Weekend, Life in the English Country House between the Wars* (London: Jonathan Cape, 2016)

Trevelyan, George Macaulay, *English Social History* (London: Book Club Associates, 1973)

Treves, Frederick, *Highways and Byways in Dorset* (London: MacMillan & Co., 1920)

Venn, John and J. A Venn, *Alumni Cantabrigienses, vol. ii, part iii, 1752-1900* (Cambridge: Cambridge University Press, 1947)

Walker, John, *The Sufferings of the Clergy during the Great Rebellion* (London: F. Nicholson, 1714)

Walpole, Josephine, *Arts and Artists of the Norwich School* (Woodbridge: Antique Collectors' Club, 1997)

Watts, Ken, *Exploring Historic Wiltshire, vol. ii, South* (Bradford on Avon, Wiltshire: Ex Libris Press, 1998)

Weld, Kit, *The Victorian Society Book of the Victorian Country House,* (London: Aurum Press, 2002)

Wilkinson, Neville R., *A History of the Coldstream Guards from 1815-1985* (London: A. D. Innes & Co., 1896)

Wilkinson, Neville R., *The Guards Chapel* (London: The Chiswick Press, 1938)

Wilson, Michael J., *The English Country House and its Furnishings* (London: Book Club Associates, 1977)

Yorke, Trevor, *Gothic Revival Architecture* (Oxford: Bloomsbury Shire, 2017)

Yorke, Trevor, *Victorian Gothic House Styles* (Newbury: Countryside Books, 2012)

Acknowledgements

I would like to thank my former supervisor Adrian Tinniswood for his encouragement, Philip Cayford for additional photography, Ann Strevens for early genealogical input and Rosina Espirito-Santo for biblical interpretations.

Research has been made easier by having expert and professional assistance from the helpful staff at the Wiltshire and Swindon History Centre at Chippenham where a considerable amount of County information is held. I would like to offer particular thanks to Ian Hicks who dealt with my endless requests for diary pages to transcribe on a regular basis, going out of his way to give support. Writing about a house on the border of three counties also required visits to the Somerset Heritage Centre at Taunton and the Dorset History Centre at Dorchester, who were equally helpful. Dorothy Treasure at the Wiltshire Buildings Record, John Davies on William Arnold and Peter Fitzgerald on Nathaniel Ireson have also been willing to pass on their expertise. I am grateful to the staff and volunteers at The British Art Library, RIBA Library, RIBA Prints and Drawings, The National Library of Australia, The Genealogical Society, The Frome Society for Local Study, and the University of Sheffield for dealing with my requests for documents and information so efficiently. As well as the libraries, others have provided me with images including Strutt & Parker, Hamptons, Northbourne Park School, Stephen Chambers and Charles Hind, which has enabled me to enhance the narrative.

Mere has a thriving reference library and museum and both the former curator Jenny Wilding and currently Rose Heesom have willingly put documents and information at my disposal Local knowledge was an important part of the story and I thank Zeals residents Alex and Katy Brydon and Colin and Clare Liddell for helping to fill me in with topographical details, Emma Chandarana, and Peter Todd for use of his collection of local photographs and letters. Dr David Longbourne and Emma Gatehouse have also extended my research.

For family and genealogical information, I was offered photographs, documents and stories from the descendants of the Troyte-Bullock family: Bill and Ann Woodhouse, Lieutenant Colonel Charles A. J. Valdes-Scott KRH, Louise Aspinall, and Geoffrey Sebag-Montefiore who gave me unlimited access to family albums.

Amberley Publishing have been creative and enthusiastic, and I very much appreciate the expert input from Connor Stait, Shaun Barrington and publicity officer Philip Dean.

Many, many thanks to you all.

Picture Credits

Introduction
Alamy, p 10.
Strutt & Parker, p 12.
Richard Colt Hoare – *History of Modern Wiltshire*, p 14.

Part I: HISTORY
Philip Cayford, p. 16.
Hoare's *Wiltshire*, pp. 21, 22, 30.
WSHC, p. 23.
Geoffrey Sebag-Montefiore, pp. 26, 34, 40.
Alamy, p. 33.

Part II: VICTORIAN
Philip Cayford, pp. 53, 55.
Geoffrey Sebag-Montefiore, pp. 57, 59.
WSHC, pp. 63, 77.
RIBA Collections, pp. 67, 74.
Northbourne Park School, p. 70.
University of Sheffield Library, pp. 72, 73, 80.
SAVE Britain's Heritage, p. 76.

Part III: THE DIARIES
Alamy, pp. 82, 124, 144, 185.
Geoffrey Sebag-Montefiore, pp. 100, 111, 118, 153.
The Library of Congress, pp. 104, 185
National Library of Australia, pp. 138, 141, 166.
SAVE Britain's Heritage, pp. 147, 163.
WSHC, p. 170.
Philip Cayford, p. 182.

PART IV: JULIA
Geoffrey Sebag-Montefiore, pp. 195, 206, 209.
Hamptons, pp. 196, 203.
Philip Cayford, pp. 200, 215.

PART V: TROYTE-BULLOCK
Geoffrey Sebag-Montefiore, pp. 211, 223, 225, 234, 235, 236, 239, 240, 243.
Stephen Chambers Gallipoli Photograph Collection, p. 228.
Philip Cayford, p. 237.
RIBA Collections, p. 246.
Bill and Ann Woodhouse, p. 248
WSHC, p. 252
Charles Valdes-Scott, p. 258.

PART VI: DEPARTURE
SAVE Britain's Heritage, p. 264.
Geoffrey Sebag-Montefiore, p. 267.
Charles Hind, p. 271.
Philip Cayford, p. 273.

EPILOGUE
Strutt & Parker, p. 275.
The Mapping Company, p. 278.
Hoare's *Wiltshire*, pp. 279, 280.
Geoffrey Sebag-Montefiore, p. 281

Index